INTERNATIONAL NIGHT

INTERNATIONAL NIGHT

A FATHER and **DAUGHTER**
COOK THEIR WAY AROUND the **WORLD**
Including More than 250 Recipes

MARK KURLANSKY
and *TALIA* KURLANSKY

BLOOMSBURY

NEW YORK · LONDON · NEW DELHI · SYDNEY

Published by Bloomsbury USA, New York

Bloomsbury is a trademark of Bloomsbury Publishing Plc

All papers used by Bloomsbury USA are natural, recyclable products made from wood
grown in well-managed forests. The manufacturing processes conform to the environmental regulations of the country of origin.

LIBRARY OF CONGRESS CATALOGING-IN-PUBLICATION DATA HAS BEEN APPLIED FOR.

ISBN: 978-1-62040-027-2

First U.S. Edition 2014

1 3 5 7 9 10 8 6 4 2

Printed and bound in the U.S.A. by Thomson-Shore Inc., Dexter, Michigan

Designed by Elizabeth Van Itallie

Bloomsbury books may be purchased for business or promotional use.
For information on bulk purchases please contact Macmillan Corporate and Premium
Sales Department at specialmarkets@macmillan.com

To Marian—there's nobody with whom we would rather have dinner

CONTENTS

INTRODUCTION
THE FAMILY RITUAL

Before it was a book, International Night started as a family game. Our daughter, Talia, who has a far better memory than mine, says that she originated it. I don't remember what the starting idea was because so many elements have been added since then that it is truly a collaborative concept. Our idea was to spin the globe once a week, and wherever Talia's finger landed, we would cook a meal from that place on Friday night.

Sometimes, though, between deciding on the recipes, shopping for the ingredients, and preparing the food, we needed more time, and Saturday or Sunday worked better. Some weeks the weekend was too packed for an International Night. Some weeks we were traveling, and more weeks I was traveling. But we enjoyed the game so much that we persisted, and eventually we had fifty-two International Nights, one for every week of the year.

Talia and I cooked the meals together, and I carefully recorded the menus and recipes for each. The dinners led to discussions about the places and their cultures, with the dialogue always beginning with geography at the globe. Occasionally Talia's finger would land on a place I had never been—ten times out of fifty-two—and then we would learn together.

Of course Talia, Marian, and I enjoyed some dishes more than others. There was never a night in which there wasn't at least one dish that pleased all of us. But I suppose that is like traveling. Some nights you eat better than others. Some nights we ate wonderfully.

I tried to accommodate certain food prejudices of Talia's, and unlike what is commonly believed by adults, all kids have their own tastes. So some kids may love things Talia hated, and the reverse. The one consistent taste is that kids like food that they grow themselves, harvest themselves, and make themselves.

Talia inexplicably loves marinated anchovies and fresh sardines, so we use them whenever possible. She usually does not care for soup, but, for example, how can you go to Quebec without potage Saint-Germain? And some soups she loved. As I overheard a teenager in Manhattan saying to his friend, "I really like soup if it's a soup I really like." Certainly not all the recipes will appeal to everyone, but like Talia, Marian, and me, most anyone will find dishes in every meal that they enjoy. Occasionally we offer alternative dishes if we suspect that our choices will not be popular. And if there was a dish that we didn't like, we reworked it another night or found a substitute. But it is always difficult to guess the tastes of others. All you can do is make good food.

We cooked wherever Talia's finger landed. If it landed on a country with widely varied regional cuisines, we tried to cook from the region on which she landed. This has led us to two very different Canadian nights, three very different French ones, and three Italian ones. We could have done more than one English, Spanish, or German night, but on those countries she landed only once. We did not do places she landed in the US because the idea was to be international. We made an exception when she landed on New Orleans and Hawaii because those places have such distinct cuisines that it tasted like going to another country. If she landed somewhere we had already been, we would spin again. For some reason she kept landing on Kazakhstan. Well, it's large and in central latitudes. But Russia is even larger and it was only after forty-seven nights that she finally landed there.

It became Marian's task before dinner to guess the country to which we were going. Since she had a whole globe's worth of countries and regions to choose from, we gave hints, small facts—when possible, geographic facts—about the country to guide her along. She guessed some countries fairly quickly, although I think she is still working on Tanzania. You will find the hints we gave for each country at the beginning of each night. You can use ours, or you can make up your own if you would like to play this game with your family too.

We tried to make each International Night an occasion. Talia would enter the dining room to announce the night, and we liked to have some music. She announced Jamaica Night to Jimmy Cliff's "Miss Jamaica," and could there have been a better accompaniment than Prokofiev's theme from the great Eisenstein film *Alexander Nevsky* when she announced Russia Night in peasant costume? If Nevsky's triumphant march into Pskov with a bass-voice chorus swearing to defend Mother Russia doesn't get you in the mood for borscht and Stroganoff, what will?

You can also create your own customs. I tried to make this both fun and an educational experience. Food is the best way to teach history and geography and most everything else.

—Mark Kurlansky

TALIA'S INTRODUCTION

"Introducing International Night!" That was my line. Before the meal was served I would march out to announce that night's country. I would be wearing an outfit designed by me to match a traditional style from that country and it was made entirely out of stuff in the house. I had an advantage—my father has traveled to most of these countries. So for Mongolia Night I could borrow a traditional hat he had brought back from Mongolia. For Ireland Night I had a leprechaun hat and red beard I got when I visited Ireland. But for other nights, like Switzerland Night, I just put together some things on my own: a straw fedora, a white shirt, my father's suspenders, shorts, and a plastic yodeling pickle that a friend had given me at a birthday party. For Argentina Night I wore a long dress, a flower in my teeth, and I danced the tango. On Hawaii Night I wore a fake hula skirt that I found in my old dress-up clothing box and a bikini top. On Senegal Night I wrapped a cotton flower print on my head.

Then the meal would begin. As each dish was about to be served, my father would tell me how to pronounce it and I would walk out introducing the food. Although sometimes my father wouldn't know how to pronounce the dish, and we would fake it.

One place kids sometimes get a chance to experience food from different countries is in a restaurant. But restaurants often give children a "kids'" menu.

Is that because children cannot enjoy sophisticated cuisine? No. They can. It's adults who think they can't! Not to say that a lot of kids don't love the (in my opinion) bland and one-dimensional food on a kids' menu; they love it because they haven't truly gotten a taste of sophisticated cuisine. It frustrates me when a waiter places a kids' menu in front of me. WHY CAN'T THE WORLD JUST ACCEPT THAT CHILDREN JUST WANT TO EAT *GOOD* FOOD?

One of my hopes for this book is that while kids are learning about all these different cuisines and cultures, they are getting a chance to *taste* these foods too. Maybe they'll sometimes prefer the more complicated flavors that come with a variety of cuisines and agree with me that international dishes can add up to some really delicious family meals.

—Talia Kurlansky

ON RECIPES

The most celebrated food writer in France for the first half of the twentieth century went by the one-word nom de plume Curnonsky. He wrote, "In cooking as in all the arts, simplicity is the sign of perfection." It is a modernist aesthetic with which I am very much in agreement.

I have tried to keep these recipes simple: of course the great early-twentieth-century French chef Auguste Escoffier always spoke of the importance of simplicity and then made everything incredibly complicated. I promise our recipes are simpler than those of Escoffier and designed for a family of amateur cooks.

With simplicity as my criterion and because I have a psychological predisposition to not follow recipes, all of these recipes ended up being my own. Some of the dishes, especially the desserts, I have made for years but until now stubbornly refused to reveal their recipes. Other recipes I found more recently and completely readapted to my style. A complete list of such sources is in the bibliography.

There is an inevitable conflict between what is authentic, what is available, and what is good. Good was always my first priority. I could have found sweet mustard comparable to the traditional Russian mustard for Stroganoff, but I don't like sweet mustard and felt confident I could do better even if I had to go outside Russia for good, seedy mustard.

I have rated these recipes on a scale of difficulty from ◆ to ◆◆◆. There are two kinds of difficulty. Some recipes take more time and effort, but also some recipes require more skill. A recipe rated ◆ takes little time, skill, or technique. A ◆◆◆, on the other hand, is more demanding. But it is wise to remember that there is very little a professional does that an amateur can't do. The professional just does it faster, with greater efficiency and in larger volume.

I have tried very hard to represent all of these cuisines around the world without using exotic, hard-to-find ingredients. Living in New York City, we can find almost everything—for Asian ingredients, for example, we go to Kalustyan's on Lexington Avenue and Twenty-ninth Street—but I do recognize that not everyone lives in New York. If you do not live in New York, you can order from Kalustyan's online. My Spice Sage is another website for spices. Many cities have ethnic neighborhoods, but if your town does not, you can search for what you need online, though you will miss the fun of shopping in an exotic store with its delicious aromas and interesting products. The reality is that you can search for almost any product online and find someone who will ship it to you.

Unless otherwise stated, the International Night recipes serve three, which is the size of our family. There are some great math exercises involved in adjusting the proportions for more than three or fewer, but Talia tells me that I am no fun when I do that. I am inclined to agree. What was that about the distance the apple falls from the tree? This may be at the root of my impatience with following recipes. To people with mathematical minds, a recipe is a formula to follow. For people with nonmathematical minds, a recipe is a series of suggestions. You can use our recipes either way you prefer.

ON COOKING *with* CHILDREN

There is an oxymoron built into the phrase "cooking with children." Cooking is an orderly pursuit. A successful kitchen is run with a strong sense of order and discipline. To cook with children, though, you are just going to have to give up that attitude, accept the fact that when it's over the kitchen may need a major overhaul, and let the kids have some fun. You can rein it in a little by cooking in stages, cleaning up before going on to the next stage, but understand that the cooking process is not going to be delicate. Kids like to play with food. They also like to eat it at every possible stage. Just relax and have fun.

Everyone has to be aware of safety, of course. Kitchen knives are dangerous and should not be handled by small children. But you can demonstrate how to use them and bit by bit accustom children so when they are older they will know how to use knives. I gave Talia very little knife work, but when we were in cooking school in Morocco—by then she was twelve—our instructors just handed her sharp knives and ordered her to chop and she did very well and still has all ten fingers intact.

Burners and ovens should be handled by the adult. Frying is not a good kids' activity because hot oil easily splatters and burns. Food processors can be dangerous. Mixers, on the other hand, can be used by children with a little instruction and guidance.

Kids especially seem to enjoy working with foods they have never handled before, like octopus and crab. They can also become enthralled with seemingly tedious tasks if they seem unusual, like skinning black-eyed peas (see p. 205).

They most especially enjoy making food that has a sense of handicraft. Making sushi is great fun, as are crepes and Indian naan. They like the magic that comes with baking breads and making pastry, filled empanadas, and Asian dumplings. Making dough, shaping dough, handling dough, eating dough . . . We tried to include such handcrafted foods wherever we could.

TALIA: *Dressing to Cook*

It's important that you wear proper clothing for cooking, for cleanliness, and for safety.

Most important is hair. If you have long hair, try to pin it back so as not to get hair in your food or in your way. Your legs and arms should be covered in case hot oil or hot water splashes on you. And you shouldn't wear anything that hangs or is floppy. For instance, if your sleeves are floppy, then when you reach over to mix something on the stove, they could catch on fire.

It's also a good idea to have an apron for protection. An apron is an extra layer that helps if things spill on you or if you need to wipe your hands. You can go with a simple white one or mix up your day with a colorful, decorative one. Personally, I have several of these and I think they "spice" up my cooking experience, so to speak!

ON DRINKS

Every International Night offers at least one nonalcoholic drink for kids. One of the few tastes that I believe is truly universal for kids is that they love drinks, especially a variety of them, preferably in a variety of colors. I still remember as a kid how my uncle used to bring us Cott sodas in a variety of weird flavors and even weirder colors. We loved it. I couldn't wait to see what he brought. I tried to find hot infusions, sparkling cold drinks, juices, and blends that were authentic to the cuisine and were better and healthier drinks than those sodas of my childhood but just as much fun.

There are also some alcohol suggestions for adults.

ON FATS *and* OILS

Some oils are healthier than others, and often a healthy neutral oil works well for frying. But different cuisines use different oils, and these oils have everything to do with the taste of the cuisine. Celts and some other northerners use butter, certain oils are best for Asian dishes, and some tropical cuisines require coconut oil. A healthy approach is moderation rather than substitution.

BUTTER AND GHEE. Butter is one of the best-tasting fats, but it is of limited use because the suspended milk solids in the oil make it vulnerable to spoilage, and also because these solids easily burn, which means butter cannot be used at high temperatures. The spoilage problem is addressed in some cuisines by adding huge quantities of salt. I do not use salted butter except when called for by tradition—for example, in some Celtic baking. For other recipes, use unsalted butter and then choose the amount of salt you prefer to add to the dish. Ghee is the Indian way of dealing with the problem of butter's low-heat threshold, as the solids are removed. Ghee can be made or bought in Indian food stores. (See India Night, p. 236, for more on ghee.)

COCONUT OIL. This is about the least healthy oil imaginable. It is almost entirely heavy saturated fat. But it also imparts the taste of Caribbean food and is almost essential for a few dishes.

CORN OIL. Corn oil is a fairly healthy oil but has a pronounced taste, one that is needed in Latin American cooking but is not a good choice as a general cooking oil.

LARD. Lard is, or should be, rendered pork fat. It is easy to make and risky to buy premade because store-bought lard doesn't taste the same, leaving you to wonder just exactly what is in it. To make your own lard, buy pork fatback, cube it, and put it in a pan with a small amount of water—about ⅓ cup water for 1 cup of fat. Cook it until the water has cooked away. When almost done, it will sizzle and splatter a lot. Then it will become silent. Cut the heat. Let cool. You can store it in the refrigerator covered for ten days or so, as my mother did with her jars of rendered chicken fat, which is the Jewish version of lard and is also a very good fat.

This kind of animal fat is not very healthy, but it is really good. A touch of lard makes pastry lighter. In France it is considered a sign of quality for pastry to be 100 percent *pur beurre*—pure butter—and when I pointed out to a French chef for whom I was working that a touch of lard would improve the dough, he was outraged. But it would have made a lighter, tastier crust. The reason fried food—fried oysters for example—is so good in New Orleans is that it's fried in lard. You can't really do New Orleans cooking without lard.

OLIVE OIL. So healthy that for a time it was sold in pharmacies, olive oil can be used at fairly high heats, though not the high heat of some Asian flash frying, and it has great flavor. The flavor, though, can be a problem, as it is distinctly Mediterranean, so it does not go with every cuisine.

PEANUT OIL. This is the oil commonly used in African cooking and is perfect for frying. Peanut oil can be heated to very high temperatures. It won't burn until 500 degrees Fahrenheit, which is almost twice as high as the burning point of olive oil. Strangely, large commercial producers such as Planters make this a neutral oil—that is, they remove the peanut flavor. Look for cold-pressed peanut oil, usually available in Asian markets, for a distinct peanut flavor. Unlike most other oils, peanut oil does not absorb the tastes of food cooked in it, so when you are done frying, you can cool, strain, and reuse the oil.

SESAME OIL. Sesame oil has good flavor, good health benefits, and heats well for frying. There is also toasted sesame oil, which not surprisingly has the taste of toasted sesame seeds. It's a great flavor and a wonderful oil for marinades but does not stand up to high-heat frying. Typically sesame oil is used in Asian cooking.

HEALTHY NEUTRAL OILS. When in doubt, canola, safflower, and soybean oil, if of good quality, are healthy oils with neutral flavor and cook at high temperatures so can be used for most anything. Just keep in mind that they don't contribute any flavor.

ON SUGAR *and* SPICE

These are seasonings that you should have on hand for the International Night recipes.

ALLSPICE. This dried berry of the pimenta tree is unique to the Americas and is grown mostly in Jamaica, where it is called pimento because the Spanish noted that the dried berries looked like peppercorns. It has a complex spice flavor and can be used in powder or seeds. It is a good idea to have both on hand.

ANISE. This plant is native to the Middle East. The seeds have a distinct slightly sweet flavor and are used in numerous liqueurs such as French pastis and Greek ouzo. Anise can be used in seed or powdered form. Star anise is from a completely different plant that contains the same flavor-giving ingredient, anethole. It is a very pleasant variation, especially in dishes that show off the attractive star shape.

ANNATTO. This is a Caribbean spice, called *achiote* in Spanish, with very little flavor but a great deal of color. It grows on a small but beautiful tree with red-veined leaves and pink flowers. The tree bears pods that are filled with small red seeds, and those are the annatto. It gives a pleasing orange tint to anything it touches: in the Spanish Caribbean it is used to dye rice yellow; in Jamaica it gives color to codfish cakes. It is also used in Mexican cooking. It is most commonly mixed with oil on the stove to create a yellow fat. It has also been used in England to make cheeses orange.

The warlike Caribs encountered by Co-lumbus used annatto to dye their skin red, and Native Americans have been called "redskins" ever since. You may have noticed that American Indians are not particularly red and wondered about this term.

BERBERE. In this book berbere, a blend of spices that typifies the taste of Ethiopian cooking, is used only for Ethiopia Night. But it is a pronounced and flavorful blend worth considering in other cooking. It is made with korarima, also known as Ethiopian cardamom. It is not cardamom, which is why it is sometimes called false cardamom: it is the seeds of a plant in the ginger family. Also included in the blend are dried rue, an herb; chili peppers, garlic, fenugreek, and white and black pepper; and ajwain, sometimes known as bishop's weed, thymol seeds, or carom seeds, a Middle Eastern spice with a powerful thymelike flavor.

BLACK MUSTARD SEED. Mustard seed, not surprisingly, is what mustard is made from. It contains glycosides, sulfur compounds that give it an acidic taste. Cabbage contains the same thing. Europeans used to make mustard from both black and white mustard seeds. Then they industrialized and designed machinery for the shorter white mustard seed, and black mustard seed was out. But it is still an essential spice in Indian cooking.

BLACK PEPPER. Black pepper is most pungent immediately after it is ground, so we keep a pepper mill filled with black peppercorns on the kitchen counter. I give all black pepper measurements by the number of turns of the mill. Of course all mills are different, so you may choose more or less.

CARAWAY SEEDS. My fondness for this spice comes from a nostalgia for my childhood passion for hot, fresh-from-the-oven seeded rye bread. It has a strong, pleasing flavor used in Mediterranean, especially North African cooking, as well as German. The plant is in the carrot family and the so-called seeds are actually dried fruit.

CARDAMOM. To be honest, this is my favorite spice. Its perfume flavor adds exotic charm to everything it touches. India and Sri Lanka are the traditional producers, with Guatemala and Tanzania now growing the spice too. Cardamom, like caraway, is a dried fruit, though it looks like a seed. The best, most delicate cardamom is green. White cardamom is simply green cardamom that has been bleached. Darker versions are from other species with a harsher flavor. Stock both whole green cardamom and powdered green cardamom.

CHILI PEPPER. The pepper is a fruit, technically a berry. It contains a group of chemicals collectively known as capsaicin. Capsaicin is the primary ingredient of the pepper gas used for crowd control. In the mouth, these chemicals immediately stimulate the pain receptors designed to detect heat, which keep you from getting burned. These receptors then send a heat-alarm message to the brain. Nothing is really happening in your mouth, but your brain is telling you there is a fire.

These chemicals are developed from sunlight and become very strong in Mexico, Central America, and the Caribbean, where the plants are native. Columbus discovered the plants on his first voyage and took some as a potentially valuable trade commodity. The Basques and the Andalusians, who made up a large part of Columbus's crews, were the first Europeans to embrace these peppers. They not only planted them at home: being engaged in global exploration, they spread them around the world. In Africa and Asia they grew to be fairly hot peppers. But in Europe, where there is not strong sunlight, they were milder. The Basque peppers, a species directly related to hot American chili peppers, have only the slightest pinch to them, though occasionally there is a summer of heat and drought and that makes the peppers a little more burning.

Scotch bonnet pepper

When we want something to be truly hot, or if we want Caribbean food to be authentic, we use habaneros, otherwise known as Scotch bonnet peppers or in Martinique as *le cul de Madame Jacques*—Madame Jacques's butt. I did a great deal of asking around and no one seems to remember who Madame Jacques was. But her anatomical gifts apparently are not to be forgotten.

My family does not like extremely hot food, and while I have more of a taste for it, in this case I agree with the French, who point out that too much heat diminishes taste. But some dishes, especially in the Caribbean, are designed for it. If you don't want that much heat, why use Scotch bonnet peppers? Because they are one of the tastiest and, despite what the French say, that taste shines through the incredible heat. But I use them very judiciously, sometimes removing them after brief cooking. You can also reduce the heat by removing the seeds and the veiny structure inside the pepper. Do not touch your face or rub your eyes after handling Scotch bonnet peppers. They are many times hotter than a jalapeño. Szechuan reds are slightly less deadly, though the Chinese compensate by using extraordinary quantities. For Indian cooking I use their traditional long, thin, green peppers, which are also of a middling heat.

No chili powders are as hot as fresh peppers. For a hot one, I use cayenne, originally from French Guiana but now also produced in Asia and North Africa. For milder chili powder, there are the European ones. Hungarian hot paprika is a little hot. Mild Hungarian paprika has barely any heat. The powder from the beautiful red-and-white Basque village of Espelette in the stunning green-velvet valley of the Nivelle River is somewhere in between, and I use it frequently. It is also useful to have some crushed red pepper, dried chilis that have been reduced to flakes but not a powder.

CINNAMON. You should stock this tree bark, native to Sri Lanka, in both sticks of bark and powdered form, though the bark is more certain to be true cinnamon and the powder may be cut with a similar bark from cassia.

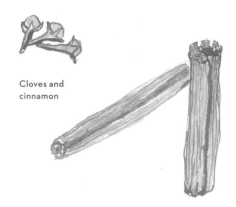

Cloves and cinnamon

CLOVES. The dried bud of an evergreen. Stock them both whole and powdered, though as with all spices the whole form imparts more flavor. Also, buy powders in small amounts because, like tennis players and chewing gum, they lose flavor with age.

CORIANDER. This is a relative of parsley but with much more flavor. It is used in this book in its three forms—the leaves, the seeds, and a powder made from grinding the seeds. Americans seem to feel that it tastes better, especially in its leaf form, if referred to by its Spanish-language name, *cilantro*.

CUMIN. To put it simply, without cumin, chili sauce would just be tomato sauce. Stock both seeds and powder.

CURRY. There are many formulas for curry powder from various regions of India and places where Indians have been. In this book two basic curries are used—a mild one from Madras, and colombo from the Caribbean. You can buy a curry and make your own alterations according to your taste or, maybe more fun, blend your own by dry-roasting the spices and then grinding in a small processor or a coffee grinder. If you use some fresh ingredients such as ginger root, chili pepper, or turmeric root rather than powder, chop them and dry them in the oven. If you don't, your curry will come out more of a paste than a powder, but that can work too.

• **Madras curry.** The usual recipe for a mild Madras curry is coriander seed, cumin, turmeric, ginger, black pepper, red pepper, cinnamon, nutmeg, cardamom, and cloves. If you want hotter Madras, as many in India do, use more red pepper.

• **Colombo.** Caribbean curry powder is made from coriander, fenugreek seeds, cinnamon, cayenne pepper, black pepper, allspice, ginger, turmeric, cardamom, mustard, and mace. All of these ingredients are available in powdered form.

FENNEL SEEDS. One of the reasons Sicily is particularly beautiful in the spring is that the wild fennel blooms with brilliant yellow flowers on the hillsides and around the ancient ruins. The seeds have an anise-like sweetness.

FENUGREEK. The seeds of this clover-related plant were once commonly used in Europe, but today they are mostly associated with India, especially with curries. They need heating to bring out their flavor and, like mustard seeds, are often briefly fried in oil or ghee at the start of a sauce. Useful in seed form and powder.

FLOWER WATERS. Rose water and orange water are commercially available. Commonly used in North African and Middle Eastern cooking, these are simply the most ingestible perfume waters, giving a blossomlike flavor to foods, usually sweet desserts.

GARAM MASALA. Masala is a spice blend. The one I use is garam masala—hot masala—which is an indispensable ingredient in the food of northern India, usually added as a finish to a dish. There are many variations, but typically it is made of cardamom, cinnamon, cloves, nutmeg, and black pepper. Some blends leave out the nutmeg, but I wouldn't. Sometimes cumin, coriander, or both are added. You can buy a premixed garam masala or other masalas and then experiment with a blend you like best. Garam masala is great for all kinds of things, not all of them Indian—spicing up stews or eggs, for example.

GARLIC. Although I know numerous good chefs, especially from New Orleans and the Caribbean, who like to use garlic powder because it is easier, I always use fresh garlic. Its flavor is incomparable and it is easily available, so why not use it?

GINGER. I feel the same way about ginger as garlic: nothing compares with the fresh root, which is easily available. Sometimes you can find young ginger, which does not need to be peeled and is slightly more gentle in flavor.

HARISSA. The primary chili mixture of North Africa is harissa, a blend made from the local hot red peppers, piri piri. It can be bought or made. Every place makes it a little differently. I learned to make it in the Tunisian city of Gabès, where fresh hot red peppers and coarse salt are layered one after another. This can be left for up to a year.

Harissa is easier to make using dried peppers. Soak a dozen medium-size dried red peppers in water for thirty minutes. Remove the seeds and any stems. Put them in a food processor with ¼ cup olive oil, four garlic cloves, one teaspoon caraway seeds, one teaspoon cumin powder, and ½ teaspoon coriander seeds. Grind into a thick paste. Add more olive oil if needed. Even with this technique, it should be made a few days in advance.

Basil

HERBS. I generally prefer to use herbs fresh. My favorites are parsley, chive, basil, thyme, rosemary, marjoram, oregano, dill, and bay leaf. Parsley, chive, dill, and basil are utterly useless when dried. Bay leaves are from the laurel tree and can be found for the picking in France and southern Europe. In Northern California and the Northwest there is a particularly tasty species of laurel. You can buy it dried, but don't keep it too long. Rosemary is an evergreen and I used to pick it along the Seine in Paris near my apartment when I lived in the 4th arrondissement. It dries well, as does oregano, and there are some very aromatic blends of herbes de Provence. Otherwise, when possible, use fresh.

MIRIN. A Japanese seasoning also used in other parts of Asia, mirin is made by fermenting sticky rice with alcohol. This recipe clearly is not rice wine, which is how it is often translated. It has about 14 percent alcohol, which chefs often cook off. Mirin is also sold with very little alcohol left in it, sometimes called *mirin-fu.* Centuries ago the Japanese stopped drinking mirin and use it only as a seasoning, which is why the alcohol content is thought of as unnecessary. It is one of the few sweeteners used in Japanese cooking. The original mirin, *hon-mirin,* is the best choice, though the alcohol should be cooked off—a natural part of most recipes anyway. *Aji-mirin,* which does not have alcohol, should be avoided because it does have other additives such as corn syrup.

NIGELLA SEEDS. These are the small, flavorful seeds in Armenian string cheese, a common spice in the Middle East from Ethiopia to Turkey to India. The Turks frequently bake them in their breads. It is the seed of the fruit of a foot-high flowering plant. In Arabic it is called *habbat al-barakah,* "seed of blessing."

NUTMEG AND MACE. These come from the fruit of a tree native to Indonesia but also a mainstay of the Caribbean island of Grenada. The fruit is edible and often eaten dried by locals, but it does not have the export value of the seed. The seed grows wrapped in fragrant red netting, which is mace. The seed, the nutmeg, needs to be shelled and grated. I always have whole nutmegs and I grate as needed: it is a favorite flavor of mine, and I use it whenever I can. Freshly grated, it is incomparably aromatic. I have never found a nutmeg grater as good as the one made from a tin can with nail holes that I bought in a market on the island of St. Lucia.

Nutmeg and mace

You need a rough grate, not too fine. When I was growing up in Hartford, Connecticut was called the Nutmeg State, referring to colonial times when goodly amounts of money were made by selling fraudulent nutmegs carved from wood. But these days states have public relations and marketing teams that have no sense of humor, so now Connecticut is the Constitution State because of the early date of its original charter. Big deal.

RED PEPPERCORNS. Not to be confused with the red phase of true black peppercorns, which redden on their way from green to black, red peppercorns are less pungent, but used whole—which they are mild enough for—they offer a cool shade of red unusual in food. When I lived in Mexico City I used to pick them in the parks.

SAFFRON. The dried stigmas of a certain species of autumn crocuses, considered the most expensive spice, saffron goes stale quickly, so buy it when you are going to use it and keep it out of sunlight. Then, despite the cost, use it generously, because what could be a greater waste of spice than using it too sparingly to taste?

SALT. Salt is just sodium chloride, a common compound found in nature. The taste of salt is not complicated; it is one of the four basic tastes on the tongue. The natural color of salt is white. Salt that is not absolutely pure white has impurities in it, usually dirt. When salt is white, it either was extremely pure in nature or it has been refined to a pure state. This is what you want. For centuries, this was what salt makers tried to achieve. In the seventeenth century, Louis XIV's minister of finance, Jean-Baptiste Colbert, who took a great interest in France's salt trade, complained about the dirt in the gray salt of Guerande in Brittany. He said that if they could clean it to be white, like the salt of their competitors in Spain and Portugal, it would bring much more money. This just shows you how much Colbert knew. Today the gray salt of Brittany is among the most expensive in the world. Artisanal salt production has combined with sophisticated marketing to convince you that the dirt in the salt is beneficial algae and minerals.

Since all pure sodium chloride tastes the same—salty—there is only one decision to be made—the size and the shape of crystals. Salt crystallizes in many different ways, and crystals melt on the tongue and stimulate the taste buds in different ways. Some may seem milder, others more harsh, perhaps saltier.

In the United States we tend to mystify sea salt because although we are the leading salt producer, we produce very little sea salt. Everyone else does, though; in fact, sea salt is the most common salt in the world. Pure sea salt is the same as pure rock salt, just sodium chloride. But if you're looking for larger crystals, sea salt tends to be a better choice because it is made through the slow process of drying in the sun, and in crystallization there is an infallible rule that the longer a crystal takes to form, the larger it will be.

So-called kosher salt is of limited use. It is not particularly kosher. Most any salt is. A correct name would be "kosherizing salt." In Jewish dietary law, blood must be drawn out of red meat, and this salt is designed for that task. The large flat crystals sit clumsily on the tongue, making kosher salt taste too harsh for most other uses.

In our family we basically use two kinds of salt: coarse and smooth. If we want the salt to just melt in and add flavor, as in pastry doughs and soups and stews, we use a common table salt, usually sea salt, but it wouldn't have to be. If we want crunchy crystals, we use a larger-crystal sea salt. Sometimes we use fleur de sel, which are crystals of sea salt that are so light that they float to the surface of a salt pond rather than sinking to the bottom. The lightness and dryness of them makes them particularly crunchy. We like crunchy salt on fried food, on vegetables, on salad, and on grilled meat and fish.

I started using crunchy salt on salad years ago. The word *salad* comes from the Roman *salada*, meaning salted. I wanted to taste what a Roman salad would be like, so I sprinkled it with larger salt crystals. Later I realized that Romans were more apt to salt vegetables than lettuce, to counteract their bitterness; they usually dressed salad with a salt brine. Too late; I was hooked on crunchy salt crystals on my salad and I have been eating salad that way ever since.

Measuring salt—I don't get too specific with salt measurements because how much salt to use is almost always a matter of personal taste. I measure with a pinch, a large pinch, and a generous pinch. A pinch is a small amount between the thumb and index finger. A large pinch is a bigger amount. A generous pinch is as much as you can hold, which is probably a little less than a tablespoon, which I sometimes call for as well. I am talking about my size fingers, not Talia's.

Japanese chefs have an excellent way of salting. They hold the pinch in their fingers high above the food and wave the hand back and forth to distribute the salt below.

SOY SAUCE. Soy sauce is at least a thousand years old and originated in China, where inventions from that epoch are considered new. It is made by fermenting soy beans and wheat and preserving it in salt brine.

Since China's Sichuan province is a traditional salt-producing area, it is also a soy sauce producer. I scoured the province looking for an old-fashioned artisanal producer, which I found in Lehzi at the Lehzi Fermented Product Corporation. When the state-run company was shut down in 1999, workers took their severance pay, sold the plant, and moved to a mud-and-stone storage building. Without equipment, they made soy sauce the old way, without heating up the beans to stimulate fermentation, instead mixing them with yeast and storing them for days on bamboo racks until the beans mold. It is then mixed with brine, poured into large clay crocks, and stored outdoors for between six months and a year. The product is black, caramelly, slightly thick, and complex in flavor. This is a Chinese ideal of soy sauce, but they also make lighter soy sauces for lighter food. The Japanese make much lighter soy sauce that is less salty, because the Japanese also add salt directly to food, something the Chinese rarely do. It is good to stock both light and dark soy sauce. The Japanese even make a "white" soy sauce: because it is not dark in color, it doesn't turn food darker.

SESAME SEEDS. First cultivated in the Middle East four thousand years ago, sesame seeds traveled to Asia. They contain sesamin and sesamolin, two fibers that scientists have been studying because they appear to lower cholesterol and may also help to prevent high blood pressure. The seeds have a much stronger flavor with toasting.

SUGAR. There are many different sugars. The following are the ones that we used.

• **Coconut palm sugar.** There are many sugars made from plants other than sugarcane, but the only one I use aside from honey and maple syrup—an increasingly precious item due to climate change and the decline of maples—is coconut palm sugar. Along with the sugar made from boiling down sap from several other types of palm such as the palmyra, it is probably the oldest form of man-made sugar—as opposed to harvested honey—in the world. It is certainly considerably older than cane sugar. It has a delicate, rich, molasses flavor. We used it for Sri Lanka Night because it is commonly used there. But I liked it so much I have experimented with it for pecan pies, gingerbread, and spice cakes. And it would probably be great for many other dishes as well.

• **Confectioners' sugar.** This is the only completely refined sugar I use. It is cane sugar ground beyond crystals to a powder, a consis-

tency that is very useful, as the name implies, for certain confections.

• **Raw sugar.** This is my basic sugar. Cane sugar is made from pressing cane, a type of grass—or actually a variety of types—and extracting a juice that is then boiled until liquid evaporates and crystals are left. Also left is molasses, a thick brown substance that has much more flavor than simply sweet sugar crystals. There is always a little molasses left in the crystals unless they are refined to a pure white. The only reason for using refined white sugar is if you are making meringues that you wish to be extremely white. Raw sugar is just slightly beige and has more flavor.

• **Brown sugar.** Theoretically, brown sugar is sugar in which the molasses has been left. But most commercial brown sugar is refined white sugar with molasses added. There are a few very good brown sugars that are natural.

• **Demerara.** A light brown sugar named after the former British colony in the Caribbean that is now the independent nation of Guyana.

• **Turbinado.** This sugar is the American version of demerara and is mostly an American product primarily made in Hawaii. Some molasses is left in turbinado so that it is the color of demerara, but it has larger crystals looking like tiny topazes. These crystals are quite hard and resistant to dissolving, so turbinado works well if you want to have some crunchiness.

• **Muscovado.** This was a famous product of Barbados but is now made in other places, such as Mauritius. The name comes from the Spanish *más acabado,* which means "more refined," which makes little sense. Dark muscovado is the most molasses-laden of sugars, with a dark, rich taste, the most flavorful brown sugar.

• **Jaggary or gur.** These words are used in India to refer to palm sugar, but they are also used to refer to an Indian cane sugar that has a yellow color that makes it look mild but has a dark molasses taste. The Hindi word *jaggary* is used in Southeast Asia exclusively to refer to palm sugar.

TURMERIC. The poor man's saffron, turmeric does not impart the taste of saffron at all, but it does give the color, and in some parts of the Caribbean it is even called saffron. It is a very strong dye and has made bright golden orange a leading color in India's culture. It is the peeled roots that are used and can sometimes be found fresh, but dried powdered turmeric is also satisfactory and doesn't turn your cutting board bright orange.

VANILLA. Vanilla is made from the seeds of the pod of a plant. The seeds work well when cooked in a liquid such as a custard or melted chocolate. In fact, vanilla was first found by Europeans when the Spanish noticed that Montezuma used it in an unsweetened drink that turned out to be chocolate. Vanilla brings out the flavor of chocolate. There are many circumstances when it is easier to use vanilla extract. Make sure, though, that it is labeled "Pure vanilla extract." By US regulations, vanilla extract must be a minimum of 35 percent alcohol, though you would never use enough for the alcohol to be an issue. It should also be expensive. Be suspicious of inexpensive vanilla. Store in a cabinet, not on an exposed rack, because it deteriorates in light.

EQUIPMENT

There are only two indispensable appliances: a mixer and a food processor.

MIXER AND ATTACHMENTS. Any good mixer such as a KitchenAid, a good one because it is strong and durable, will come with three attachments—a dough hook for mixing doughs, a whip for whipping air into something such as egg whites or whipped cream, and a paddle for beating mixtures that you do not want to whip air into.

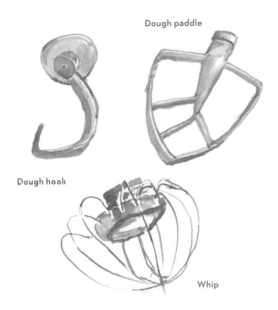

Dough paddle

Dough hook

Whip

FOOD PROCESSOR. Any food processor will do, as long as it has at least one chopping attachment and one grating attachment.

BEATERS. Always use hand whisks, not those weird implements with the revolving handle.

WOODEN SPOONS AND RUBBER SPATULAS. These are inexpensive and always useful. You should have about eight wooden spoons and four rubber spatulas standing by.

CAST-IRON SKILLET. Ideally a cast-iron skillet should never be touched by soap. When it is new, it should be washed with a wet sponge and then rubbed in cooking oil. After the first few times you use it, heat the pan after rubbing in the oil. As the pan gets black and resistant to sticking, less has to be done, but detergent will ruin this carefully laid seasoning.

EARTHENWARE OVEN DISHES. Called *cazuelas* in Spanish, these are good for baking and also for marinating, as food marinated in metal or plastic will develop undesirable flavors.

ZESTER. The zest is the colorful part of the peel of citrus fruit. It is the most flavorful part of the fruit, much more so than the juice. This little tool with tiny ring-shaped cutters on the end is the most efficient way of lifting the zest.

SIFTER OR STRAINER. Wooden hoops with a screen at the bottom are the most efficient sifters. Sift by tapping the wood. Dome-shaped strainers also work well.

SPRINGFORM PANS. These are the only cake pans I use. Open the spring and remove the outer sleeve and the cake is out without having to turn it upside down.

TART PANS. These are metal pans with crinkled rims and a bottom that is not attached and just sits on the rim.

SPATULAS. You should have at least two of these and they should both be long enough to pick up a fish fillet.

POTATO MASHER. I am talking about that old-fashioned tool with the zigzag metal and the wooden handle. They really mash, which is why they are still made, though the new ones usually don't have those nice wooden handles.

MEXICAN BEAN MASHER. This was a tool I picked up in Mexico, but you can find it in many kitchen shops. With its wooden handle and cylindrical wooden head, this tool has endless uses.

LIME SQUEEZER. This is another tool I picked up in Mexico, but there are variations on it everywhere. It consists of a metal cup with holes and a hinged top. A half lime or lemon is placed in the cup and the hinged top flips over it. You squeeze the two handles like a pair of pliers.

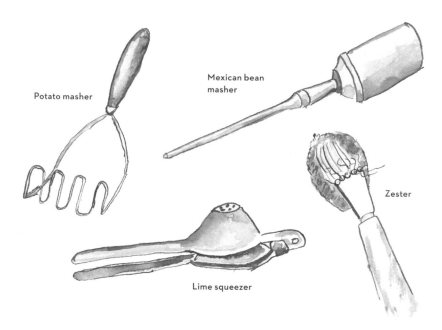

Potato masher

Mexican bean masher

Lime squeezer

Zester

A SLIGHTLY NUTTY WAY *to* OPEN *a* COCONUT

After a decade as a journalist in the Caribbean, engaged in every aspect of coconut life, including learning how to get water to drink by knocking them out of the tree (and not on your head), I have developed my own curious method for opening a coconut. I would be surprised to see this technique anywhere else, but it works very well. All that is needed is a corkscrew and a hammer.

There are three eyes in a coconut, round indentations near the top. You have to open at least two—all three is better—to be able to pour out the coconut water to save for later use. You can do this by drilling into each eye with a corkscrew and, when all the way through, pulling the corkscrew straight out to make a hole. Pour out the coconut water and then place the coconut on a hard surface such as a tiled terrace or bathroom floor and crack it open with a few sharp blows of a hammer.

ON SALT COD

Since the development of refrigeration, salt cod has lost popularity in American cuisine. But it has remained important to numerous cultures around the world. Europeans tend to use better-quality salt cod when the dish involved is served as a piece of fish with a sauce and not mashed up. There are exceptions, such as Provençal *brandade*, which calls for high-quality salt cod. In West Africa and the Caribbean, where salt cod was introduced as an inexpensive slave food, lower-quality salt cod is traditional for dishes that mash up the fish and disguise the quality.

This is worth keeping in mind when shopping for salt cod, as there is a considerable price range. The best salt cod is dry and hard and stiff as a board. It has become fashionable, particularly in France, to use a light cure—salted but not dried, and requiring much less soaking time. This fish is not nearly as good.

To prepare salt cod for cooking, it must be both desalinated and rehydrated. This is done by long hours of soaking. French merchants used to buy salt cod in the port of Bordeaux and drag it behind barges that went up the river. Two days later they would deliver it to markets with the fish ready to cook. But this practice fell into question with the pollution of the rivers in the twentieth century. In 1947, in preparation for an important banquet, a prominent politician in the Aveyron—the remote inland region famous for Roquefort cheese—asked his valet to regularly flush the toilet, one of those old contraptions with a water tank that hung high on the wall. When it was time to cook the meal, the valet was told to reach into the tank and retrieve the salt cod, now ready for cooking.

If you do not have that kind of toilet, a bowl of water kept in the refrigerator and changed every two hours works well. You can also put the bowl under the faucet with a slight trickle of water. But it will take between twenty-four and forty-eight hours, and you do not want the fish out of refrigeration, especially in a warm climate, for that long.

When it is ready to a degree depends on your palate. The Basques have very salty pal- ates and leave their salt cod quite salty. It is a matter of taste, but don't soak until it has no salt, or you'll lose the taste of salt fish. After twenty-four hours, start periodically breaking off a small piece to taste until the fish is at the point you like.

ON VEGETABLES

Parents who find that their children do not like vegetables should ask themselves why Chinese families don't usually have trouble getting their children to eat vegetables. What is the Chinese secret? There are two. One is that vegetables are such an integral part of the cuisine that a meal without vegetables is unimaginable. The second is that the Chinese are experts in balanc- ing tastes. The dominant taste of vegetables is bitter. Research has shown that children have extremely powerful bitter receptors, meaning that they taste bitter very strongly. As we get older, we get desensitized to bitter and find it more palatable. Most kids prefer milk chocolate to dark chocolate, find the taste of coffee un- bearable, and often don't like vegetables. The other tastes—salty and sweet and sour—diffuse bitterness, so this should be kept in mind when serving vegetables.

Vegetables should be cooked quickly so that they are crisp and bright. There are two ways to do this—either steam them or blanch them. Blanching means plunging them into salty boil- ing water and removing them quickly. Put your kids in charge of making vegetable dishes. We always prefer food that we make ourselves. You can trust it.

ON DESSERTS

A great many people, and especially a great many children, expect a dessert at the end of a meal. But dessert, from a French verb for clearing plates, is a Western concept, a European style, and a fairly modern one at that. The idea was popularized by the French in the eighteenth century and originally came with an emphasis on what it looked like, an elaborate pyramid or some other construction of sweets to be placed on the table after a meal. To this day many cultures in the world, especially in Asia and Africa, do not serve desserts. It makes no sense in Chinese culture, where dishes are served together to contrast tastes, to then follow with a dish that is merely sweet. The Japanese do have a tradition of desserts, although hip modern Japanese often prefer Western desserts. A Japanese businessman visiting New York wanted to show me a great Japanese meal and took me to a Japanese restaurant in midtown Manhattan. Nothing but Japanese was spoken in this restaurant. The menu was printed in Japanese only. The food was exquisite. But I was curious to see if there would be a dessert and what that might be. He said something to the waiter in Japanese. It sounded as if he had ordered something with miso. He explained to me through our translator that he had ordered dessert. Some sort of miso dessert, I imagined. But when it came it was tiramisu, the Italian dessert that dates back at most only fifty years.

I tried to come up with a dessert for every dinner. Sometimes I had to stretch things a bit, though never as far as my Japanese friend did. Sometimes it's a fairly recent invention from foreign influence concocted out of local products. Sometimes it's a traditional sweet, though not one that's traditionally served after a meal.

BASIC RECIPES

I used to make everything myself, including pasta. But good fresh pasta became easily available, so that work seemed pointless except for inventing fillings for homemade raviolis. So now Talia and I only occasionally make our own pasta for the fun of it, though I have to admit it is still better than what I can buy. I made my own pâtés, but this involved so many ingredients that I ended up with a pâté for eighty. I made my own jams and preserves, brined my own olives, put up my own pickles. But there are acceptable, even excellent versions of these foods commercially available.

All of the foods in this Basic Recipes section can be bought premade, but for purists who want to do it themselves—which after all is one of the pleasures of cooking—here are some basic recipes.

MAYONNAISE. Mayonnaise can be made well by hand with just a bowl and a whisk as I did for years until food processors became popular.

Mayonnaise, like chocolate, is a solid suspended in an oil. Like chocolate, it requires careful handling, but homemade mayonnaises are infinitely better, though more fragile, than commercial ones.

4 egg yolks
a large pinch of salt
oil
lemon juice, lime juice, or vinegar

Put egg yolks in a food processor with a large pinch of salt. Whip them together with the spinning blade and continue whipping as you carefully add oil *one drop at a time.* Typically you would use a neutral oil like canola or sunflower, unless an oil with a pronounced flavor was needed for a particular dish, such as olive oil for Mediterranean cooking. You should spin a minute between drops. If the oil is added too quickly, the eggs won't thicken; if this happens, the best thing to do is to throw it out and start again. The thicker it becomes, the faster the oil drops can be added. When it is reasonably thick, add acid. This is normally lemon juice, but lime can be nice, and various vinegars are sometimes used. This will liquefy the mixture again. Add just enough acid so that it begins to liquefy, which should only take a few drops. You don't want the mixture to be watery. Return to the procedure of slowly beating in oil and it will thicken quickly. All kinds of ingredients are added to mayonnaise for certain dishes—herbs, shallots, garlic, mustard, red pepper. But this is the basic recipe.

PASTRY DOUGH. The International Night recipes call for many types of dough and batters, but there are three that come up often—puff pastry, short pastry, and rising dough ball.

• Puff pastry. This is difficult to make well, so keep in mind that frozen puff pastry is perfectly adequate. In fact, when I worked as a pastry maker, I would make large batches of puff pastry and freeze them. Freezing is good for most doughs. By chance, I discovered that French butter has less water and makes better puff pastry. I first realized this difference when I moved from New York to Paris and suddenly my puff pastry was so good that I was wrapping everything in puff pastry. The ideal surface for rolling puff pastry is a marble top, because it stays cool and keeps the butter from getting too soft.

If you get very good at making puff pastry, yours will be better than the commercial product. Otherwise I would recommend buying it—a considerable time savings. But if you want to try making it, here is the recipe. You must make it at least a day in advance. Making a good puff pastry is a very satisfying experience.

This recipe, which I have been making for many years but was originally adapted from one by the Paris pastry maker Gaston Lenôtre, will make almost three pounds, which is a lot, but it is easier to make large amounts, and you can always freeze what you don't use.

Slightly less than 1 cup water
2 teaspoons salt
3¾ cups flour
6 tablespoons warm, soft butter
2¼ cups refrigerated butter, or 500 grams if a
  French packet

In a glass, mix the water with the salt and

stir it until the salt is dissolved. Put the flour in a mixer with a dough hook, add the warm, soft butter, and mix well at a moderate speed. Then add the salt water and continue mixing until it is a completely homogenous dough ball. Take the ball, carve an X on the top with a knife, wrap it, and refrigerate it for at least three hours.

Place the refrigerated butter on a sheet of parchment paper. Knock it gently with a rolling pin or slightly roll it until the butter forms about a ½-inch sheet.

Flour the table. Throughout this process you will have to constantly flour both the table and the rolling surface of dough. If the dough sticks to the table or roller, this can ruin your pastry—however, too much loose extra flour will also ruin the pastry, so use as little as you must to avoid sticking.

Roll the dough out into a rectangle that is not too thin but big enough to wrap around the butter. Place the butter in the center. Fold the dough over the butter so that the butter is completely covered by the dough.

Placing the dough so that folded edges are at a right angle to you, flour the rolling pin and check if other flouring is needed on the table surface. Gently roll the dough into a long rectangle about ¼ inch thick, then fold the dough in thirds as you would a letter.

Cover it well and refrigerate for an hour. Again, with the folded edges perpendicular to you so that you are always rolling with the folds, roll and fold twice more. Then cover and refrigerate. When you are ready to use, roll and fold two more times. You will also need to roll and fold twice after thawing if frozen. After the two more folds, refrigerate again for one hour, and then it is ready to use.

• **Short pastry.** This is a basic dough that I have been using for years for pie and tart crusts. It is really a cookie, and as a matter of fact, Talia and I roll it out and use appropriate cookie cutters and sparkles to make butter cookies for Halloween and Valentine's Day. There is no magic formula to this dough, and you can play with it as you will. Make it saltier, make it sweeter, add cinnamon, add lemon zest, add powdered almonds, but this is the basic formula. The important thing, as with most baking recipes, is to do everything in the right order—flour, butter, sugar, salt, flavorings, eggs.

3 cups flour
¾ pound cold butter
1 cup sugar
a generous pinch of salt
a splash of vanilla extract
2 eggs

Put the flour in a mixing bowl with a dough hook. Add the cold butter chopped into square pieces the size of a brussels sprout. When the flour has become the consistency of coarse meal with no visible chunks of butter, add sugar. Mix well. Add salt. Then mix in a splash of vanilla and two whole eggs, one at a time. It should all come together into a ball of dough.

• **Rising dough ball.** This recipe, adapted from one by Jeff Hertzberg and Zoë François's excellent book *Artisan Bread in Five Minutes a Day,* is used in many kinds of breads. After making, tear off the amount you want and freeze the rest or adjust the quantities to the size you want.

1 tablespoon fresh yeast or 1 packet dry yeast
2 cups warm water
1 tablespoon salt
4¼ cups flour

Add yeast to warm water—not hot, just a little warm. Add salt. Mix well. Mix in flour. Put it in a mixer with a dough hook on low speed until completely mixed. This should take only a few minutes. Put it in a container with a lid but not an airtight seal. Let the dough rise at room temperature until it begins to flatten on top. It is ready to use, though if you store it overnight in a lidded container it will be easier to work with.

STOCKS. Stocks are a simple thing for a restaurant but more of a project at home. Restaurants have lots of scraps to throw in the pot and enough space for a really big pot and a free burner to keep working on off hours. At home you have to go out and buy most of the ingredients, cannot use a big enough pot for a huge supply, wouldn't have the freezer space for it anyway, and it is difficult to find a few hours to leave it simmering on a spare burner with no staff to watch over it. So keep in mind that perfectly adequate beef, chicken, and vegetable stocks can be bought. But for the die-hard do-it-yourselfer, here are two recipes.

• **Beef stock.** Take a few pieces of leg bone with marrow. Roast them for half an hour and put them in a tall stockpot with a little olive oil, 2 tablespoons salt and 5 turns of black pepper, and a pound of beef short ribs, 5 scraped carrots, 2 leeks with greens, 1 yellow onion peeled and cut in half, 3 bay leaves, 3 sprigs of thyme, several sprigs of parsley, and 3 heads of garlic. Fill the pot with water. Bring to a boil and reduce to a very slow simmer and cook with the liquid moving slightly for eight hours. The longer you cook it, the stronger it becomes. Eventually it cooks down to an intense dark jelly called glace de viande. But you can stop it as soon as it becomes a dark soup and strain out the solids. They can be eaten with coarse salt and crusty bread and called pot au feu, but if you are going to do that put a little more meat in the stock.

• **Chicken stock.** The short and long recipes. First the short. Make your grandmother's chicken soup and drain out the solids.

The long recipe: take one whole chicken cut in quarters. Add all the ingredients for the beef stock except the beef and bones. Add water. Bring to a boil. Simmer for four hours. Strain.

PRESERVED LEMONS. This is a North African condiment but so good you should think about using it in other soups and stews. Also, in a nice large sealed preserving jar they keep for years and look attractive. I learned this recipe in Tunisia.

Mix salt and water in a bowl. Test the saltiness by putting in one raw egg still in its shell. Keep adding salt until it floats slightly. Old North African cookbooks in French used to say that the area of the egg exposed above the water's surface should be the size of a ten-centime coin. Centime coins have been done in by the euro, but a ten-centime coin was about the size of an American dime. Wash the lemons and arrange them in a large preserving jar. Once the brine is the appropriate salinity, cover the lemons with it and seal the jar. Wait at least six weeks.

In Morocco I learned a completely different

recipe. The lemons are slit in quarters but not completely cut through. Coarse salt is jammed in the cracks and these lemons are crammed into the jar so tightly that they have to be forced. After a day the jar will be three quarters filled with lemon juice. Top the rest with olive oil and keep it a few months before opening. After the lemons are gone, Moroccans sometimes use the juice like a vinegar in salads. The Tunisian version is simpler and, it seems, more pure, but some argue that the Moroccan version is better. I keep both.

TOMATO SAUCE. I have never liked the conventional thinking about tomato sauce, which is that seed and skin are bad, so plunge the tomatoes into boiling water to remove a fourth of the flavor along with the skin, then squeeze them to remove the seeds: the juice and the gel around the seeds are where most of the flavor lies. All those elements that you are removing are part of the tomato. Some argue that they are bitter, but they are what tomato is supposed to taste like. Here are two recipes for tomato sauce. The first is smoother in texture and sweeter and less pungent in flavor than the second, and there are any number of good commercially bottled sauces, sometimes even local ones, that can serve as well. There are times that you want the first sauce, either because its texture blends better with the dish, its flavor blends better with strong spices that you're adding, or, as in the case of Morocco, it is simply the regional tradition.

Sauce #1—Cut 6 tomatoes in half and burn the skin side either on a grill flame or a stove flame. Let them cool and just pull the skins off. Quarter the tomatoes and pull out the seeds and gel. Gently sauté in olive oil 5 sliced garlic cloves, a generous pinch of salt, 3 turns of black pepper, 8 basil leaves, and the leaves from 3 sprigs of fresh oregano. Put in a food processor with the tomatoes and puree. Then gently simmer for 10 minutes, stirring occasionally with a wooden spoon.

Sauce #2—Mince 1 yellow onion and 5 cloves of garlic. Sauté in olive oil with a large pinch of salt, 3 turns of pepper, the leaves of 3 sprigs of oregano, 4 finely chopped basil leaves, and 6 chopped ripe unskinned tomatoes. Gently sauté together, stirring with a wooden spoon, until the tomatoes fall apart into a chunky sauce.

ON COOKING TEMPERATURE

I was taught that good cooks use low heat. Most cooking is done on fairly low heat, but a few things, especially frying, require high heat. If the temperature isn't specified for a particular recipe, cook on a low heat.

PHILIPPINES NIGHT

HINT: A REPUBLIC OF 7,107 ISLANDS.

It seemed propitious that the very first place Talia's roving finger landed was the Philippines. My father had been in the medical corps among the troops that liberated the Philippines from the Japanese in 1945. They treated wounded and horribly abused prisoners of war in Manila. I was born three years later, and although he declined to share many details, he brought up the Philippines often during my childhood. When in my early thirties I was sent there as a journalist, the first thing I did was call my father to tell him I would be going.

When I arrived, another war was going on—a mean, hidden guerrilla war in the northern part of the island of Luzon against the dictator Ferdinand Marcos, who was from that region. While there, I met up with a small guerrilla band of the New Peoples Army and traveled with them briefly. They ate food so strange to me I could not identify much of it. A lot of it was uncooked. Though I am one of those fortunate people who can eat almost anything with impunity, this food did me in. I had intense pain and felt as though I would faint at any moment.

I could not take time out; I only had two weeks to research articles. I left the guerrillas and traveled to the majestic rice terraces of Banaue, where I met indigenous Ifugaos who played sweet songs through their noses on bamboo flutes. And then, somehow, I ended up at a cockfight. I accomplished all this with the aid of Coca-Cola, something I had never drunk but that I now discovered eased the pain of whatever it was I was going through. By the time I got to the cockfight I felt barely conscious, leaned against a pole, held money in one hand and the Coke in the other, and managed to bet because in the Philippine language that everyone was speaking, Tagalog, numbers are the same as in Spanish. After each desperate chicken contest, more money would be thrust into my hand.

But I also had wonderful eating experiences, especially a creature called a coconut crab, a crab that lives on coconut palms. A relative of the hermit crab, it is the largest land-dwelling member of the arthropod phylum, which includes scorpions, crustaceans, and other crawly things. It can grow to be more than a foot long, and can break open coconuts with its mighty claws and feed on them, which may explain why it is the most succulent crab I have ever tasted. There

Coconut crab

were also many strange things like the crispy pata, literally a crisp paw. It is the deep-fried leg of a pig, an enjoyable dish until someone points out to you that you must inspect the foot to make sure it isn't from a dog or cat.

The country has about 170 languages, but the leading one, Tagalog, is Austronesian, which is to say native to the region in the family of Malay languages. But there is Spanish and English mixed in. There are many influences in the Philippines, which has often been controlled by other people, including the Spanish, the Americans, and the Japanese. The food, too, is a mixture: Malay-Japanese-Chinese-Spanish-American.

PICKLE
◆ SINGKAMAS (PICKLED JICAMA)

Singkamas is a pleasant accompaniment to this meal, but must be made at least one week in advance. Jicama, the big, round root from a native Mexican bean plant, is one of many foods the Spanish learned about from the Aztecs and brought to the Philippines.

3 cups water
3/4 cup salt
3 cups peeled and grated jicama
1/2 white onion, thinly sliced
3 garlic cloves, sliced
2 tablespoons peeled and grated
    ginger

1/2 green bell pepper, minced
1/2 red bell pepper, minced
1/2 Scotch bonnet pepper, minced
1 cup white vinegar
1/3 cup sugar

Leave the grated jicama to soak overnight, unrefrigerated, in a bowl with well-mixed salt water. Then rinse the jicama and drain it to remove all salt and water. Place in a two-pint pickling jar with onion, garlic, ginger, and peppers. In a non-aluminum pot, boil the vinegar and sugar, then reduce to a simmer for a few minutes. Pour the vinegar mixture over the vegetables, and when it cools, close the lid. The pickles will be ready to eat in a week.

APPETIZER
◆ KILAWIN ISDA (FISH KILAWIN)

This dish, which dates to the pre-Spanish era in the Philippines, must be made three days in advance. *Kilaw* is thought to come from the word *hilaw*, meaning raw. Filipinos eat a lot of raw food, which is probably why I got sick. In the tropics, without refrigeration, raw food can be dangerous, but in a modern home it is not. The moral is, when traveling with a guerrilla army, decline the hilaw. But this dish, kept in a refrigerator, is not to be missed. It should also be noted that applying something acidic to food, such as lemon or vinegar, creates the identical chemical reaction as applying heat, so in reality this dish, like ceviche, is cooked, but without heat.

1½ pounds fairly white-fleshed fish
   fillet, such as flounder
1 cup rice vinegar
3 garlic cloves, peeled and chopped
1 white onion, chopped
6 black peppercorns, crushed
a pinch of salt
⅓ cup water
1 green mango, grated
cayenne pepper

Place the fish in an earthen casserole with the rice vinegar, garlic, onion, crushed peppercorns (you can smash them with a bottle or a hammer), salt, and water. Cover and keep in the refrigerator for one to three days. Serve with grated green mango. The mango grates well with a food processor's grating attachment, but make sure the mango is truly green, hard, and unripe. Sprinkle cayenne pepper over the entire dish.

MAIN COURSE
◆ ADOBONG BABOY (PORK ADOBO)

Adobo is a Spanish word for a uniquely Filipino cooking style of stewing in vinegar. When the Spanish came to the Philippines in the sixteenth century, the locals were already cooking this way. It remains one of the most common methods of cooking in the Philippines and is used not only for pork but also for liver, seafood, chicken, beef— most anything that can be stewed. Squid adobo, adobong pusit, is another very good dish, and it can be cooked in the same way, but without the bananas or with plantains instead. There is a lot of room for creativity in a Filipino adobo, as long as you stew with vinegar.

6 garlic cloves, peeled and sliced
4 thin slices peeled ginger root
3 bay leaves
1/2 cup rice vinegar
a large pinch of salt
2 tablespoons Japanese soy sauce
1/2 cup water
3 turns of black pepper

1 1/2 tablespoons turbinado sugar (or light brown sugar if turbinado is not available; see On Sugar and Spice, p. 15)
1 1/2 pounds pork shoulder
1/4 cup sesame oil
2 ripe yellow bananas, sliced

Mix the garlic, ginger, bay leaves, rice vinegar, salt, soy sauce, water, pepper, and turbinado sugar in a bowl.

Cube the pork shoulder, mix well into the marinade, and leave unrefrigerated for 30 minutes. Then simmer the meat in the marinade on low heat for one hour.

Heat the toasted sesame oil in a skillet, drain the meat with a slotted spoon, and brown it in the oil. Also brown the bananas. When everything is browned, arrange the meat and bananas on plates. Discard the ginger slices and bay leaves.

Put the marinade in the skillet that browned the meat and cook it over high heat until it is reduced to about half the volume and is looking brown and a bit thickened. Pour over meat. Serve with rice.

VEGETABLE

◆ SITSARO AND TOFU (SNOW PEAS AND BEAN CURD)

about ¼ cup sesame oil
8 ounces firm bean curd (tofu) cut into
    cubes about ⅓ inch
3 garlic cloves, peeled and minced
1 white onion, thinly sliced
1 tomato, chopped
½ pound shrimp, peeled, deveined,
    and chopped

½ pound snow peas, tips and string
    along sides removed
½ cup coriander leaves (cilantro)
a large pinch of salt
3 turns of black pepper

Heat the oil in a skillet. Add the cubed bean curd, then toss the garlic into the skillet while the bean curd is browning. Once bean curd is lightly browned on all sides, add onion and then tomato. Then toss in shrimp. Add snow peas. Stir with wooden spoon for a few minutes. Just before removing from pan, add cilantro and salt and pepper.

DESSERT
◆ TROPICAL COOKIES

These cookies reflect the American influence that turns up often in the Philippines, where English has replaced Spanish as the second language.

1 short pastry recipe (see Basic
    Recipes, p. 23) plus 1 teaspoon
    baking soda
2 ripe yellow bananas
½ cup shredded coconut

1 tablespoon peeled and grated fresh
    ginger
¼ cup turbinado sugar
¼ cup candied ginger (found at most
    Asian stores)

Make a batch of short dough, but when adding the sugar, also add one teaspoon baking soda. Break the dough into two parts; use half for each recipe.

COOKIE ONE

Preheat oven to 350 degrees. Mash the bananas and mix with the shredded coconut. Mix in with dough and break into dollops and place on a baking sheet. Bake for 15 minutes, or until the cookies have puffed up but are still soft.

COOKIE TWO

Preheat oven to 350 degrees. Puree the ginger in food processor. Mix it with the dough, turbinado sugar, and small pieces of candied ginger. Break into dollops and place on baking sheet. Bake for about 20 minutes.

DRINK
◆ BUKO JUICE

This is simply the water from fresh green coconuts (see A Slightly Nutty Way to Open a Coconut, p. 19), a longtime favorite in the Philippines.

PROVENCE NIGHT

HINT: A REGION FAMOUS FOR HERBS AND SUNLIGHT.

Provence is possibly France's most loved region and that is probably because it is the sunniest region in a rainy country. The early-twentieth-century British writer Ford Maddox Ford in his 1935 book on Provence said that life is so good there that sin "would be superfluous." When I think of Provence, like most people I think of olives, aromatic herbs, garlic, and anchovies. But I also think of birds—the exotic birds from North Africa, like the great pink flamingos that fly over to fatten on the tiny brine shrimp that cluster around the salt pans at Aigues-Mortes, one of Europe's great sea-salt producers. Also the hawks and eagles and woodpeckers and the fluffy long-beaked black-and-white pied avocet, known aptly in French as the *avocette elegant*, that live in the swamps of the Camargue, still the home to wild white horses. But of course there is a lot more to this famous region immortalized in the paintings of its native son Paul Cézanne. There is the dry and rocky land with steep outcroppings covered with scrubby brush, those hilltop towns with winding streets and mountain views, sometimes clear to the Mediterranean sea.

Provence is an official region of France. There are twenty-two such regions in mainland France. Provincial governments control public schools and raise taxes for them and a few other local institutions but have considerably less power than a US state. Though provinces are usually about the size of a small New England state, they often include several cultural groups and frequently have more than one style of food within the region.

France, like most European countries, was put together over centuries from various kingdoms and duchies acquired through military conquest, treaty, or marriage. The regions often reflect these earlier nations. Provence became a part of France not by conquest but because after a series of deaths, King Louis XI of France inherited Provence in 1486.

Provence originally covered all of what is today Mediterranean France, from the Alps to the Pyrenees, but over the century bits got carved off. It still extends from Italy through about half of France's Mediterranean coast. Provençal is a distinct culture reflected in music, literature, fabric designs, food, and its own language, actually a dialect of another language called Occitan, which is still spoken in the nearby region of Languedoc. In Occitan *óc* means "yes," so *Languedoc* means "the language where they say *óc*."

While most of France is a rich green, a lushness the French pay for by living with constant rain, Provence is one of France's driest, sunniest regions, with a rocky yellow terrain covered with scrubby brush. Some of this scrubby growth is fragrant—thyme, rosemary, oregano, marjoram—the famous herbes de Provence. And this, along with the olives and olive oil typical of warm, dry Mediterranean places, characterizes the region's cooking.

APPETIZERS
◆ TOMATE FARCI

This typical Provençal dish is made with anchovies, which have historically been an important part of French Mediterranean cultures. The men would row out in small wooden-hulled boats, and the women would stay on shore curing and barreling the catch. Then, in the 1920s, the fishermen found a way to significantly increase their catch: they started mounting spotlights on the sterns of their boats, attracting the anchovies so they could easily scoop them up. This was the first of numerous practices that have led to a much smaller Mediterranean anchovy population—although it is a rapidly reproducing little fish, so its fortunes rise and fall quickly, some years seeming plentiful and others threatened with extinction.

3 ripe tomatoes
1 pound pitted black olives
4 cured anchovy fillets from a can
3 garlic cloves, minced
3 tablespoons capers
5 tablespoons olive oil
juice of ½ lemon

1 tablespoon fresh chopped basil
¾ cup toasted croutons, soaked in
    ½ cup heavy cream
9 small toast rounds
6 marinated artichoke hearts
about 6 ounces marinated anchovies

Preheat oven to 350 degrees.

Cut centers out of ripe tomatoes.

To prepare the tapenade (this black olive condiment can also be found in jars, often imported from Provence), spin the olives, anchovy fillets, garlic cloves, capers, olive oil, and lemon juice in a food processor for about 30 seconds—enough for it to be pastelike but still a little coarse and chunky.

Put half the tapenade in a mixing bowl. Add the basil and cream-soaked croutons. Stuff inside the tomatoes and bake for thirty minutes.

Serve surrounded by toast rounds with extra tapenade, some marinated artichoke hearts, and some marinated anchovies.

◆◆ BRANDADE DE MORUE

I did not make this Provençal appetizer on Provence Night, but I often serve it to family and guests. I first started making the dish when I was researching my *Cod* book. In it I wrote:

> Some believe *brandade de morue* began in Nimes, but it is more commonly associated with Provence. It was originally called *branlade*, meaning "something which is pummeled," which it is . . . Since salt cod has become expensive, potatoes have been added—*brandade de morue parmentier*. Antoine-Auguste Parmentier was an eighteenth-century officer who popularized the potato in the French Army, and his name has ever since meant "with potatoes." In 1886 *brandade* was decreed an official part of the enlisted man's mess in the French Army. As the price of cod has risen, so has the amount of potatoes in the *brandade*. Sometimes the dish simply seems like fishy mashed potatoes.

Good brandade has no potatoes. My favorite recipe for it was published in Marseilles in 1910 by the great nineteenth-century Provençal chef J. B. Reboul. It is particularly good because of the inclusion of the skin. The only change I make is that where he calls for milk, he is talking about a much more cream-rich product than most of today's homogenized milk, so I substitute light cream—though you should keep in mind Reboul's gentle advice: "If we were health advisers, we might counsel you to use this dish in moderation."

Also while he suggests twelve hours of soaking, I find most salt cod requires about twenty-four hours soaking, or even more. (For soaking instructions, see On Salt Cod, p. 19.) Reboul wanted the cod very salty for this dish, but twelve hours' soaking usually leaves the fish almost unbearably salty.

There are only four ingredients:

½ pound dried hard salt cod with skin
 still on
1 cup olive oil

6 garlic cloves, minced
1 cup light cream

After soaking the salt cod, cook it in simmering water with the skin left on. After about 20 minutes cooking, place it in a skillet with the olive oil and minced garlic. Reboul then tells us to work it with a wooden spoon, but I find it more effective to use an old-fashioned potato masher. Work in, a little at a time, light cream and then olive oil, alternating the two in the skillet over low heat until it is a smooth, well-incorporated spread. Serve with toasted crusty bread.

MAIN COURSE

◆ GRILLED LAMB WITH HERBES DE PROVENCE

Herbes de Provence is a contemporary commercial label for packages of herbs popular in Provence. Until recently there was no set combination, but rosemary, thyme, and savory are most typical. Others can be added.

3 loin lamb chops
3 generous pinches of herbes de
    Provence

3 pinches of salt

Sprinkle the herbs generously on the lamb chops with a pinch of salt, then grill or broil them under high heat to your taste. For me, twenty minutes grilling a thick chop is about perfect, still red in the center, but others may prefer longer. Serve with ratatouille.

Tomatoes and herbs

◆ RATATOUILLE

Ratatouille, like herbes de Provence, is a contemporary packaging of a traditional combination. Perhaps such commercialization occurred because of the high volume of tourism in Provence. The word originated in the eighteenth century from the verb *touiller*, which means to stir, and it referred to a country stew. But for the past eighty years or so, *ratatouille* has come to mean a sauté of typical Provençal vegetables.

1 cup olive oil

3 medium-sized ripe red tomatoes, cut in quarters

1 large unpeeled eggplant, cut in cubes

1 large zucchini squash, unpeeled and cut in disks

1 red bell pepper, cut in strips

1 green bell pepper, cut in strips

½ yellow onion, thinly sliced

6 garlic cloves, thinly sliced

a large pinch of herbes de Provence

a large pinch of salt

4 turns of black pepper

Preheat oven to 400 degrees. Heat some olive oil in a large skillet and add the tomatoes. Toss lightly for about five minutes until the tomatoes are slightly wilted, and then place the tomatoes in an ovenproof casserole dish. Add olive oil as needed to the skillet. Add the eggplant to the skillet and toss for about five minutes and place the eggplant in the casserole dish as well. Add the rest of the ingredients to the skillet with more oil if needed and sauté about five minutes until the onions and peppers are wilted and the garlic turns golden. Add to the casserole dish and mix everything thoroughly; then place the casserole in the oven. Bake for ten minutes.

DESSERTS
◆◆◆ CHOCOLATE RASPBERRY SOUFFLÉ

Okay, this is not so much a Provençal dessert as a French one, but there is a lot of French food in Provence. Besides, my family loves this dish, and I like to make them happy. Soufflés seem to have developed in Paris in the late eighteenth century—but then again, everything in France appears to have come from Paris, because everyone with an idea took it there. The great eighteenth-century restaurateur Antoine Beauvilliers, who was one of the first to make soufflés, was Parisian, not from Provence. If you are a stickler for authenticity, an alternative is offered below.

6 tablespoons unsalted butter
1½ cups granulated sugar
4 whole eggs, separated
4 tablespoons flour
1½ cups heavy cream
1 split vanilla bean

5 ounces dark semisweet chocolate,
    grated
1 cup raspberry preserves
1 pint fresh raspberries
½ cup confectioners' sugar

Preheat oven to 350 degrees.

Thoroughly brush a soufflé dish with melted butter and dust its sides and bottom with granulated sugar, tapping the dish upside down against your palm to knock off excess. Make a collar with folded aluminum foil that rises two inches above the height of the soufflé dish.

In a mixing bowl, beat 2 egg yolks and ¼ cup sugar.

Melt 2 tablespoons butter in pot. With a wooden spoon, slowly incorporate an equal amount of flour until you have a white paste. Add ¾ cup heavy cream and 1 vanilla bean and heat, stirring to make it thick until it begins to boil and rise, and then quickly pour into the bowl with egg yolks and beat together. Scrape the vanilla seeds off the pods with a spoon, stirring them back into the mixture, and throw out the pods.

Add the chocolate and melt it into the mixture.

Whip 2 egg whites in mixer with 2 tablespoons sugar, dip your finger in, and when a peak is formed that holds its place and doesn't collapse, begin to fold the egg whites into the chocolate mixture.

Folding is very important. Add one third of the egg whites, slowly turning the bowl with your left hand, while with your right take a spatula, dig deep into the bowl, and move the contents gently up and over. Keep doing this as the bowl turns until there are no pockets of egg whites, then add another third, and then the last. Folding is much slower and also more vertical in motion than stirring. It takes practice, but it is a great skill for kids to learn because they will take pride in it when they get it right. Put the folded mixture into the soufflé dish, which should be half full.

Now repeat the process: in a bowl beat the 2 remaining egg yolks with ¼ cup sugar, then melt the butter and stir in the flour and cream, and combine once the mixture rises. This time, instead of chocolate, add the raspberry preserves. Whip the remaining egg whites and sugar and carefully fold into the raspberry mixture.

Gently place the fresh raspberries on top of the chocolate mixture in the soufflé dish, then cover with the raspberry mixture. It should come up to the beginning of the aluminum collar. Carefully place in oven and bake for almost an hour until the soufflé rises in a dome above the collar. Remove. Place the confectioners' sugar in a strainer and thoroughly dust the top with sugar by tapping the strainer. Unpeel the aluminum collar and serve soufflé immediately, scooping out portions with a large serving spoon.

TALIA: *The Art of Separating an Egg*

(When you read this you will understand why washing hands is strongly recommended before cooking.)

It's fun. You get to do something that, if it weren't part of cooking, would be considered weird. It's messy. Try to think of any other time you can squish and just go crazy, make a mess, and not feel bad or in trouble. If you're a kid, that's a feeling that is hard to resist.

First you crack the egg over a bowl. Let the entire gooey mess from inside the egg drip into your hand and throw out the shell. Then carefully pour the goo into your other hand, then back into the first hand. Just keep doing this, passing the yolk from one hand to the other, and feel the groove of the white oozing through your fingers and into the bowl. Soon you will have nothing in your hand other than the shiny yellow ball of the yolk. You've separated the egg—ta-da!

◆◆ STRAWBERRY TART

An easier and more authentically Provençal dessert is *tarte aux frais*. Provence, especially the region Carpentras, is famous for its strawberries. I created this recipe based on a tip from Nice mayor Jacques Médecin. Combined, Médecin and his father ran Nice for sixty-two years. Médecin was passionate about everything Niçoise and much preferred talking about the local food—he even published a cookbook—to talking about the disappearance of city funds, which eventually led to his fleeing to Uruguay, where he died in 1998. According to Médecin, "Fruit tarts are made everywhere in France. What makes them special in Nice is the perfume of orange-blossom water."

2 cups flour	a splash of vanilla extract
1 pound butter	2 ounces orange-blossom water
2 pinches of salt	1 cup heavy cream
1½ cups sugar	1 vanilla bean, split
5 eggs (1 whole, 4 yolks)	1 pound fresh strawberries

Preheat oven to 400 degrees.

In a mixer place the flour, then add the butter in one-inch pieces, beating with the palette until the mixture looks like coarse meal. Add salt and 1 cup sugar. Continue mixing and beat in one egg, the vanilla extract, and 1 ounce of the orange-blossom water. The mixture should now be a solid dough. Press it into a French-style tart pan, the kind where the bottom pops out. Place dough in ball in the center, flatten toward the edges, and press the dough against the ridged outer ring.

Beat the yolks in a bowl with ½ cup sugar. Cook the heavy cream in a saucepan with the vanilla bean and 1 ounce orange-blossom water. Heat until it boils and starts to rise, then pour over egg-yolk mixture. Scrape vanilla beans with a spoon, stir in the seeds, and remove the husks. If the mixture is not thick, put it back in a pot over medium heat and beat constantly until it thickens. Do not overcook, or it will curdle. Take it off the heat the instant it thickens. Pour into tart. Bake at 400 degrees for 10 minutes and then 30 minutes at 350 degrees. Let it cool, then carefully push tart out of the ring. Put confectioners' sugar in a strainer and tap it as you move it around the tart until the top is white. Arrange fresh strawberries over the custard and chill.

DRINK
◆ CANTALOUPE JUICE

1 cantaloupe   honey
water

Cavaillon, the wonderful little sweet and juicy melons whose flesh resembles cantaloupe, are named for the rugged subregion where they are grown. Though they have a more colorful skin and are much smaller than cantaloupes, that they are related is confirmed not only by the similar taste but by the fact that the original cavaillon seeds brought to Provence in the fourteenth century came from the Italian town of Cantalupo.

Puree ¼ cup of ripe cantaloupe in a food processor or blender with an equal amount of water plus some honey the amount depending on how sweet you want the drink. Strain and chill before serving.

On the other hand, for adults there are many excellent but not famous—so not overly expensive—Provençal red wines, plus the best rosés in the world.

KAZAKHSTAN NIGHT

HINT: THE LARGEST LANDLOCKED COUNTRY IN THE WORLD.

This is how the game of International Night works. Sometimes Talia's finger lands on a place such as Provence that I know well and has an extensive and celebrated cuisine. My struggle is how to choose from all the possibilities. Then sometimes she lands on a place such as Kazakhstan, where I have never been, where the cuisine seems limited and little is written about it. Now my struggle is to come up with a meal. I would need a statistician, an expert on the laws of probability, to explain why, without exaggeration, Talia's finger lands on Kazakhstan at least once in every five spins. Does this have to do with its latitude in relationship to her height and the height of the globe? I don't know. Or is it because with more than 2.7 million square miles of territory, it is a fairly large country? On the other hand, Russia is much larger, and it took more than fifty spins before we landed there. The third time we spun the globe, Talia's finger landed on Kazakhstan, and since that was the first time, we were committed to, as Talia always liked to say, "Introducing—KAZAKHSTAN!" Miraculously, reading up on the country and its culture and cuisine, I came up with several delicious dishes.

I should announce up front that my Kazakh dishes are not 100 percent authentic, as instead of the traditional mutton or horse meat, I switched to lamb or beef. Kazakhs are proud horsemen with a tradition of roaming the wilds on horseback. In fact, the word *Kazakh*, which means free spirit, relates to their image on horseback. Horse meat, along with mutton, is one of the few meats available in Kazakhstan. Horse meat, though, is not commercialized in the United States and is hard to come by. The French, until very recently, always had one shop in every market area that exclusively sold horse meat. The meat is dark and bloody and looks extremely meaty, if you think of meat as a bad word. Its chief virtue was that it was cheap. Not cheap enough: even in France it is disappearing. As for mutton, the reason sheep are slaughtered as lambs is that if you wait until they are grown, the meat, mutton, is not very good. So where I saw horse I thought beef, and mutton became lamb.

The Kazakh language is Turkic, from the same family as Turkish and numerous other central Asian languages. But Russians have been an important part of Kazakh history since the early nineteenth century. Kazakhstan did not become independent from Russia until 1991, and a fourth of the population is still ethnically Russian. The Russian influence can be seen in the food—for example, in gutap.

APPETIZER
◆◆ GUTAP-KAZAKH

1 cup flour
½ pound butter
2 tablespoons salt
warm water, as needed
3 sprigs parsley, chopped

3 sprigs dill, chopped
3 garlic cloves, peeled and chopped
1 cup canola oil
sour cream

Place the flour in a mixer with dough hook attachment. Add the butter and salt. Beat until the mixture is the consistency of coarse meal. Slowly add warm water while beating until the mixture becomes balled up into workable dough on the hook. Roll the dough into 5-inch-long ovals. Sprinkle the chopped parsley, dill, and garlic on the center of each oval. Wet the edges and fold over the ovals and seal the edges by pressing. Heat canola oil very hot, and fry the pastries on one side until slightly golden, then flip them and fry the other side. Drain on paper towels. Serve with sour cream.

MAIN COURSE
◆ BASTURMA

1 pound lamb shoulder
2 cups red wine vinegar
1 yellow onion, thinly sliced

¼ cup vegetable oil
2 fresh tomatoes, sliced
1 cucumber, peeled and sliced

This dish is supposed to be made with mutton marinated in apple cider vinegar, but, trust me, use lamb: cube it and marinate it in red wine vinegar with thinly sliced yellow onion.

After at least 5 hours—overnight would be good—sauté the lamb in vegetable oil, though if you really want to cheat, olive oil would be better. Cook to whatever color you like lamb. Then remove to a platter and add sliced tomatoes and the peeled, sliced cucumber.

DESSERT
◆ CHAK-CHAK

2 eggs
2¼ cups sugar
5 tablespoons butter

½ to 1 cup flour
½ cup water
½ cup honey

Beat eggs with ¼ cup of the sugar. Add 2 tablespoons butter, melted. Slowly work in enough flour for it to become a dough. Let the dough rest for 40 minutes.

Roll out dough flat and slice into noodles. Melt the rest of the butter in a skillet and sauté the noodles.

In a pot, dissolve the rest of the sugar in the water. Stir until dissolved into a syrup. Add the honey. Set aside a glass of cold water. From a wooden spoon, drip one drop of the syrup into the water. The drop should roll into a soft, malleable ball. If it doesn't form a ball, the syrup is not hot enough; if the ball is hard, cool down the syrup. When the syrup forms a soft ball, toss the noodles in the syrup and spread them out on a serving plate to cool.

DRINK
◆ PEACH KEFIR

3 ripe peaches
3 cups kefir
a splash of vanilla extract

a pinch of sugar
a pinch of powdered cinnamon

Puree fresh peaches and mix with kefir. Add vanilla extract, sugar, and cinnamon. Mix well.

SWEDEN NIGHT

HINT: A LAND THAT SERVES UP PRIZES AND BURIES FISH.

During my one trip to Sweden, to the Gothenburg Book Fair, I landed in Stockholm first and traveled across Sweden to Gothenburg on the opposite side of the country. Fortunately Sweden is a long and narrow country and it is not too distant a journey from Stockholm, on the Baltic Sea across from Estonia, to Gothenburg, between Denmark and Norway and at the beginning of the Skagerrak, which opens to the North Sea across from Great Britain.

Along the way I ate a lot of traditional dishes involving pork and a lot of salted food. Salt has always been important to cold northern countries with a short growing season and a long winter to provision. Nobel Prize–winning poet Tomas Tranströmer wrote that Sweden in winter looked like "a bleached unrigged ship." The weather is not suitable for drying sea salt, which is only economically viable if evaporated in the sun. The Swedes acquired a Caribbean island, Saint Barthélemy, for the purpose of making sea salt, but the meager amount of salt produced there was mostly used up in curing herring shipped back to the island to feed slaves.

People were always looking for light salt cures to conserve salt. By the sixteenth century, Baltic herring was given a light cure and became known as surströmming, which is still a Swedish delicacy. One way of preserving fish without using a great deal of salt was to lightly salt it and then bury it in the ground. This was the origin of gravlax, literally buried salmon. Most modern Swedes would probably not relish this dish if it had not been modernized through the use of refrigeration. It is also now cured with both salt and sugar. Swedes are so passionate about the salt-sugar blend that they have their own word for it, *sockersaltad*. It is used not only for salmon and herring but for cakes and even candy, especially salt lakrits, salted licorice candy, which is a Swedish passion.

APPETIZER
◆ GRAVLAX

1 medium salmon fillet (a wild-caught
    salmon, such as Alaskan sockeye,
    would be excellent)
½ cup coarse salt

½ cup sugar
½ cup chopped fresh dill
1 tablespoon ground white pepper

Take the salmon fillet and place it skin side down. Cover with salt, sugar, chopped dill, and ground white pepper. Place a second piece on top with the skin up. Wrap the fish well in plastic wrap. Put a platter or board on top with something heavy on top of it. Press like this in the refrigerator for 48 hours. Eat with dark rye bread and butter.

MAIN COURSE
◆ PORK AND APPLES

1½ pounds pork shoulder
4 tablespoons butter
3 apples, sliced

a large pinch of salt
3 turns of black pepper

Cube pork shoulder. Sauté in butter over medium heat with apples, salt, and pepper until pork is cooked and apples caramelized—about 30 minutes. Boiled potatoes go well with this dish if you like.

VEGETABLE
◆ RED CABBAGE

3 tablespoons butter
1 white onion, thinly sliced
3 apples, peeled, cored, and chopped
½ tablespoon cloves

1 teaspoon allspice
½ head red cabbage, shredded
¼ cup brown sugar
½ cup apple cider vinegar

Melt butter in a skillet over low heat. Add onion, apples, cloves, and allspice, and sauté together. Add shredded cabbage, brown sugar, and vinegar. Simmer until the cabbage is wilted, approximately five minutes.

DESSERT
◆ GIFTA

2 cups bread crumbs
½ cup melted butter
1 cup heavy cream, whipped

1 cup cranberry sauce with whole
  cranberries

Mix bread crumbs with melted butter, setting aside half a teaspoon, and layer in bottom of dessert cups, one for each person. Add a layer of whipped cream to each cup, then a layer of cranberry sauce, setting aside a few whole cranberries for garnish, then a layer of whipped cream. Dust with bread crumbs and place a cranberry on top of each dessert. Chill in the refrigerator 24 hours.

Cranberries

DRINK
◆ GLÖG

This is drunk both warm and cold throughout Scandinavia. Heat unsweetened berry juice and add cinnamon sticks, a few cloves, and a few cardamom seeds. Sugar can be added to whatever sweetness you enjoy. After being heated but not boiled for one hour, it can be served warm or chilled.

NIGER NIGHT

HINT: A COUNTRY NAMED AFTER THE SECOND LONGEST RIVER IN THE WORLD TO HAVE A COUNTRY NAMED AFTER IT.

When I was living in Paris in the early 1980s, the *International Herald Tribune* asked me to do a series of articles on West Africa. The editor suggested that as a starting point, I speak in Paris to the ambassadors of the various countries I would be visiting. The only one of these conversations that I still remember was with Niger's ambassador to France. We met in his embassy, which was very modest by Paris standards, and we spoke French, a language with which we were both comfortable but was not the first language of either of us, which is a situation that often leads to accidents. His government, a military dictatorship, had withstood a coup d'état attempt only days before. I thought that to ease the tense conversation, I would talk about tourism. Governments always like to talk about tourism, and West African coun-tries at the time were trying to build tourism, particularly with French tourists. But Niger's ambassador to France did not want to talk about tourism. He assured me that there was "absolutely no tourism in Niger." I was startled at how emphatically he stated this. But then I realized that while I was talking about *tourisme* he was talking about *terrorisme*.

Largely desert, Niger is one of the poorest countries in the world. Goods are brought in by boat along the Niger River to the capital, Niamey. The only river longer than the Niger to have a country named after it is the Congo.

There are limited products available and the cuisine is simple. As in most of West Africa, mangoes and pineapples and peanuts are plentiful. The chicken-and-peanut-butter dish below is typical of a number of West African countries.

Peanuts

SALAD
◆ MANGO SALAD

2 mangoes, sliced
10 slices fresh pineapple

½ cup apricot nectar
juice of 6 limes

Arrange slices of ripe mango and pineapple on dishes. Mix apricot nectar with lime juice and pour over the sliced fruit.

MAIN COURSE
◆ PEANUT CHICKEN

4 skinless chicken breasts
3 cups chicken stock (see Basic
    Recipes, p. 24)
5 garlic cloves, peeled and chopped
½ yellow onion, thinly sliced
½ cup peanut oil
½ cup tomato sauce #1 (see Basic
    Recipes, p. 25)

¾ cup peanut butter (preferably hand
    ground, nonhomogenized, and
    without additives)
½ to 1 whole Scotch bonnet pepper,
    chopped

Poach the chicken breasts in chicken stock for 20 minutes. In a skillet, sauté the garlic and onion in peanut oil. Remove chicken from pot and mix broth with tomato sauce, peanut butter, and Scotch bonnet pepper and cook on low heat, stirring with a wooden spoon until smooth. Add the sautéed onions and garlic. Pour over chicken and serve with rice.

VEGETABLE
◆ GREENS PILI PILI

If you cannot find collard greens, turnip greens or beet greens can be substituted. The pili pili sauce can be made in advance and kept for a long time in a jar.

5 tomatoes
½ cup white onion, minced
3 garlic cloves, minced
½ to 1 whole Scotch bonnet pepper,
   depending on your tolerance for
   pain
1 tablespoon premade horseradish
   sauce
1 pound collard greens, thoroughly
   washed
¼ cup water

Cut tomatoes in half and burn the skin side either on a grill flame or a stove flame. Let them cool and pull the skins off. Quarter the tomatoes and remove the seeds and gel. Chop the tomatoes and add all the other ingredients except the collard greens and water. Pour into a jar. This is the pili pili sauce.

Heat the water until it steams, add the collard greens, and cook at less than a boil for about five minutes, or until the greens are wilted. Serve hot with pili pili sauce on top.

DESSERT
◆ CAAKARI, CHAKERY, OR THIAKRY

2 cups couscous
2 cups water
a large pinch of salt
4 tablespoons butter
1 cup heavy cream
1 cup sour cream
a splash of vanilla extract
½ cup sugar
½ cup crushed raw pineapple
a small handful of raisins
2 sprigs of mint

Cook couscous in water until the water is absorbed, about five minutes. Add salt and butter. Stir well and let cool. Mix in the cream, sour cream, vanilla extract, sugar, pineapple, and raisins. Chill a few hours or, better, overnight. Garnish with mint leaves.

DRINK
◆ TART APRICOT NECTAR

Mix apricot nectar with lime juice, as in the salad, but at a ratio of 3 parts apricot nectar to 1 part lime juice.

CHINA NIGHT

HINT: THE BIRTHPLACE OF PAPER, NATURAL GAS, GUNPOWDER, PASTA, MOVABLE TYPE, AND THE SPINNING WHEEL.

Although the legend of Marco Polo bringing pasta back from China and introducing it to Italians is probably not true—there was pasta in Italy before Marco Polo—the Chinese probably made it before anyone else. They were certainly the first to make paper, to use paper money, to make gunpowder—a staggering list of inventions. When I was in rural China, peasants in fields sometimes called me over with my translator to say, "We invented many things." Then they would start listing them.

The first time I went to China, I arrived in Beijing on the train from Moscow. In Siberia three Frenchmen got on and I befriended them. We all agreed that when we arrived in Beijing, our primary goal would be to sample real Chinese food. But how would we order? Since my friends spoke only French and I spoke several languages, they assumed that I could conquer any linguistic hurdles despite the fact, as I kept explaining, that I spoke not a word of any of the several Chinese languages. We got to our first restaurant in time for lunch, a busy little place with fish tanks from which to select your meal while it was still alive. No one spoke anything but Chinese. We were seated at a large round table and handed menus in Chinese. A waiter walked up to us, and the Frenchmen looked at me.

"Tsingtao," I said in what I imagined to be an impressive accent. The waiter left imme-diately and returned with beer for everyone. The Frenchmen were properly impressed, but all I had done was order us Tsingtao beer, a brand I had learned of in Chinese restaurants in the US.

I was out of tricks, so we started drifting around the restaurant pointing to foods on other tables that looked good. In this manner we ordered a wonderful meal. There is no place in the world with better food or more food-conscious people than China.

But the next time I went to China, which was to research my *Salt* book, I hired a trans-lator, and in this way I could talk to Chinese chefs about their food. These conversations were often about the complex Chinese ideas of how to put together a meal. Balance is the key. According to Chinese cooking, there are five flavors that must be balanced: *la*, the burn of hot peppers; *tian*, sweetness; *suan*, sourness; *xian*, saltiness; and *ku*, bitterness. Each flavor must be enriched with others. Saltiness enhances sweetness or sourness. Salty and hot is another favored combination, which is why soy sauce with red peppers is sold commercially. In Sich-uan, where some dishes are extremely *la*, spicy, only a *tian* dish, something very sweet, can save your burning mouth.

In addition to the balance of flavors, there must be a balance between hot and cold foods, based not on their temperature but on their es-sential attributes. Fatty meat, spicy food, and alcohol are all considered hot. Vegetables and fruit are cold.

Most of these ideas also existed in the West, in Europe, but have now vanished. Once the seventeenth-century French removed sweet from the main meal and started serving it as a special course afterward, the multicourse meal took hold in the West. Ideas of hot and cold hung on longer. Although in China the idea of hot and cold is said to stem from the fourth century BC belief that the world operates with two opposing forces, yin and yang, in Greece Hippocrates had written about warm and cold food a century earlier. And some indigenous Americans had this belief in hot and cold foods before the arrival of Europeans. The Roman Catholic Church kept vestiges of this idea until the twentieth century. Hot food was thought to lead to lustful thoughts and so was banned on holy days, which in the Middle Ages was half the days of the year. By modern times, all that remained of these beliefs was the eating of fish rather than meat on Fridays, which has also now been abandoned.

Most of the dishes for China Night are designed to be served at the same time. Only the soup is a separate course at the end of the meal. The dinner moves from a bite of one to a bite of the next. In restaurants in China, the meal is often served on a revolving tabletop like a big lazy Susan. In China, as opposed to most Chinese restaurants outside of China, rice is generally not served with a meal unless it is a specific part of a dish. Rice on the side is generally for the very poor. Our menu combines dishes that are spicy, sweet, salty, or bitter—*la*, *tian*, *xian*, and *ku*—four out of the five flavors. It is not unusual for a meal to miss one or two of the five flavors There are four hot dishes and one cold one (tofu and peanuts). A grander meal might have two courses—one for cold foods and one for hot.

MAIN COURSE
◆◆ HUIGUOROU

This dish was taught to me by Huang Wengen, a cooking instructor at what at the time was the only accredited cooking school in China, in Chengdu, a small city by Chinese standards of white tiled modern buildings and streets full of bicycles that is the capital of Sichuan Province. The recipe calls for a pork leg, an uncured ham that is boiled and then sliced perpendicular to the bone. This cut is often hard to find, but other pork cuts, such as a loin thinly sliced, will also work. The recipe calls for douban, which is a paste of fermented beans and spices, and dousi, which is a black paste from fermented yellow beans. Both can be bought in Chinese stores or ordered online. This is a Sichuan dish, and Sichuan soy sauce is dark and thick. Do not use Japanese soy sauce; use the heaviest Chinese soy sauce you can find.

The original recipe calls for MSG. The Chinese do not understand why Americans do not want to use MSG. Liu Tong, another instructor at the school in Chengdu, told me, "It is not a chemical. It is made from the fermentation of cereal." This is true. MSG is fermented wheat gluten or sugar beet molasses. But some people are allergic. Don't worry, though; the recipe works very well without the MSG.

¼ cup sesame oil
1½ pounds pork, thinly sliced
2 tablespoons douban
2 tablespoons dousi
a pinch of sugar
2 big splashes of Chinese soy sauce
small handful garlic greens (or onion greens)

In a wok or large skillet, heat sesame oil over high heat and then reduce to medium. Stir-fry the pork until it begins to curl. Add the douban and dousi. Stir with a wooden spoon until it becomes a reddish sauce, then add a pinch of sugar and a large shot of soy sauce.

Before serving, sprinkle chopped garlic greens on top. If you can't find them, onion greens will also work.

◆ BROCCOLI

Chinese broccoli, *kai-lan,* tastes like a bitter version of the vegetable we know. If you do not have a Chinese store nearby, broccolini is a suitable substitute; it tastes like a cross between kai-lan and broccoli. Or you can substitute broccoli rabe.

½ cup canola oil
1 tablespoon Chinese soy sauce
2 slices ginger, peeled and minced
1 tablespoon mirin (see On Sugar and
    Spice, p. 12)

2 garlic cloves, peeled and minced
1 pound Chinese broccoli

Heat the oil in a skillet or wok until hot. Toss in all the ingredients and stir quickly until the broccoli becomes a bright color. Transfer to a serving platter.

◆ HOT SHRIMP AND NOODLES

5 ounces very thin Chinese noodles
about ¼ cup sesame oil
12 shrimp (preferably whole with the
    heads still on)
4 garlic cloves, peeled and sliced

chopped red chili pepper (as hot as
    you want, but in China this would
    be very hot—see On Sugar and
    Spice, p. 9).
8 snow peas, tips snapped off and
    strings pulled out
2 green onions, chopped

Boil a pot of water and cook noodles for about a minute, until limp. Strain in colander.
In a wok or large skillet, heat sesame oil. Add shrimp, garlic, and chili pepper. When almost done—a few minutes stirring—add snow peas and green onions. Place over cooked noodles in a serving bowl.

◆◆ TIAN SHAO BAI

Literally this means "sweet white stew." It is a popular Sichuan dish, and though the idea of sweet and fat together may seem unappealing, over the course of a spicy Sichuan meal it is the perfect antidote to a burning mouth. Within a meal, a bite at a time, it is a delight, even though you would never eat it by itself.

First you must buy or make red bean paste. It is sold in Chinese stores or available to order online. To make it, you need red beans. You could use a number of types of red beans, but the right one is the tiny, red oblong bean called *adzuki*, which can be found in Chinese or Asian specialty stores or online. Soak the beans overnight and then simmer for more than an hour until they are soft. Run in a food processor with half as much brown sugar. Sauté the paste in vegetable oil while stirring with a wooden spoon until all the liquid cooks off the top and it is thick. Then let it cool.

The Chinese have their own style of air-dried bacon, but you could also use a smoked, thickly sliced bacon.

2 cups red bean paste
6 thick slices Chinese or smoked
    bacon

1 cup uncooked sticky rice

Spread bean paste thickly on three strips of bacon, cover each with another strip, and broil so that they are cooked but not crisp. In Sichuan this is served over sweet rice, also sometimes called sticky rice or glutinous rice or *naw mai*. It has very stumpy-looking grains and is not sweet but is so named because it goes with sweet food. Soak the rice in cold water for 3 minutes with the grains completely covered before turning on heat. Cook for about 10 minutes at a medium heat until the water is gone except for bubbles dancing between the grains on the surface. Turn off heat, cover the pot, and let stand covered another 5 minutes.

◆ TOFU AND PEANUTS

5-6 mustard greens leaves
½ cup peanut oil
¾ cup raw peanuts
1 firm bean curd cake (tofu), cut into
    rectangles about 1 inch by ½ inch

2 cups coriander leaves (cilantro),
    chopped
¼ cup Chinese soy sauce
a pinch of sugar
2 tablespoons toasted sesame oil

Using tongs, dip mustard greens leaves in boiling water one by one for only a second each. Place on serving platter.

Heat peanut oil in skillet until very hot. Add raw peanuts. Stir for 1 minute, then turn off heat but continue stirring until the peanuts turn from white to golden. Then place them on paper towels.

Reheat the oil and put in bean curd. Cook on each side until golden and then place on paper towels as well.

When well drained, place the fried bean curd on top of the mustard greens on platter. Stir-fry the coriander very quickly in the hot oil. Remove the instant the leaves brighten and put them over the bean curd. Place peanuts on top.

Mix together the soy sauce, sugar, and sesame oil to make a dressing. Drizzle this over the dish.

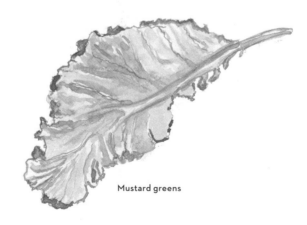

Mustard greens

◆ BOK CHOY IN CHICKEN STOCK

Chinese meals do not end with a sweet dessert, but after putting your mouth through its paces from sweet to spicy, a simple soup such as chopped bok choy in chicken stock can be enjoyed at the end of the meal. Bok choy is in the cabbage family, and so while it bears little resemblance to Western cabbage, it is often referred to in the West as "Chinese cabbage." In Mandarin it is called *pak choy*, which means "white vegetable," and it is a staple in most parts of China. The best bok choy is picked young, when it is smaller and whiter.

Simply heat the chicken stock (see Basic Recipes, p. 24) and add chopped bok choy.

HAWAII NIGHT

HINT: ONE OF ONLY TWO INTERNATIONALLY RECOGNIZED INDEPENDENT NATIONS THAT BECAME US STATES.

The other, by the way, is Texas. Hawaii was granted independence in 1900, but an oligarchy of landowners from the US ruled, importing cheap foreign labor, until the laborers, angry about their mistreatment, gained control. Hawaiian food, like its culture, is a blend of Polynesian, Asian, and American influences.

A confession: I have been to forty-nine states. Hawaii is the only one I have missed. Perhaps by the time you read this I will have corrected the matter, since I am under intense pressure from Talia, who has longed to go there since she was five years old.

So when her finger landed on the Hawaiian Islands, she was very happy. At least she could go to Hawaii for one evening. It was a good evening. For Marian and me, the highlight was ahi poke. Talia liked it too: the popularity of sushi has accustomed a lot of American kids to eating raw fish. But for Talia, the best part of the night was chocolate haupia pie—and our own Hawaiian punch.

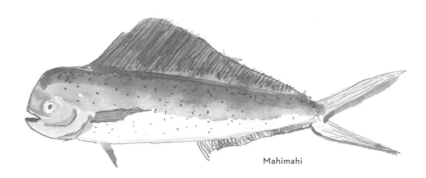
Mahimahi

PICKLE
◆ TAKUWAN

This is pickled daikon, a Japanese standard that is also popular in Hawaii. It must be made at least three days in advance. Daikon, a Japanese word meaning "large root," is the most abundantly produced vegetable in Japan, which is why, though it is grown all over Asia and even in Texas and has many names, it is usually referred to in the US by its Japanese name. In Japan, daikons are grown to enormous size. I once saw a woman by the roadside in Japan selling a daikon that was almost a yard tall: she was only slightly taller. Although it was brought to Hawaii by the Japanese, it is generally agreed that daikons did not originate in Japan—little did—and candidates for authorship range from China to the Mediterranean. Daikons are a dream health food. They barely have any calories, are loaded with vitamin C, and are said to improve digestion.

¾ cup water
½ cup sugar
4 tablespoons salt
¼ cup white vinegar

2 cups daikon, peeled and chopped
    into ¾-inch pieces
chopped dried red chili pepper
    according to taste (see On Sugar
    and Spice, p. 9)

Heat water with sugar, salt, and vinegar until salt and sugar are dissolved. Then let the mixture cool. Place the daikon and red peppers in a pickling jar, pour the cooled liquid over them, and tighten the lid on the jar.

APPETIZER
◆ AHI POKE

2 tablespoons sesame seeds
1 pound very high quality yellowtail
    tuna, cubed
2 green onions, chopped

2 teaspoons cayenne pepper
2 teaspoons toasted sesame oil
5 tablespoons Japanese soy sauce

Toast the sesame seeds in the broiler of a toaster oven until slightly brown. Add them to the fish along with the other ingredients. Mix well and refrigerate for several hours before serving.

SALADS
◆ OGONORI AND CUCUMBER SALAD

Ogonori, in Hawaii often called ogo or the Hawaiian name, *limu manauea*, is a delicate seaweed with pinkish filaments available in stores that sell Chinese, Japanese, or Hawaiian products, or from Tao Nature International or other online retailers. It is usually sold salted, which makes it ready for use in this dish.

3 cucumbers
¼ cup salt
1 cup ogonori
¼ cup rice vinegar

½ tablespoon fresh ginger root,
    peeled and minced
2 tablespoons sugar

Slice the cucumbers, place them on a plate, cover with the salt, and let sit unrefrigerated for 30 minutes. In the meantime, boil a pot of water. Place the seaweed in a strainer and plunge it into the boiling water. Remove it after a few seconds and let it drain well. Chop it into half-inch pieces.

Mix vinegar, ginger, and sugar in a bowl. Drain the water from the cucumber and press the slices a bit with your fingers to squeeze out excess water, then rub off excess salt. Pour vinegar mixture over cucumbers in a serving dish. Mix in the seaweed.

◆ WATERCRESS SALAD

This is an alternative to ogo and cucumber if you cannot find ogonori. Rachel Laudan, in her wonderful book *The Food of Paradise*, offers a similar recipe with wilted watercress, which is accomplished by quickly dipping the watercress in boiling water and then squeezing the water out of it. This is probably closer to the traditional dish, but we prefer the watercress fresh and crisp.

1 tablespoon sesame seeds
1 pound watercress, broken into
    pieces
1 tablespoon sugar

3 tablespoons Japanese soy sauce
1 tablespoon mirin (see On Sugar and
    Spice, p. 12)

Lightly toast the sesame seeds and then mix together all of the ingredients.

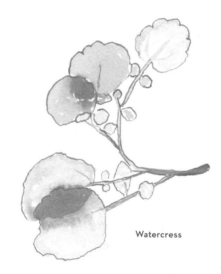

Watercress

MAIN COURSE
◆ MACADAMIA-CRUSTED MAHIMAHI WITH PAPAYA SAUCE

Mahimahi used to be called dolphin fish in the US, but confusion with the mammal of the same name upset people, so the Hawaiian name is now commonly used.

1½ pounds mahimahi fillet
about ½ cup flour
3 eggs, beaten
3 cups crushed macadamia nuts
½ cup canola oil
1 large mango

1 small papaya
about 2 cups chicken stock (see Basic Recipes, p. 24)
a large pinch of cayenne pepper
¼ cup heavy cream

Cover the fish in flour, dip it in the eggs, and cover it in macadamia nuts. Fry it in the oil for about 5 minutes on each side or until golden.

Chop the mango and papaya and put them in enough chicken stock to barely cover. Cook until sauce begins to thicken. Add the cayenne pepper and heavy cream. Stir briskly with a wooden spoon until thickened. Remove from heat and pour over fish.

DESSERT
◆◆ CHOCOLATE HAUPIA PIE

1 short pastry recipe (see Basic
    Recipes, p. 23)
1 can coconut milk
1 cup whole milk
1 cup sugar

½ cup cornstarch
½ cup water
½ cup grated bittersweet chocolate
½ cup shredded coconut
1 cup heavy cream

Preheat oven to 350 degrees. Press short pastry dough into a 10-inch pie plate and bake for 40 minutes or until golden.

Beat together coconut milk, whole milk, and sugar. Boil the mixture, then reduce to a simmer. Dissolve cornstarch in water, then slowly stir into the simmering mixture. Set aside half the mixture and add the grated chocolate to the half of the mixture still simmering. Stir until chocolate is completely melted and mixed in. Then pour the chocolate mixture into the pie shell and refrigerate for at least 20 minutes, until it is set. In the meantime, add shredded coconut to the reserved half of the mixture and cook on low heat until the first half is set. Then pour this half on top and return to the refrigerator. Let set 24 hours or longer. Whip the cream and cover the pie with the whipped cream before serving.

DRINK
◆ PUNCH

Stir together equal parts passion fruit, pineapple, and guava juices, ginger ale, and a touch of grenadine. This is also good for adults with a shot of gold rum added.

SAUDI ARABIA NIGHT

HINT: THE BIRTHPLACE OF A MAJOR RELIGION.

The Prophet Muhammad founded Islam here in the seventh century AD. Because of the harsh desert climate, the tribes of the area did not coalesce into a country until the twentieth century. But it is the largest country on the Arabian Peninsula, and the word *Arab* was originally used to refer to someone from this peninsula. The country is named after Abdul al-Aziz Ibn Saud, who conquered Riyadh in 1902 and spent the next thirty years gaining control of the rest of the peninsula.

Saudi Arabia is a tradition-bound country; its diet and cooking have changed little over several thousand years. One of the newer innovations, only a half millennium or so old, is the use of spices, especially cardamom, coriander, and black pepper. Of course, a still newer arrival is American-style fast food, which young, wealthy Saudis seem to be passionate about. But let's not even think about that.

Saudis eat yogurt often in the form of a drink called laban, and it's also a frequent ingredient in sauces for meat. They grow and eat hundreds of millions of pounds of dates every year. Coffee and dates is a common snack and the traditional way to break the religious fast of Ramadan. In earlier centuries the coffee was ground and roasted with a few cardamom seeds in front of the guest. Today it is usually prepared in advance. Saudis are the world's largest consumer of chickens per capita—almost ninety pounds of chicken per person annually. But for holidays and special occasions they prefer lamb. They are one of the world's largest importers of lamb and goat meat. But Islamic law is strictly observed, so there is no pork or alcohol, and animals must be slaughtered under religious supervision.

In Saudi Arabia, our Saudi Arabia Night would probably be a Saudi Afternoon: Saudis eat big meals during the day and a lighter meal at night.

APPETIZER
◆◆ AL MOTUBAG

Make the dough the day before from the rising dough ball recipe in Basic Recipes, p. 23.

rising dough ball
3 tablespoons olive oil
1 tomato, chopped
½ yellow onion, chopped
1 pound ground lamb
a pinch of salt
5 turns of black pepper

½ tablespoon cumin powder
½ tablespoon cardamom powder
juice of 1 lemon
3 parsley sprigs, chopped
3 sprigs of coriander (cilantro),
    chopped
½ pound spinach, chopped

Preheat oven to 350 degrees.

In the olive oil, sauté the tomato, onion, ground lamb, salt, pepper, cumin powder, and cardamom until the lamb is just browned. Add lemon juice, parsley sprigs, coriander, and spinach.

Roll out dough into disks. Place filling on half, then fold over and seal edges. Bake for about 40 minutes or until dough is golden and risen.

MAIN COURSE
◆ AL ROAZ AL-ZIRBYGEN (ZIRBEYAN RICE)

¼ cup olive oil
1 chicken, quartered
½ yellow onion, chopped
3 tablespoons turmeric powder
a pinch of salt
1 tablespoon powdered cumin

1 cup commercial tomato sauce
    or tomato sauce #1 (see Basic
    Recipes, p. 25)
½ pound spinach, chopped
1 cup Greek-style yogurt

In olive oil, sauté the chicken, onion, turmeric, salt, and cumin until chicken is golden brown, about 20 minutes. Add tomato sauce and spinach. Cool slightly and add yogurt. Serve over rice.

VEGETABLE
◆ CAULIFLOWER AND TAHINI

Tahini, which is widely available in the US, the Mediterranean, the Middle East, and Asia, is probably an Arab invention dating far back into the Middle Ages. *Tahini* is an Arab word meaning "ground," which makes sense: it's made of hulled sesame seeds ground into a paste. *Cauliflower*, on the other hand, is a word of Latin origin meaning "cabbage flower," but it, too, probably is from Arabia, since the earliest mentions of it are in twelfth-century Arab scientific writing.

1 small cauliflower, broken into florets
3 garlic cloves, chopped
½ cup tahini
1 teaspoon ground cumin
juice of 1 lemon

a generous pinch of salt
3 turns of black pepper
1 ½ tablespoons cayenne pepper
½ cup chopped parsley

Cook the cauliflower in a vegetable steamer until it yields slightly to a fork. (If it is soft, this means it is overcooked.) Drain.

Mix the garlic with the tahini, cumin, and lemon juice. Season with salt, pepper, and cayenne. The mixture should be no thicker than a cream sauce, so if it is a heavy paste, add one or two spoonfuls of water to thin it a little. Then add it to the cauliflower.

Sprinkle a little more cayenne pepper on top with the chopped parsley and serve.

DESSERT
◆ MANGO ROSE PUDDING

½ cup cornstarch
1 cup mango juice
1 fresh mango, chopped
3 cups milk

3 tablespoons sugar
2 tablespoons rose water
½ cup heavy cream
2 tablespoons crushed pistachios

Dissolve ¼ cup cornstarch in the mango juice and stir in the chopped mango. Fill dessert cups halfway, one per person. Let set in the refrigerator for at least one hour.

Mix the milk and 2 tablespoons sugar in a small saucepan over low heat until sugar is completely dissolved. Then add the other ¼ cup cornstarch to the mixture, stir until dissolved, and remove from heat. Add the rose water. Pour into the dessert cups on top of the mango mixture. Let set for 24 hours in freezer. Before serving, top with whipped cream beaten with rose water and a large pinch of sugar. Sprinkle chopped pistachios on top.

DRINK
◆ MINT ICED TEA

Arab mint tea has caffeine in it, as it is made from Chinese green tea, so it is not recommended for children. People often think that by putting less tea in the water, the amount of caffeine is decreased. The opposite is true. Steeping time is what brings out the caffeine: if you use less tea, you have to steep it longer, so there'll be more caffeine. If you put in a lot of tea, it steeps very quickly, and there's actually less caffeine.

Children often love the flavor of mint, so instead you can buy a mint infusion—that is, herbal tea that consists only of dried mint leaves. A mint infusion can also be made by steeping fresh mint leaves in simmering water. Brew the mint with a few pods of cardamom. After brewing the mint tea, add honey according to your taste and chill the drink. Serve with ice. If you want to be Saudi, you might accompany it with a plate of dates.

For a more elaborate mint tea recipe, see Morocco Night, p. 117.

Mint

MEXICO NIGHT

HINT: CREATED BY CONQUEST AND HALF LOST TO CONQUEST.

When you look at a map of North America and realize that all of the southwestern US, from California to the Louisiana state line, was once a part of Mexico, you begin to understand the complicated feelings Mexicans have about the United States. On the other hand, with almost 80 percent of the population at least partly related to the indigenous people whose lands were taken by the Spanish, there are not warm feelings about the Spanish, either. In the masked dances of traditional folk festivals, Hernán Cortés, the Spanish conqueror, is usually portrayed as a blue-eyed devil.

Mexico is a complicated society with sixty-two indigenous pre-Spanish languages still in use. Culturally and gastronomically, Mexico is still divided along the same lines as it was before Cortés arrived. The Mayans dominate the south, the Aztecs dominate the central highlands, and the northern desert is inhabited by scattered nomads. What Americans tend to think of as Mexican food comes either from the north or from the American southwest, whereas most Mexican food is actually rooted in the cooking of the Aztecs, Mayans, and other pre-European cultures.

When I lived in Mexico City, I shopped weekly at downtown markets with floors so filthy with garbage and muck that I wore boots—Mexican army boots, in fact. But the food was a wonder.

One of my favorites was a fish that is found only in Mexico, *blanco de Pátzcuaro,* named after a lake in the central state of Michoacán that is the only place where this white-fleshed freshwater fish is found. In 1519, when Cortés arrived in Tenochtitlan, today's Mexico City, at the time one of the largest, most developed cities in the world, it was built over a lake with a series of causeways and canals and a central market not far from where I shopped. That lake also had these fish, but it was eventually filled in by urban sprawl and no longer exists.

I used to buy freshwater crayfish, known by the Maya word *piguas,* as big as lobsters from southern rivers. There were goats and pigs and lambs from the north. There were all the unique cheeses of Mexico. There was a huge variety of tropical, subtropical, and desert fruit, some of which I have never seen anywhere else. There was a wide variety of edible cactus, and a black

Chilies

fungus called *huitlacoche* that appears on corn ears during the rainy season and makes an incomparable black sauce. And among the huge variety of vegetables were table after table of different types of chili peppers—fresh, smoked, and dried.

After two years of cooking only Mexican food, I left Mexico. I realized that I would never be able to make these foods again because I would not be able to find the products. At least I could bring with me some of the dozen types of dried peppers I had learned to use. But I was driving to the US. Would these treasures be confiscated at the border? I decided as I packed to slip a pepper or two randomly in the pockets of my clothes.

For the next several years, at a social event or a press conference, I would reach into the pocket of a coat or jacket that I hadn't worn in a while, looking for a pen, and to my surprise and sometimes embarrassment I would pull out an old dried Mexican chili pepper.

TORTILLAS

The essential of any Mexican meal is tortillas. They are often the primary utensil, used to scoop food off the plate. Tortillas are made from corn. The wheat-flour tortilla, and for that matter wheat, is an American thing only found in the north and only used for a few *Norteño* dishes. Corn tortillas are widely available in the US, although, unfortunately, they are almost always machine made. This is true in Mexico as well. About the time I arrived there, in the early 1980s, tortilla-making machines had started to become widespread and it became increasingly difficult to find the thick and corn-rich handmade ones. More than one young campesino told me that what he was looking for in a wife was someone who made good tortillas by hand.

APPETIZERS
◆ GUACAMOLE

Avocado is a native Mexican fruit, specifically from the state of Pueblo, and technically it's a very large berry. But it is an unusual fruit because it ripens only after it is picked. It must be ripened to a soft creamy state to be used for guacamole. Both the words *avocado* and *guacamole* come from Nahuatl, the language of the Aztecs. Today the best avocados for making guacamole are grown in the state of Morelos and are of the dark bumpy variety known in the US as Hass—after Rudolph Hass, the Californian who first bred them in the 1930s. Happily for guacamole lovers, it is the most common type of avocado in the world.

As far as I am concerned, the following simple recipe is *the* recipe for guacamole, and I rate all guacamoles by how close they come to this.

3 Hass avocados
⅓ white onion, finely chopped
3 sprigs coriander leaf (cilantro), finely
    chopped

½ to 1 whole serrano pepper, finely
    chopped

Cut the avocados in half, remove the pits, and scoop out the flesh. Mash it with a fork but let it remain a bit chunky. Add the onion, coriander, and the serrano pepper. Serranos are small, fresh, green medium-hot peppers very commonly used in Mexican food and widely available. How much you use depends on your taste and the pepper. Some serranos are hotter than others. Serve the guacamole with tortilla chips.

Avocado

◆◆ TACO DE HAUCHINANGO

There is a raging debate in the US about the origin of the fish taco. Many believe it to have originated near California, probably in Baja California; some say in Ensenada, and others say San Felipe.

Like many debates in the US, though, this one is a bit odd to Mexicans because their people have been eating fish tacos since before the Spanish arrived, possibly for more than a thousand years.

This discrepancy is explained by the fact that Americans and Mexicans do not mean the same thing when they say "taco." The American idea of a taco is something developed in southern California with the invention of the industrial "hard taco," the crisp tortilla that can be bought bent into a half moon shape ready for stuffing. Since this taco needs no cooking, shredded lettuce and other greens that shouldn't be heated can be placed in it. The trendy fish tacos made with these hard-shell tortillas stuffed with shredded lettuce are not the fish tacos in the recipe below.

Mexicans usually do not choose between a hard or soft tortilla. Tortillas are soft, and if you want them to be hard you fry them, which means that fresh crisp greens will not work.

The green tomatillos used in the recipe are not unripe tomatoes but a husked fruit in the gooseberry family. They turn yellow when ripe, but are usually used in their unripe green state. They are also called cascara, fresadillas, and green tomatoes. They have become widely available outside Mexico.

1 fillet of red snapper	3 garlic cloves, peeled and minced
½ cup corn oil	a pinch of salt
½ yellow onion, finely chopped	½ to 1 whole serrano pepper,
2 sprigs oregano	chopped
6 green tomatillos, chopped	6 corn tortillas
1 tablespoon powdered cumin	

Chop the snapper fillet into pieces and sauté in ¼ cup hot corn oil with the onion, the oregano leaves, and the green tomatillos. Add cumin, garlic, salt, and the chopped serrano pepper according to taste. Place some of this filling onto each tortilla, then roll the tortillas into cigar-shaped tacos. Fry them in corn oil to crisp them.

SALAD
◆ LEAFLESS MEXICAN SALAD

In the two years I lived in Mexico, I never experienced the stomach ailments for which that country is famous. I attribute that to an extremely durable stomach and a few precautions. I boiled water for more than twenty minutes, peeled all fruit and vegetables, and I never ate any lettuce. Instead, from Mexican traditions, I created numerous leafless salads. This is one of them.

The bumpy sour orange—Seville orange, or bitter orange—called for in this recipe is difficult to find in the US: usually it's available in winter, if at all. All oranges originated in Asia and came to the West via the Arabs. But the sour orange came first, introduced by Arabs to the Mediterranean around the year 1000. Sweet oranges didn't arrive for almost another four centuries. Sour oranges endure chiefly because their durable rootstock is used for cultivating sweet oranges, and in the US and Europe its peel is used in making marmalade. But in the Caribbean basin, the juice is commonly used in cooking. If you can't find sour oranges, substitute the juice of one lime.

¼ pound trimmed green beans
about 1 pound peeled jicama, cut in
   quarter-inch strips
a large pinch of coarse salt
2 tablespoons fresh cilantro, minced

¾ cup sour-orange juice (or ½ cup
   fresh-squeezed lime juice)
½ cup regular orange juice
a pinch of cayenne pepper

Steam green beans for about 10 minutes until they become bright. Put the jicama in a bowl and add a pinch of salt. Mix the sour-orange juice (or lime juice) with the regular orange juice. Pour the juice mixture over the vegetables and sprinkle lightly with cayenne pepper.

MAIN COURSE
◆ POLLO CON MOLE

This is a very simple dish—if you have the mole. There are an increasing number of Mexican specialty shops in the US—one of the delights of living in a country enriched by immigration—so you may be able to find one in your area that carries moles; you can also buy online. There are many different types of mole: green, black, yellow, red. It is not unusual to have more than two dozen ingredients in one mole, and many recipes date back to the ancient Aztecs. Chocolate is sometimes used for its bitter flavor. The Aztecs, who invented chocolate making, never sweetened it. Seeds, chilis, and many other ingredients are also used. Moles are sold as pastes.

3 chicken breasts
1 carrot
1 yellow onion, sliced in half

2 sprigs oregano
2 tablespoons salt
about ½ cup mole

Place chicken parts, carrot, onion, oregano, and salt in enough boiling water to cover and cook for about 15 minutes. Remove chicken and use liquid as chicken stock.

In a separate pan, add the simmering chicken stock to the mole a little at a time until it dissolves and the mixture is the consistency of a chocolate sauce. Serve it over the boiled chicken.

If you can't find a mole, try making this simple one:

PIPIAN ROJO

This recipe calls for two different dried Mexican chili peppers, ideally anchos and mulatos—beginning to see why I stuffed so many in my pockets?—but see what you can find. These have to be reddish, dark chilis and should not be hot peppers. A lot of dried chilis are showing up in markets these days, especially in Mexican neighborhoods. And a number of websites offer them.

2 dried ancho chilis
2 dried mulato chilis
10 garlic cloves, peeled
¼ cup sesame oil
1 cup shelled pumpkin seeds

¼ cup toasted sesame seeds
a pinch of salt
½ cup chicken stock
3 tablespoons corn oil

Remove the seeds and veins and stems from all of the chili peppers and crumble them into a food processor. Brown the garlic in oil and add it to the food processor. Put the shelled pumpkin seeds in a skillet with a little oil. This is tricky because you have to move the seeds a bit to keep them from burning, but you also need a lid on the pan or they will pop out. So move the pan up and down occasionally by the handle. Peek in every minute or so, remove the seeds when they're golden, and add to the food processor. Finally, toast the sesame seeds in a broiler and add to the food processor along with the salt and chicken stock. Grind together.

In a frying pan, heat the corn oil. Fry the sauce for about ten minutes, then pour over chicken.

VEGETABLES
◆ STUFFED SQUASH BLOSSOMS

A favorite when I was in Mexico was to stuff a zucchini blossom with Oaxaca cheese, which is halfway between Armenian string cheese and Monterey Jack. Oaxaca cheese is sold in the US, and on occasion you can even find fresh squash blossoms.

6 ounces Oaxaca cheese
6 zucchini blossoms
½ cup flour

3 eggs, beaten
1 cup bread crumbs
½ cup corn oil

Place strips of cheese in the center of the blossoms. Cover the blossoms with flour, dip them in beaten eggs, cover them with bread crumbs, and fry them in hot corn oil until golden but not too dark on all sides.

◆ STUFFED CHILI

If you can't find squash blossoms, try to find poblano chilis, which are long, fresh, green, only slightly hot peppers.

3 poblano chilis
6 ounces Oaxaca or Monterey Jack
    cheese
½ cup flour

3 eggs, beaten
1 cup bread crumbs
½ cup corn oil

Broil the peppers until the skin blisters, then take them out of the heat and place in a plastic bag to cool. The skin should then easily come off. Remove the stems, veins, and seeds and stuff each pepper with cheese. Roll each in flour and dip in beaten egg. Cover with bread crumbs. Fry in hot corn oil until golden on all sides.

DESSERT
◆◆ BUDÍN DE CAMOTE

"CA-MO-TE!" I can still hear that high-pitched cry, each syllable held an extra beat. In the late afternoon, a cold wind blows out of the high mountains just outside Mexico City. Pushcart vendors appear, selling either hot roasted sweet potatoes—*camotes*—or steamed tamales wrapped in corn husks and stuffed with either sweet or savory fillings. But in homes this pudding is made with camotes.

2 sweet potatoes	4 eggs, separated
½ cup brown sugar	¼ cup sugar
2 tablespoons powdered cinnamon	12 walnut halves
1 dash vanilla extract	

Preheat oven to 350 degrees. Roast the sweet potatoes. Peel them, mash them, and mix them in a baking dish with the brown sugar, cinnamon, vanilla extract, and egg yolks.

In a bowl, beat the egg whites to a soft peak and mix in the sugar. Fold the whites into the sweet potato mixture, arrange walnuts on top, and bake for 30 minutes or until it rises.

Serve hot. We broke with tradition and put a scoop of dulce de leche ice cream on top, although vanilla would have worked well too.

DRINKS

Mexicans have their beer and various alcohols and some very good, underrated wines, but what Mexicans are truly passionate about is nonalcoholic cold fruit drinks served in huge pitchers and called licuados and aguas frescas. They are often in brilliant colors and Mexicans are fond of setting a table with several large glass pitchers with these colorful drinks. We chose pink and red and green for ours.

◆ STRAWBERRY LICUADO

In the US, licuados are confused with smoothies. They should not have yogurt or crushed ice. They are simply fruit, water, milk, and sugar. How much sugar is a personal taste. Mexicans tend to like sugar a lot—Marian and me much less so, Talia in between.

2 cups fresh strawberries
2 cups milk

2 tablespoons sugar (more if you like)

Puree the strawberries in a blender or food processor. Keep beating and add milk and sugar. Pour into a pitcher.

◆ WATERMELON AGUA FRESCA

Without the milk licuado becomes an agua fresca.

3 cups seeded or seedless
    watermelon
3 cups water

1 lime
4 tablespoons sugar (more if you like)

Puree the watermelon in a food processor or a blender. Strain through a fine sieve. Add lime juice and sugar. Chill and serve.

◆ LIME AGUA FRESCA

juice of 12 limes
equal amount water

½ cup sugar (more if you like)
club soda

Squeeze the juice from about a dozen limes. Mexicans make the best lime squeezers—a cup-shaped tool resembling a garlic press. Mix the lime juice with an equal amount of water and sugar according to your taste. Top with a splash of club soda.

BRAZIL NIGHT

HINT: AS CLOSE AS AMERICA GETS TO AFRICA.

Brazil is a former Portuguese colony, and the Portuguese brought African slaves to work there. But the easternmost point of Brazil is also literally the closest point to Africa in the Americas. Today more than half the population has some African blood. The country is only slightly smaller than the United States, and although it is known for its huge tracts of tropical rain forests and its tremendous natural resources, most people—80 percent—live in cities. Cities such as Rio de Janeiro seem crowded, but in the northern interior, running across another human being feels like an event. In an attempt to move the population into a sparsely populated area, Brazil decided in the 1950s to build a new capital city in an unpopulated zone. Construction of the city of Brasília, currently with a population of about three million people, started in 1956 and was completed in less than four years. But Brazil is also a country of villages where only a handful of people live along wide black rivers that run deep into the interior, villages that can be reached only in a small boat, where people catch and eat huge freshwater fish unknown to the rest of the world.

The maracuja dessert should be made the day before.

Palmetto tree

SALAD
◆ HEARTS OF PALM SALAD

Hearts of palm are the tender core of young palms known as sabal palmettos. They are not unique to Brazil, and in fact the tree grows abundantly in Florida. There, though, it was regarded as poor peoples' food because it is a tough tree to chop down and was disdained with the name "swamp cabbage" until the Depression, when in desperation the tender shoots were commercialized and became labeled "millionaire's salad." There must have been more millionaires than you would think, because the plant was soon endangered, protected from harvest by the state, and is now the state tree of Florida. In Brazil, on the other hand, it is a staple food and, with few calories and almost no cholesterol, an extremely healthy one.

1 can hearts of palm
2 ripe tomatoes
about 12 marinated anchovy fillets

juice of ½ lemon
½ cup olive oil
black pepper

Cut hearts of palm stalks into disks and place them on a plate with tomato wedges and marinated anchovies. Pour lemon juice and a touch of olive oil on top, along with a small amount of fresh-ground black pepper.

MAIN COURSE
◆◆◆ FEIJOADA

Feijoada is said to be the Brazilian national dish. Although it was originally slave food, today it is eaten regularly by most Brazilians. The dish is Portuguese in origin and is still eaten there, but with different beans. The word *feijoada* comes from the Portuguese word *feijão*, which means beans, though today in both Portugal and Brazil, as well as other former Portuguese colonies, it is made with meat. In Brazil often the entire pig is used, including the ears, snout, tail, and feet. But this is not absolutely necessary, and restaurants catering to squeamish tourists skip these parts, which in any event can be hard to come by. If you can find a pig foot, it is a flavorful addition. This is the recipe that we use, which is slightly modified so that it can be easily made outside of Brazil, but it takes most of a day to prepare. Portuguese linguica sausage can be found anywhere that Portuguese or Azorean immigrants live. It is common in coastal New England. If you can't find it, use chorizo instead, but linguica is worth a search.

This dish must be made in a very large pot and will feed a number of people: it would be very difficult to make it any smaller.

1½ pounds black beans, soaked
    overnight
½ pound pork belly
1½ pounds pork butt
1 rack pork ribs
2 smoked ham hocks

2 pig's feet
5 two-inch pieces of Portuguese
    linguica sausage
1 sweet orange, thinly sliced
2 green onions, chopped

Leave the black beans soaking in water the day before.

Cut the pork belly into one-inch cubes. Heat in a pot until they render enough fat to brown the pork butt and rack of ribs. Fill a large stockpot with water about halfway, and when it's well heated, add all the meat, including the ham hocks and pig's feet. Drain the black beans and add them to the pot.

Simmer over low heat, so that the water is barely trembling, for three hours.

Add the sausage. Cook slowly for two more hours.

Serve with thin slices of fresh orange and chopped green onions on top.

DESSERT
◆◆ MOUSSE DE MARACUJA (PASSION FRUIT MOUSSE)

This is one of the most common desserts in Brazil, where passion fruit is a native plant. Passion fruit is sometimes available in the US. If you can't find it, unsweetened concentrate of passion fruit juice is commonly available in stores or online. Although the juice will save you considerable work, it does not provide the seeds with which to decorate the top. Passion fruit seeds are used as a garnish on all sorts of desserts in Brazil.

14 passion fruits or ½ cup
    unsweetened concentrate
4 egg whites
a pinch of salt
½ cup superfine sugar (sometimes
    called baker's sugar)

½ envelope unflavored gelatin
    powder, a little more than 1
    teaspoon
½ cup evaporated milk
fresh passion fruit seeds for garnish

Cut the fruit in half and strain the pulp through a fine sieve, rubbing to remove the pulp from the seeds. Wash the seeds in water, then dry on a paper towel.

In a medium bowl, beat the egg whites and salt to soft peaks. With the mixer running, gradually add ¼ cup sugar and beat until the meringue is stiff and glossy.

Place 2 tablespoons of the purée or juice concentrate in a saucepan and sprinkle with the gelatin to moisten. Heat the mixture over medium-low heat, stirring, just until the gelatin is dissolved. Remove from heat and place the mixture in a medium-size bowl. Add the remaining juice to the bowl and stir to combine. Add the evaporated milk and the remaining ¼ cup sugar and stir until dissolved. Add a large spoonful of the egg white mixture to the chilled passion fruit mixture and gently stir until thoroughly combined. Fold in the remaining meringue very gently.

Spoon the mousse into individual dessert cups and chill overnight in the refrigerator. Sprinkle with passion fruit seeds before serving.

SWEETS
◆ BRIGADEIRO

These are extremely popular, especially with children. It began in the 1940s when Nestlé began selling chocolate powder and condensed milk in Brazil—key ingredients in a confection that would be featured at rallies for air force marshal Eduardo Gomes's unsuccessful 1946 campaign for president. Thus the treat got its name and gained popularity—at least more than the general, who also lost again four years later.

Brigadeiros probably predate the general and are sometimes called *negrinhos*, little black ones. They may even predate Nestlé. Brazil is, after all, a leading cultivator of cocoa beans, and there was probably a longer homemade process before the Nestlé products arrived. There is a version that uses coconut instead of chocolate known as *brinquinhos*, little white ones, but these too used condensed milk, which was probably from Nestlé.

In all of Gomes's involvements with various coups d'état and elections, he never gained the kind of dominance of brigadeiros, which seem to become ever more popular. Once a homemade sweet for children's parties, they are now sold in fashionable stores in São Paulo. Brigadeiro stores have also been opening in New York, and there is even one in Montana. There are now many variations, including mint, almond, coffee, cashew, cherry, and dulce de leche.

The following is a simplified recipe from Ana Maria Cecelia Simonetti dos Santos from São Paulo, who makes them this way for her daughter Stefania and Stefania's schoolmates, including Talia. It makes thirty or forty brigadeiros.

1 can (14 ounces) sweetened condensed milk
1 tablespoon butter

2 tablespoons chocolate drink powder (like Nesquik; you can also use sweetened cocoa powder, but half the quantity, otherwise it gets too "chocolatey")
chocolate sprinkles

In a bowl, mix the condensed milk, butter, and chocolate drink powder. Place the bowl in the microwave for 4 minutes at full power.

Mix and return to the microwave for another 3½ minutes at 60 percent power. Take it out of the microwave as soon as it is finished. The mixture will be quite bubbly. Mix vigorously with a wooden spoon until you get a smooth mixture; take care not to burn your fingers, as the bowl will be very hot. The mixture needs to be stiff enough so that it keeps some shape and does not completely flatten in the bowl. If you don't want to use the microwave, you can cook the mixture in a pot until it is stiff enough to show the bottom of the pot when stirring. Leave the mixture to cool for around 30 minutes so that you can handle it.

When the mixture is cool, put the chocolate sprinkles in a clean and dry soup bowl and grease your hands with a bit of butter. Get a bit of the mixture with a teaspoon and, with your hands, roll a little ball slightly smaller than a Ping-Pong ball. Put the little chocolate ball in the bowl with the chocolate sprinkles and roll it until it's completely covered. Put each in a paper cake cup.

DRINK
◆ CAIPIRINHA

The name of this drink comes from the word *caipira*, meaning a country bumpkin. This does not necessarily mean it is a drink for hicks, but instead probably refers to the people who grow the lime and sugar it's made from; both are major agricultural products in Brazil. In fact, Brazil is the largest sugar producer in the world and has been using its sugar leftovers to produce ethanol, now a major source of energy there.

at least 12 limes, quartered	sugar to taste
water	cachaça (for the grown-ups)

Squeeze the limes and leave a few of the quarters in the juice. Add an equivalent amount of water and sugar to taste, and you have a refreshing nonalcoholic drink over ice. But for a real caipirinha for the grown-ups, add cachaça, which is a Brazilian alcohol made from sugarcane. Cachaça is said not to be rum because it is made directly from distilled cane juice, whereas rum is made from distilling the leftover molasses. However, in the French Caribbean islands they do make alcohol directly from cane juice, and they call it *rhum agricole*. It's rum, and it's identical to cachaça.

SICILY NIGHT

HINT: AN ISLAND IN A PRIME LOCATION WILL OFTEN BE CONQUERED.

Sicily is a sentimental favorite because Marian and I went there for our honeymoon. We were married in April, which is the perfect time of year for Sicily, although I have been there at other times that were beautiful as well. But at Easter time the sky is bluer than cornflowers, the wild fennel is in bloom with bright yellow blossoms that seem to flourish especially around the ruins of ancient Greek temples, and the shop windows are decorated with colorful scenes fashioned from marzipan.

Italy is a country made up of many distinct regions, but there is no part of Italy more different than Sicily. They speak a dialect that sometimes seems to be a completely different language than Italian. It is an island that has been occupied by the Phoenicians, the Carthagenians, the ancient Greeks, the Romans, the Arabs, the Ostragoths, the Normans, the Germans, the French, the Spanish, the Austrians, the Americans. It is a land of many ruins, and scuba divers report finding a sea strewn with the detritus of would-be empires.

Sicily at times seems Italian but at times seems North African, and other cultural influences are present as well. And the food is that way too. North African couscous is as popular as Italian pasta, and Sicilians season with unsweetened chocolate the way the Aztecs taught the Spanish. The four dishes that follow are all family favorites. The dessert should be made the day before.

APPETIZER
◆◆◆ SARDINE PIZZA

1 rising dough ball (see Basic Recipes, p. 23)
½ cup chopped white onion
¼ cup olive oil
3 cups tomato sauce #2 (see Basic Recipes, p. 25)

6 whole fresh sardines, gutted and scaled
2 sprigs fresh oregano
a large pinch of coarse salt
3 slices provolone cheese

Make a rising dough ball and let it rise overnight in the refrigerator.

Sauté the onion in olive oil at low heat but do not let it completely wilt. Add to the tomato sauce.

Place the sardines on a hot grill seasoned with the oregano and salt. Grill for only about four minutes on each side.

Fillet the grilled sardines: take one of the sardines and carefully, with a knife, make an incision along the back and another cut just before the tail and slide the knife gently, with the blade flat, toward the head and lift off the fillet. Then lift the bone by the head off the bottom fillet. Each fish will have two fillets, a top and a bottom. Move to the next fish. If the fish is well grilled, the fillets will lift off the bones easily. You can gently touch the meat with an index finger and feel for stray bones, which can then be picked out.

Preheat the oven to 400 degrees. Roll out the dough and cut it into three 6-inch-diameter disks and place on a cookie sheet. Leaving a half-inch lip around the edge, cover each with sauce. Place 4 sardine fillets on each one, then cover with a slice of provolone cheese. Bake for 30 minutes or until the crust has risen and the cheese melted.

SALAD
◆ FENNEL SALAD

This salad always reminds me of the flowering fennel on Sicily's tough, rocky hillsides. It is not only full of flavor, but also beautifully bright in the Italian colors.

Pecorino is a hard Sicilian sheep-milk cheese that is widely available.

2 heads fennel
9 cherry or grape tomatoes
3 sprigs fresh oregano
1 generous pinch of coarse salt

½ cup olive oil
juice of ½ lemon
pecorino cheese

Chop the fennel into 1-inch pieces. Place on three salad plates with tomatoes and oregano leaves plucked off their stems. Add salt, drizzle with olive oil, and top with fresh-squeezed lemon juice and shaved pecorino.

Fennel

MAIN COURSE
◆ PISCI SPATA (SWORDFISH)

Sicilians, being an island people, are fish eaters. But after centuries of overfishing, they risk running out—especially of their favorite giants, swordfish and bluefin tuna. In his great 1881 novel, *Il Malovoglia*, the Sicilian writer Giovanni Verga tells the story of brave fishermen in eastern Sicily risking their lives with sails and oars, forced to go ever farther out to sea because there are too many fishermen. With engine-powered boats the situation has gotten even worse in the Mediterranean, and big fish are becoming scarce. So before you buy swordfish for this recipe, you may want to ask how it was caught. If it was caught by harpoon, buy it. If it was caught by net or longline—a line with many hooks—keep looking.

½ cup pine nuts
½ cup olive oil
2 cups yellow onion, chopped
6 garlic cloves, peeled and chopped
a large pinch of salt
4 turns of black pepper
2 tablespoons capers

½ cup green Sicilian olives, pitted and chopped
2 cups tomatoes, chopped
a splash of balsamic vinegar
2 tablespoons unsweetened cocoa powder
¼ cup raisins
1¼ pounds swordfish

Place the pine nuts in a skillet with a tablespoon of the olive oil and keep them moving in the pan over medium heat until they are golden but not burned. Set them aside and add the rest of the olive oil. Sauté the onion, garlic, salt, pepper, capers, olives, tomatoes, and balsamic vinegar. After the tomatoes have cooked down to a chunky sauce, add the toasted pine nuts and the cocoa powder.

Place the raisins in a strainer and plunge them into boiling water; remove and drain immediately. Add them to the mixture and stir well with a wooden spoon.

Grill the swordfish for about 10 minutes on each side—less if thinner than half an inch and longer if thicker. Put on serving plates and pour the sauce on top. Serve with steamed asparagus.

DESSERT
◆◆ SICILIAN CHEESECAKE

I have been making this cake for many years. The recipe is completely of my own invention but the ingredients and concepts are Sicilian, so while you probably wouldn't find this cake in Sicily, you will find many desserts like it.

3½ cups sugar
½ cup water
2 lemons
2 limes
1 orange (I have always used a sweet orange, but this is an instance where a sour orange would be wonderful if you had one)
2 pounds almonds
¼ cup flour
¼ pound butter, cut into 2-inch cubes

a large pinch of salt
a splash of almond extract
a splash of vanilla extract
6 eggs
2 pounds ricotta cheese
3 tablespoons orange-blossom water
8 ounces dark or semisweet chocolate, chopped into chips
confectioners' sugar
zest of ½ lemon, ½ lime, and a few pieces of orange peel

Preheat oven to 350 degrees.

Melt 2 cups sugar in the water in a skillet over medium heat. Peel the lemons, limes, and orange. Cut the peel into small cubes and cook in the sugar syrup slowly over low heat for an hour. Then let cool for an hour in the syrup. (It is important not to let the syrup get too hot at any time, or it will cool into a solid.)

Roast the almonds until brown, but be careful not to burn them. Grind them into powder in a food processor, then combine the powder with the flour in a mixer. Using the dough hook, add the butter, one 2-inch cube at a time, until the mixture has the consistency of coarse meal. Mix in the salt and 1½ cups sugar, then add the almond and vanilla extracts and beat in 2 eggs, one at a time. When the mixture becomes a solid dough, dust your hands with flour and press the dough into the bottom and sides of a 9½-inch springform pan.

Mix the ricotta cheese with 4 whole eggs and add the candied peel and syrup, the orange-blossom water, and the chocolate. Mix well and pour over the dough in the pan. Bake for 40 minutes or until filling is solid. Cool and then dust the top with powdered sugar, which is best done by putting the sugar in a screen strainer and tapping it against your palm over the cake. Sprinkle lemon, lime, and orange zest on top.

DRINK
◆ SPUMA DE LIMONADA

You can order this in most cafés throughout Italy, but Sicily is the heart of lemon country. The lemons there can be literally the size of grapefruits. Sicilian and Italian cafés and roadside stands are often equipped with an ingenious machine for squeezing oranges and lemons that has made the fresh juice available everywhere. It looks like a large metal box and has a wire basket for the citrus fruit sitting on top. Press a button and a single fruit drops down and hits a blade that instantly cuts the fruit in half. The two halves fall to either side on spinning domes that quickly press out the juice and release the peels to be tossed into a discard pile. The machine can thus juice several fruits a minute but unfortunately is too large and too expensive to be a household appliance.

at least 12 lemons	sugar to taste
water	

Squeeze lemons into a pitcher. Add a nearly equal amount of water and sugar, according to everyone's taste. Add 5 or 6 slices of lemon and some ice cubes. In the hot months in Sicily the juice is poured over finely crushed ice to make a *granite di limone*.

For adults, there are good, hearty Sicilian red wines. Sweet wine from Marsala on the west coast of Sicily is pleasant with dessert, with an espresso afterward.

JAPAN NIGHT

HINT: A VERY CROWDED ISLAND NATION WITH THE WORLD'S LONGEST LIFE EXPECTANCY.

Japan has more than six thousand islands, but most people live on the four largest ones. Almost three quarters of the land is mountainous forest and unsuitable for farming, so the Japanese are crowded into coastal areas. Greater Tokyo, with more than thirty million people, is the most populous metropolitan area in the world. But despite all this crowding, the Japanese live longer than everyone else. Some have suggested it is their diet, which is high in protein and low in fat. The Japanese also drink a great deal of green tea, which various laboratory studies have suggested fights cancer, diabetes, strokes, and heart disease, lowers cholesterol, helps burn fat, and helps fight dementia.

Japan, currently one of the world's wealthiest countries but a nation that has been poor for most of its history, has a minimalist aesthetic rooted in simplicity. The traditional house has rooms divided by handmade paper panels that let in light, because for a very long time Japan produced little sheet glass for windows. Shoes are kept outside, and the Japanese live on mat-covered floors. The only artwork on the wall of a traditional home is a scrolled watercolor in an alcove especially reserved for the house painting. The painting is always a landscape, and more affluent people change the painting once a month with the seasons. Sometimes a special painting will be put out for a special guest. The paintings are in a style adapted from ancient Chinese painting, with black ink and occasional splashes of color. The eleventh-century Chinese writer Kuo Hsi wrote in a famous essay on landscapes, "If one approaches them from the sympathetic spirit of a nature lover,

Sea bream

the quality is high; but if one approaches them with the eyes of pride and extravagance, their value is low."

This also describes the Japanese approach to cooking. The Western fad of celebrity chefs has reached Japan, but for the most part Japanese cooking is not about splashy individualism but about tradition, respect for nature, modesty, and simplicity.

Not only painting, but much of Japan's culture and many of its foods, including rice, soy sauce, and bean paste, come from China. But in cooking, the Japanese have their own distinct style, which is much more restrained than that of Chinese cooking. Japan has limited land and limited resources. It cannot even produce enough salt for the nation's needs, which is why its soy sauce is lighter and less salty than that of China. But the Japanese have turned their deficiencies into an art form, developing a cuisine that is lean, delicate, and extraordinarily creative. A bean can be a vegetable or a pickle or a sweet dessert.

The sea is the primary source of food for the Japanese, and they eat everything edible from plant to animal—a wide variety of seaweeds, every imaginable shellfish, fish eaten raw, smoked, dried, or cooked, and even, to the anger of much of the rest of the world, whale meat. From their mountains they gather wild shoots and vegetables and dozens of wild mushroom varieties. In recent years they have been grazing cattle on the mountain slopes and now produce the best beef in the world, marbled in fat and tender as bean curd.

The Japanese, like the Chinese, love to eat and love to talk about food. On the many efficient trains by which people move through

Kelp

their country, it is a pleasure to watch people enjoying all the good things they brought for the trip. Even the box meals that you can buy from the wagon on the train are good.

In fact, food is almost always good in Japan, full of strange, unrecognizable things. Don't ask too many questions and pop it in your mouth. It will often be surprising and always delightful. You'll find yourself saying, "That was delicious! I wonder what it was."

Twenty years ago I would have said that Japan would be one of the most difficult cuisines to interest children in, but of course I would have been completely wrong. As Japanese food has become more and more popular in the US, children have become among its biggest fans. Also, a lot of it, especially sushi, is fun to make. But there is much more to Japanese food than sushi. For Japan Night I relied primarily on dishes I learned to make in Japan. But I was also inspired and informed by Shizuo Tsuji's great book *Japanese Cookery: A Simple Art*, which was my introduction to Japanese food years ago.

In Japan I learned from a number of sources

including Hasegawa Shigeki, whose small, fashionably stark restaurant, Haseshigein, opened in 2008 in the old port city of Yokohama. He serves a style of cooking called kaiseki, which comes from the tradition of tea ceremonies in Kyoto. These tea ceremonies, dating back to the seventeenth century, take between two and four and a half hours, during which a tea master directs a few people in the ritual drinking of matcha tea, a tea dried and crushed into a powder so that the drink is strong and bitter and resembles espresso. But the ceremony is also about the craft of hosting and the art of conversation, with certain subjects such as politics and money forbidden. Participants sit on the matted floor in a room filled with softly diffused light from the paper paneling, or shoji. The food of a tea ceremony consists of a soup and three other dishes.

Green tea

The food, kaiseki style, is based on the season, and the preparations are simple to bring out the freshness of the food. It is similar in principle to the French nouvelle cuisine of the 1970s, except that in Japan the style goes back centuries.

The Japanese sometimes serve everything at once, Chinese style. A family might do this so that the woman of the household does not have to constantly hop up. But when a guest is invited, this changes. The cold dishes are put out first, together, and the hot dishes brought out one at a time.

The traditional order of a Japanese meal is:
Appetizer
Soup
Sashimi or sushi
Broiled or grilled food
A stew or something cooked in a pot
Fried food
Dessert

As Hasegawa Shigeki explained, "The hardest thing in Japanese cooking is the preparations." If you try to do as much as you can in advance, the evening's dinner will be easily accomplished.

We decided to make Japan Night in six separately served courses—seven dishes from several different cooking traditions—rather than the all-at-once family style. To the Japanese aesthetic, serving in courses is a bit more formal, but also more festive.

◆ DASHI (SEAWEED STOCK)

The first three recipes are from Hasegawa Shigeki, and they all start with the same stock, a soup that is the base for many of his dishes. A small amount is also used in the spinach and sesame dish and the sea bream, which are not Shigeki's recipes. The stock, called dashi, can be bought commercially bottled, but when basing an entire dinner on it, it is worth making yourself. The base is kombu, dried kelp, which can be found in Asian stores, health-food stores, or online. Kombu was traditionally associated with the cuisine of Osaka, but it is considered a great source of umami, which has been a growing obsession in modern Japanese cooking. Up until 1908 the Japanese, like many Westerners, thought of four basic tastes, the tastes of the tongue—salt, bitter, sweet, and sour. But in 1908, Kikunae Ikeda, a chemist, discovered that there was a certain flavor produced by glutamates for which there are receptors on the tongue just as there are for the other four basic tastes. This is why the Chinese season their food with monosodium glutamate. Although controversial in the US, this fermented cereal has long been made by the Chinese because they find that it adds "flavorfulness," a loose translation of Kikunae Ikeda's word, *umami*. Seaweed, but also tomatoes and meat and other foods that are high in glutamates, have this flavor. The Japanese prefer to introduce umami more naturally by using foods high in glutamates—in Shigeki's case, with a seaweed stock.

13½ cups water
1 piece of kelp (kombu), 4 by 6 inches

3½ ounces dried bonito flakes

Place the water in a large pot and add the dried kelp, letting it soak for about 2 hours. Shegaki suggests less soaking on a hot summer day. Then place the pot on high heat. Remove the kelp when bubbles begin but before it reaches a full boil.

After the water reaches a boil, reduce the heat to low and add the dried bonito flakes, which are usually available from the same sources as kelp. After 5 minutes of simmering, skim off any froth that has formed, remove from the heat, and strain through cheesecloth. This should be enough broth for the following five recipes that use dashi.

SAKIZUKI
◆◆ ROASTED WHITE ASPARAGUS AND GRAPE TOMATOES

Sakizuki is is the Japanese word for a small dish to serve at the beginning, before the appetizer. This recipe was given to me by Hasegawa Shigeki. It should be made the day before dinner is served, along with the aspic for the appetizer below.

6 white asparagus stalks
3 grape tomatoes
4 cups dashi
5 tablespoons light soy sauce

5 tablespoons mirin
1 heaping teaspoon powdered gelatin
3 tablespoons lukewarm water
6 edamame beans

Peel the asparagus stalks with a vegetable peeler and roast them in a hot skillet for a few minutes until they begin to brown. Plunge the grape tomatoes into boiling water and quickly remove them to cold water. The skins will easily peel off.

Make the marinade for sakizuki and the aspic for the appetizer: Heat the dashi with the light soy sauce (Shigeki likes to use white colorless soy sauce so that it doesn't darken the soup, but the lightest you can find will work) and the mirin (see On Sugar and Spice, p. 12) until it boils. Then immediately cut off the heat.

Pour about half over the asparagus and tomatoes and refrigerate overnight. Mix the remaining stock with the gelatin dissolved in lukewarm water. Refrigerate this overnight for appetizer dressing.

Cut tomatoes in half for serving and arrange on plates with asparagus. In his restaurant, Shigeki adds a few fermented soy beans for a touch of green. We added two beans from edamame pods to each dish.

APPETIZER
◆◆ GREENS IN UMAMI ASPIC DRESSING

Shigeki's recipe is notable for completely rethinking salad dressing. The key to this dish is using the freshest possible greens: Shigeki's recipe calls for twenty red-beet leaves. That is because the Japanese do not eat beets, so they pick them young with small tender leaves, which is the only part of the plant that interests them. But small, young beet leaves are hard to find here. We instead used a few torn chard leaves. Chard and beets are the same species, with beets bred for their roots and chard for their leaves, so I think chard makes a good substitute.

3 green onions, cut into 2-inch pieces
1/3 head of green leaf lettuce, torn
    into bite-size pieces
leaves of 1 head of endive, torn into
    bite-size pieces

4 torn chard leaves
1 lime
aspic dressing (see previous recipe)

Arrange the ingredients on plates. Stir the aspic to break it up and place on top of each dish, along with a little grated lime zest. Squeeze lime over the salads and serve.

SOUP
◆ OYSTER ZOUSUI

The Japanese, who seem to us to eat almost anything, are distrustful of *kaki*, the oyster. On the coast of what is known as the Inland Sea, a body of water with a graceful island-strewn coastline between the three main Japanese islands, the oysters grow bigger and plumper in a year than most American oysters in three years. But, odd for a people who eat most everything raw, most Japanese will not eat raw oysters, believing them dangerous and unhealthy. The less their oysters resemble oysters, the better they feel about them. They fry them or grill them. They even have a machine that presses them with bean curd into a wafer-thin crisp cracker, *kaki sembei*. The crackers are great, but it's a shame, really. I visited my friend Satoru Urabe, the largest oyster producer in Japan, at his Maruto Suisan Company in Maruto port, an area along the Inland Sea where he farms his oysters. He shucks them, washes them, steams them, freezes them, and sells them sealed in plastic. But he let me taste his oysters directly from the tanks while still raw and alive. They were the largest one-year-old oysters I have ever seen. Normally, warm water makes oysters grow fast but also makes them bland. The Inland Sea is fairly cold, especially when I was there in late February; the oysters are farmed along a stunning stretch of islands in the Harima bay of the Inland Sea. The bay is especially rich in phytoplankton and nutritious sediment from the floors of the dark and green nearby forests. So while most oysters take two to three years to get to a marketable size, these are quite large after one year and incredibly plump and briny-tasting, with a sweet aftertaste, like a cold-water oyster. The best oysters I ever tasted in Japan were shucked standing in front of Urabe-san's tank. But if you want a Japanese way of eating them, this recipe from Shigeki's Haseshigein restaurant is excellent.

He begins his recipe, "Wash the shucked oysters in water containing a 1 percent ratio of salt . . . " This is a typically Japanese way of dealing with the dreaded oyster, but while I greatly admire Japanese chefs on all non-kaki matters, I urge you not to do this to your oysters. Washing them, they feel, removes bacteria, but I think it removes flavor. In fact, there is no need to salt them if you don't wash them.

8 plump oysters
4 shiitake mushrooms
1 green onion
14 ounces rice
4 cups dashi
a generous pinch of salt

2 teaspoons Japanese soy sauce
3 eggs
1 small sheet nori, cut into thin strips
½ cup mitsuba or parsley, minced
seven-pepper blend (shichimi)

Shuck the oysters and cut them into approximately ½-inch pieces. If there is some watery liquid left in the shells, pour it into the soup pot, making sure not to include shell fragments.

Mince the shiitake mushrooms and green onion.

Cook the rice in an equal volume of water until all that is left of the water is bubbles dancing on the top. Cut the heat and cover for 5 minutes. Fluff the rice with a fork and place it in a colander. Wash with cold water and drain thoroughly. Pour the dashi into a pot over low heat. Make sure you put aside a few cups for the spinach and sea bream recipes that follow. Add salt, soy sauce, mushrooms, and onions and cook over very low heat for 3 minutes. Add the oysters and continue cooking on low heat. After a few minutes, add the rice and bring heat to medium. When the soup starts to boil, turn it back down to low.

Beat the eggs, then slowly beat them into the soup a little at a time. (In Japan this is done with large chopsticks, a great kitchen tool.) Pour the soup into small bowls and garnish with nori (see sushi recipe below), finely cut into slivers, and mitsuba. If mitsuba—sometimes known as Japanese parsley—is not available, parsley may be substituted, though parsley has a less complicated flavor. Sprinkle with some Japanese seven-spice blend. This common Japanese table condiment has many names in Japan, including shichimi, and is mostly red chili pepper, but it also includes roasted orange peel, black and white sesame, ginger, hemp seed, and nori. It is available online and in some stores.

◆◆◆ TUNA SUSHI

When people in the rest of the world think of Japanese food, they think of sushi, a word that has at least five different spellings in the Japanese language, each reflecting subtle linguistic differences in the concept but all generally meaning "fish." You can eat wonderfully in Japan without ever going near sushi, which is not served in most restaurants. The best place to have sushi in Tokyo is at the Tsukiji (pronounced *skeeji*) market—the largest wholesale fish market in the world—in the dark of early morning for breakfast. At about five every morning hundreds of frozen, beheaded giant bluefin tuna are auctioned off there—a bit shocking for those of us who believe bluefin is in danger of extinction. There is a lot that is shocking at this market—undersize fish taken before they have a chance to spawn, such as quarter-inch baby sardines that are dried to add a crunchiness to salads, and one-inch abalones. Cans of whale meat are sold there. If you are going to eat endangered species, can't you do better than canning them?

There is an alley of sushi restaurants at the market, each the size of a railroad car, with one long counter and little space to pass behind the customers seated at the stools. If you get there before the market opens to the public at nine A.M., you can avoid long lines. The sushi are placed in front of you on a long green haran leaf faster than you can eat them. You can have five kinds of tuna sushi with different degrees of fattiness, a huge pile of uni (sea urchin), steamed freshwater eel—unlike the roasted eel you find elsewhere—and a bulbous pile of something soft and white and rich tasting. I asked what the last was and the translated response came back as "testosterone of cod." My guess is that it is the organ that produces the sperm, but as I said, one of the secrets of enjoying Japanese food is not to ask too many questions.

Sushi making takes a bit of practice, but it is not as daunting as you might suppose, and it's fun for kids. Shari, used for making sushi, is a short-grain rice often sold as "sushi rice."

Nori is a type of red algae made into sheets by the same process as the ancient Chinese craft of paper making that Buddhists brought to Japan about 500 AD. The seaweed is raised from seed on off-shore platforms, washed, chopped, mixed with water, then poured through a screen that forms it into a thin layer that can be pressed and dried. Like paper, some nori is still made by hand, but most by machine. The machines toast the sheets to make them crisper, which also makes them lighter and greener. In Kisarazu, a town on the nori-making coast on the Pacific east of Tokyo where the machines were introduced fifty years ago, the old-timers still speak with nostalgia about the old-time nori. One older woman complained that "the machines chop it too fine. The handmade was not as fine and retained more flavor and more nutrients." Handmade nori is thicker, softer, and blacker, but it's expensive and extremely difficult to find, even in Japan.

Traditionally tuna sushi is made with bluefin tuna, but this huge migratory animal is in such danger that I do not feel comfortable using it and so recommend yellowfin tuna, preferably not caught by longline. I ask at the store.

1½ cups short-grain rice
3 tablespoons rice vinegar
3 tablespoons sugar
2 teaspoons salt

1 large sheet nori
½ pound raw yellowtail tuna, cut into
    ¼-inch slices
3 ounces wasabi

Put the rice in a pot with an equal volume of water. Bring it to a vigorous boil for 2 minutes, then cover it and leave it on medium heat for about 10 minutes or until liquid is gone. Then turn off the heat and let the rice rest covered for 10 minutes.

After the rice is cooked, add the rice vinegar, sugar, and salt. Japanese cooks always salt food from their fingers held high above the food to make sure the crystals are evenly distributed. In Japan, salt is never wasted.

Put the rice in a bowl and cool it by stirring it with big horizontal strokes with a wooden paddle, while someone else—in my case, Talia—fans the rice with a cardboard until it is cool. This seems like an elaborate ritual, but it is the only way to get the rice to the right flavor and consistency for successful sushi. If you really want to embrace the tradition, use a Japanese hand fan.

Spread out a sheet of nori. Spread the rice on the center third of the nori sheet in an even layer the long way. Place slices of raw tuna on top.

Sprinkle lightly with wasabi, a paste made from the root of a Japanese plant of the same name and widely available. Roll up the nori and seal the ends by wetting the edges and pressing them together.

Chill, and then cut into 1-inch slices.

TALIA: *On Sushi*

Kids love using their hands. That's one reason making and eating sushi is so much fun. There is also a sense of luxury in sushi. It's special. Many kids like acting older or more sophisticated; that's why it's fun to play dress-up. Sushi feels like dress-up food.

At Japanese restaurants, the chefs at the sushi counter work so fast and skillfully that it all looks very difficult. But actually, you can learn to do it and it's not as difficult as you might think. The first thing you need to know is the right rice to use, but that's easy because it's often marked "sushi rice." However, you have to make it exactly right, cool it right, fan it—the whole process really takes two people. Once you get the rice right, it's quite simple. You just spread it on the seaweed, place thin strips of fish in the middle, and add some wasabi. (Be careful, wasabi can be very spicy and too much can make you cry, so use it sparingly and to your own preference.) Then you just roll the seaweed up tightly, slice it up into pieces, pick it up with your hands, and eat.

MAIN COURSE
◆◆ HORENSO NO GOMA-AE (SPINACH AND SESAME)

1 pound spinach
a splash of sesame oil
a splash of soy sauce

a splash of dashi
dashi

Steam spinach and chop in slices. Dress with sesame oil, soy sauce, and a splash of the same dashi used in the earlier recipes.

◆ TAI MESHI (SEA BREAM AND RICE)

Sea bream is a fish found in the Pacific but only on the European side of the Atlantic. Nevertheless, it is flown in and commonly available in US fish stores.

1 sea bream, gutted and scaled but left
    whole with the head and tail still on
1 cup rice
1 cup dashi

a pinch of salt
2 splashes of soy sauce
1 ounce mirin
2 green onions

Place the sea bream in a casserole dish on the stove with rice almost covered with the dashi, salt, soy sauce, and mirin (see On Sugar and Spice, p. 12). Bring to a boil for 2 minutes, then cook for 20 minutes, covered well, over medium heat. Turn off the heat and let it rest for 10 minutes. Remove the head, tail, and bones, which should come off easily. Stir the fish and rice together and place in a bowl with chopped green onions on top.

DESSERT
◆◆ STRAWBERRY MOCHI

The Japanese love sweets. They have huge shops of them, pretty pastel edible ornaments. Most are made of some combination of beans, rice, and sugar. Mochi uses all three. The word actually refers not to a finished dessert but to pounded sweet rice, which is then filled with a variety of treats, not all of them sweet. At the Nozaki mansion, a well-preserved 1827 estate of a wealthy salt merchant in Kojima—the opulence of which even today gives some idea of the importance of salt in Japan—there are stone tubs two feet wide with huge wooden mallets that were used to pound the rice to make mochi. Today it is sometimes made the same way with almost identical tools. In home cooking, the rice is not pounded as much, so some of the shape of the grains is still discernable in the paste.

High in the mountains, steep and snowcapped as the northern Rockies, I was invited to a home where they pounded their own rice for mochi—in fact, they even grew their own rice for pounding. Then they stuck large balls of it on a pair of chopsticks, rolled the balls in a paste of ground black sesame with sake, sugar, and soy sauce, and lightly grilled them (using their homemade charcoal, of course). The sweet shops sell more elegant versions of mochi, sometimes stuffed with fresh fruit. In the late winter, strawberry mochi appears. The berries, though raised in hothouses, are extremely sweet and juicy. When you buy strawberry mochi in the shops they tell you, "They must be eaten in twelve hours," though in my case they get consumed in less than one hour. They hold up very well in the refrigerator for twelve hours, but not much longer.

This dish—easy and tactile, like working with modeling clay—can be made entirely by supervised children. The trick here is to use very sweet, juicy, not-too-large berries.

½ cup sugar
1¼ cups water
3 cups sweet rice or glutinous rice flour

6 perfect ripe strawberries, stems removed

Boil the water and sugar and stir until the crystals are melted. Pour the liquid into a mixer with the hook attachment and add sweet rice or glutinous rice flour (see China Night, p. 54). Mix on a slow speed. You may have to add a little more water if it is too thick to come together. Eventually you should have a malleable dough ball around the hook. As it cools it will become less sticky, but you can dust your fingers with leftover rice powder to prevent sticking. Roll dough into a ball big enough to hold your strawberry, press a large hole in the center with your thumb, and insert strawberry.

Work the dough over the strawberry to encase it, or, as we did, leave a heart-shaped opening with the berry showing.

There are a lot of variations of this in Japan. In Kyoto I had them with a little whipped cream placed in the hole before the strawberry. Orange segments with the membrane removed are a popular filling. In the Tsukiji market I found them with the dough mixed with the juice of cooked blueberries, rolled into small purple balls and filled with bean paste (see China Night, p. 54). If you are fast and nimble fingered, you can fill them with small balls of ice cream and put them in the freezer. Ginger, red bean, or green tea are traditional ice cream flavors, but use what you like, including, perhaps, strawberry ice cream.

DRINK
◆ GREEN TEA

It seems in Japan that when there is any occasion during which you are seated, someone will bring you a cup of green tea. The more accustomed to it you become, the more you enjoy it. The flavor that is usually sought is called "grassy," an apt name for a taste that resembles the scent of fresh-cut grass. For our meal we drank karigane kukicha, a very grassy green tea prized in Japan and made from stems rather than leaves of the gyokuro variety, grown exclusively in the shade in the Kyoto region. After dinner we sipped hojicha, a tea from the Kyoto region also made mostly from stems. It is roasted, so, while technically a green tea, it is brown. Stem teas have less caffeine than leaf teas. Green teas should be steeped with hot but not boiling water. If the water is too hot, the tea becomes bitter.

AFGHANISTAN NIGHT

HINT: A NATION RICH IN OIL, NATURAL GAS, SALT, COPPER, IRON, AND PRECIOUS GEMS, IT REMAINS ONE OF THE POOREST IN THE WORLD, LARGELY BECAUSE OF CONSTANT WARFARE.

Afghanistan's history is one of constant invasions, most of which have failed. Among the few with lasting impact was the seventh-century Arab invasion that left the country Muslim, the eleventh-century invasion by the Turks, who for a moment made it the center of Islam, and the sixteenth-century invasion by Afghanistan's ruler, Babur, a descendent of Gengis Khan, into parts of India. The food reflects the invaders, especially the Arabs, the Turks, and the Persians (Iran). But a rich and varied cuisine has failed to flourish because this mountainous country, one of the first agricultural countries in the world, has worn out its soil. The tribalism and warfare that has kept the economy from growing has also inhibited sound farming practices, and arable areas are increasingly turning into deserts.

But that is not to say that Afghanistan does not offer an interesting array of dishes, and with a vegetarian appetizer, a meat and soup main course, and a sweet dessert, we greatly enjoyed this meal—somewhat to our surprise, since we could not pronounce a single dish.

The dessert should be started the day before.

APPETIZER
◆ BOURANEE BAUNJUN

1 eggplant
salt
1¼ cups olive oil
1 onion
½ green bell pepper, chopped
2 tomatoes, chopped

1 tablespoon cayenne pepper
3 garlic cloves, peeled and chopped
¼ cup chicken stock (canned or see Basic Recipes, p. 24)
1½ cups plain Greek-style yogurt

Slice the unpeeled eggplant. Salt it heavily and let it sit 20 minutes. Wipe the salt off and cook lightly in very hot olive oil. Add onion, bell pepper, tomatoes, cayenne pepper, and garlic.

Sauté until wilted, then add chicken stock. Simmer slowly for 5 minutes. Cut heat. Stir in yogurt. Mix well.

MAIN COURSE
◆ KOFTAD NAKHOD (CHICKPEA MEATBALLS)

2 cups canned chickpeas
1 yellow onion, chopped
6 ounces ground lamb
a large pinch of salt
4 turns of black pepper

1 tablespoon powdered cinnamon
1 cup bread crumbs
2 eggs
2 cups chicken stock

Purée chickpeas in a food processor with the onion. Mix in the ground lamb. Add salt, pepper, cinnamon, bread crumbs, and eggs. Mix well. Form balls the size of golf balls. Simmer in chicken stock for 30 minutes. Serve with rice, if you like.

VEGETABLE
◆ SABZI (SPINACH)

olive oil as needed
½ white onion, chopped
5 garlic cloves, peeled and chopped
2 teaspoons coriander powder
6 coriander seeds

3 tablespoons chopped fresh dill
3 tablespoons chopped fresh
coriander (cilantro) leaves
1 pound spinach

Sauté onion, garlic, and coriander powder and seeds in olive oil. Add dill, coriander leaves, and spinach. Stir and cook quickly until spinach wilts.

Spinach

DESSERT
◆◆ ASABIA EL AROOS (BRIDE'S FINGERS)

3/4 cup water
1 cup sugar
juice of 1/2 lemon
a generous splash of rose water
2 cups shelled pistachios

2 1/2 cups sugar
3 eggs
5 sheets phyllo dough
1 stick melted butter
1-2 egg yolks

The day before, heat water and melt sugar in it. Add lemon juice and rose water. Chill the syrup.

The next day, preheat oven to 400 degrees. Place shelled pistachio nuts, sugar, and eggs in a food processor and grind to a paste.

Unfold a sheet of phyllo dough. (You can buy this frozen and then thaw it.) Brush it with butter, fold it in half, and brush with butter again. Continue this process until you have a 5-inch square.

Put a line of the pistachio paste on the dough square and roll it up. Repeat. You should have enough paste for 4 or 5 fingers. Brush with beaten egg yolk, sprinkle with sugar, and bake for 15 minutes. Pour cold syrup over these before serving.

DRINK
◆ SHOMLEH

2 cups Greek-style plain yogurt
1 1/2 cups water

5 fresh mint leaves

Put all the ingredients in a food processor or blender and mix until mint is completely pureed. Chill and serve.

MOROCCO NIGHT

HINT: THE WESTERN KINGDOM IN ITS REGION.

The original Arab name for Morocco was al-Mamlakat al-Maghribiyyah, "the westernmost kingdom"—westernmost, that is, in the Maghreb, an area of Arab North Africa that includes Libya, Tunisia, Algeria, and Morocco. These countries have much in common in culture and cuisine, but Morocco is the region's gastronomic star, the part of North Africa with the most flair in its cooking, and some say the country with the best food in all of Africa. When Talia's finger landed on Morocco, I already knew a few Moroccan dishes, especially since I had studied cooking in neighboring Tunisia. But when I learned that for the first time in history there was a cooking school in Morocco, I decided that Talia and I had to go there.

The school is in a beautiful boutique hotel in the medina, within the ancient walls of the earthen red town of Marrakech, a city known for its cooking and culture that lies on the yellow plains before the rugged black Atlas Mountains. The hotel has a history of firsts. In 1946, two French women, Hélène Sébillon-Lorechette and her daughter Suzy, who had been living in Marrakech since the 1930s, obtained permission from the pasha of Marrakech, Thami El Glaoui, to establish not only the first restaurant open to foreigners inside the medina but also the first business in Morocco run by women. More than permission, he sent a cook from his palace to teach them Moroccan cuisine.

The part of Marrakech frequented by foreigners lay primarily outside of the medina in a turn-of-the century French colonial neighborhood with such institutions as La Mamounia, said to be one of the world's most luxurious hotels. But the women were able to bring such luminaries as Winston Churchill, Jackie Kennedy, and Charles de Gaulle into the medina—with its crowded markets, snake charmers, and winding streets and alleys—and to their restaurant, La Maison Arabe.

In 1995 Fabrizio Ruspoli di Poggio Suasa, an Italian aristocrat who had fallen in love with Morocco while spending his summers in his grandmother's home in Tangier, bought the restaurant and the riad, the traditional urban home, next door. Another first, this was the first riad to be turned into a hotel, a practice that is becoming widespread.

Fabrizio indulged his personal taste in every handwoven rug, every lamp, every doorknob, creating a stunning Arab setting for his restaurant and hotel—even hiring students of North Africa's most celebrated oud player to perform Arabo-Andalusian guitar and oud music. (The oud is an Arab invention, the predecessor of the lute.)

In this haven of Arab and Berber culture, he established Morocco's first cooking school in a well-furnished room of marble counters with a dozen cooking stations.

A charming woman, Wafaa Amagui, one of seven children who learned cooking from her mother, ran the school when we visited. Our program was rigorous, but she would graciously offer me a glass of wine before our hours of serious cooking began. Moroccan wine, by the way, long a horror sold to the poor in France, has become more than drinkable; it is actually quite good.

We studied under dadas. A dada is what Morocco had, until recently, instead of cookbooks. They are women trained by their mothers who pass on the crafts and secrets and recipes of Moroccan cooking from one generation to the next. They are still the best archive of Moroccan cooking knowledge. We worked with two dadas: Fatiha and Ayada.

Fatiha feigned an aura of sternness, barking out orders in French and English and addressing me sharply as "chef," which amused Talia, who was not in the least intimidated. We

Tagine

could see that Fatiha was actually a warm and sympathetic woman. She had learned cooking from her mother, who, far from a simple country cook, had been adopted at the age of eight by the pasha of Marrakech, Caïd El Ayadi, an important figure in Moroccan politics until his death in 1964. Fatiha's mother worked with the palace dadas from a young age. She became known as a superb cook, and palaces and leading homes in Marrakech would hire her to oversee major events. She would do this with her daughter Fatiha, the youngest of ten children, and so Fatiha learned the finest in Moroccan cuisine.

Our other dada, Ayada, was a large woman with an appropriately large belly laugh that erupted regularly and was somewhat unnerving to me because she spoke only Arabic—so unless Wafaa explained, I never knew what she was laughing about. Wafaa and Ayada had regular disagreements. Since Ayada was working for La Maison Arabe, she was supposed to be teaching their recipes. But Ayada had her own variations, and when Wafaa objected, Ayada would simply say, "This is my personal creativity." These were minor variations, such as adding the tomato at the beginning of the soup rather than at the end. But such variations amounted to a dada's secrets, and when a dada revealed a secret, it was always worth listening.

We cooked with the dadas for three or four hours a day. The rest of the day was spent beyond the sheltering walls in a grimy, fascinating world of street acts, monkeys and snakes, men and women in exotic clothes, small shops and stalls selling rugs, jewelry, hand-carved wooden tools, clothes, and food. We also saw some of the great examples of medieval Arab architecture and the fabulous gardens built by Yves Saint Laurent.

Moroccan cuisine, like the Moroccan people, is a hybrid. It is part Berber, the original inhabitants who are still the majority; part French, since France controlled Morocco for almost half of the twentieth century; and part Arab, since the Arabs conquered Morocco in the Middle Ages and controlled it for centuries. Through the Arabs there is also a noticeable Turkish influence, such as the use of phyllo dough, one of Turkey's most widespread inventions. Phyllo was brought to Morocco by the Moors, the Spanish Arabs who also brought the beautiful oud music. Another important influence is Jewish. Morocco used to have one of the largest Jewish populations in the world, though today most Moroccan Jews have moved to Israel, France, the United States, Canada, and other places. Preserved foods, such as preserved lemons, are said to be Jewish inventions.

It is an old-fashioned kind of cuisine with no shortcuts. "The secret of good cooking," said Ayada, "is taking time." Food is rarely chopped. It is minced extremely fine, even if this means ten minutes of chopping. At La Maison Arabe, Talia learned how to use knives, something I had been afraid to teach her at home. In Morocco food tends not to be left in a natural state. Tomatoes and peppers are skinned. Seeds are removed from tomatoes. Nothing is left whole. It is not a fat cuisine. Oil is used sparingly, usually olive oil or peanut oil, fitting choices for a crossroad between Europe and Africa.

The Moroccans don't use machines. The only machine I ever saw used was a food processor for grinding almonds, though the origi-

nal tool for this purpose, two round, heavy grinding stones, one on top of the other with a wooden stick in a hole for turning, was still in the kitchen. As with Indian food, the elegance of Moroccan food is in the careful blending of herbs and spices. Wafaa repeatedly emphasized that the cuisine started with black pepper, ginger, and turmeric. Instead of fresh ginger, they generally used powdered ginger, which I don't think is nearly as good. They agreed, but said fresh was hard to get. Another important spice is cumin. When they want something a little hot, never burning, they use harissa, a blend of red chilies, garlic, and cumin, either as a powder or made into a paste with olive oil. (See chili pepper in On Sugar and Spice, p. 9.) Fresh parsley and coriander (cilantro) are also frequent ingredients, as are finely minced garlic and onions. Saffron is also important but expensive: it is the stigma of one variety of crocus, with each long purple flower having only three deep red stigmas, so it takes 150,000 flowers to make one kilogram (2.2 pounds) of saffron. And there are only three or four flowers on a plant. In Morocco it is produced only in Taliouine and harvested only in October. So it is used sparingly.

And as with all spicy cuisines, there is a special blend of spices, Ras el Hanout, which literally means "the head of the shop." Different spice makers make it slightly differently, and good Moroccan cooks are careful where they buy their blend, but it generally includes cardamom, mace, red pepper, galingale (the stalk of the ginger tree from which cardamom comes), nutmeg, star anise, ginger root, cinnamon, cloves, belladonna berries, orris root (locally known as *oud el amber*, from an iris valuable in perfume making that grows in the High Atlas

Mountains), lavender, black pepper, rosebuds, and a few other ingredients, several of which are believed to be aphrodisiacs.

What I most loved about the cooking style of the dadas was that they never measured. "Take a handful of this, a pinch of that, some of this." Cooking, after all, involves personal choice, not scientific formulas. Wafaa said to me, "I teach that food is not measurements." But most Westerners have been raised on cookbooks that encourage measuring, so I have tried to come up with measurements to help you out.

One of Ayada's secrets is to begin candying the oranges for the tagine the day before (see Lamb and Candied Orange Tagine on p. 114). The Zaalouk Salad (p. 119) is also best made the day before.

A WORD ON ALMONDS

Almonds are a constant ingredient in Moroccan cooking, and they are almost always blanched. In Morocco, blanched almonds are rarely sold. It is believed that almonds that have been pre-blanched lose flavor and texture. The dadas, who do everything the hard and best way, always blanched almonds for each dish that they used them in. To do so, plunge the almonds into boiling water, leave them for a few minutes, chill in cold water, towel dry, and skin by squeezing between your thumb and first finger. It's a bit time consuming, but kids sometimes enjoy this task, squirting the white almond from their fingers . . . or you could simply buy blanched almonds.

TALIA: Our trip to Marrakech

The first thing my dad and I did when we got to the hotel in Marrakech was go to its soothing courtyard and have some of Morocco's famous mint tea and La Maison Arabe's assortment of homemade cookies. The beautiful plants, the birds chirping will stay in my memory forever.

The hotel was an architectural masterpiece, a traditional Moroccan-style home but with all of the modern conveniences and a courtyard in the middle of the building with a relaxing breeze and a small fountain filled with rose petals. In the center of another courtyard, a beautiful pool majestically beckoned you to swim in it. Since we were in the old city, it was short walk every morning to shopping in the souk.

Our cooking classes with the dadas were so much fun. We prepared many tagines, which are in a way a Moroccan version of a stew. They can be sweet or sour, vegetarian or with meat. We also experimented with drinks, including an almond milk drink that was extremely tasty. We learned to make desserts, which are always fun to make (and eat!). And we made salads that I wouldn't exactly call leafy, but that were nevertheless delicious. We even learned how to make our own bread similar to pita bread.

And of course I learned to make a tomato rose. If you skin a tomato in a spiral starting at the top, carefully so as not to peel the skin too thin and therefore cause it to break, you will have a long strip of tomato skin. Then, as if you are rolling up a rug, roll the skin into a cylinder. You want the skin to be rolled tight in the center and looser as you continue. Voilà . . . you have a delicious red rose.

While on this trip I went up a level in my cooking skills. Before, if a difficult job came up, such as something involving a flame or heavy use of a knife, my dad would swoop in to help. However, while in Morocco I learned to slice, dice, chop, and mince my way through the kitchen. I was careful, and the experience was so much more satisfying when I was really able to do everything on my own. But of course you need to start off with some assistance when you start using fire and knives.

Another ingredient of this magical trip was the atmosphere of the city. Most nights we ate the food we had spent the afternoon cooking, which completed the process and made it even more memorable.

We realized that we had too many dishes we wanted to make for just one dinner, so we had two Morocco Nights. You could eliminate some of the dishes and have one night, but what would be the fun of that? Why not just have a whole Moroccan weekend? .

FIRST NIGHT
◆◆ BATBOUT BREAD

We began every class by making bread, because it is essential to Moroccan food. While the Maison Arabe has ovens, few Moroccans have ovens in their homes. They either make the bread in a skillet or take it to a communal baker. One such communal baker was around the corner from the Maison Arabe. A small doorway led to a step down into a cavelike shop with a magenta-and-white tile floor and, at the far end, in the darkness, a red-hot wood-burning fire, next to which the breads were baked. The man in the dark wearing a black woven skullcap and a white-striped cotton djellaba, the traditional robe, was a master baker, a title that takes at least ten years to earn. People bring their uncooked breads and he not only bakes them perfectly, but remembers whose is whose without labeling. There is a kind of social order to bread, and people's economic standing can be seen in the quality of flour they use.

The bread—very similar to bread I learned to make in Tunisia—is made in a flat-bottomed bowl, a gsaa, an ingenious North African invention. When you are finished, all you have to do for cleanup is wash the bowl. In both countries the wooden bowl is found in country kitchens, and in a city such as Marrakech a glazed ceramic one is used.

The dadas blended two types of flour, a standard white and a higher-quality darker one. But you can use any kind of flour. They used fresh yeast, which is always best, but the recipe will work with dry yeast also. It works better in a warm room than a cold one, which is why Moroccans say the bread is better in the summer.

1 tablespoon fresh yeast
3 cups flour
a large pinch of salt

a large pinch of sugar
warm water
1 or 2 tablespoons peanut oil

Mix yeast with flour, salt, and sugar. Little by little, mix with warm water until you have a slightly sticky but kneadable dough. If you use fresh yeast, crush it between your fingers as you mix. If you use dry yeast, dissolve it in a little warm water before mixing in the other ingredients. Knead well for at least 10 minutes, pressing a thin layer against the bottom of the bowl with your palm, folding it over, turning, and repeating. Shape dough into a ball and coat with a little peanut oil so the surface is smooth but not dripping in oil. Sprinkle lightly with flour and cover with a cloth. After about 30 minutes, the ball will have expanded. Break off pieces and flatten into pancakes about five or six inches in diameter.

Heat a small skillet very hot. Place a disk of the dough in the skillet and turn every few minutes until it is slightly browned on both sides with a few dark spots.

APPETIZER
◆◆ BAKED SARDINES

This is a family favorite and the only dish for Morocco Night that does not come from our Marrakech cooking classes. Moroccans eat a lot of sardines, but not in Marrakech, which is far inland.

5 fresh whole sardines, scaled and gutted
1 cup white onion, minced
¼ cup olive oil
4 cups tomato sauce #1 (see Basic Recipes, p. 25)
3 tablespoons powdered cumin
1 tablespoon harissa (or cayenne pepper)

3 garlic cloves, peeled and finely minced
½ cup coriander leaves (cilantro), finely minced
½ cup Italian parsley, finely minced
7 black olives
1 Moroccan preserved lemon, chopped (see Basic Recipes, p. 24)

Preheat oven to 350 degrees. Grill the sardines. Fillet them (see Sicily Night, p. 85, and Aquitaine Night, p. 210). Sauté onions in olive oil and add tomato sauce. Add cumin and harissa (or cayenne pepper if you don't have harissa). Put half of the sauce in a small, ovenproof casserole. Place 5 sardine fillets in the sauce, skin-side down, in a neat row. Mix garlic, coriander, and parsley and place the mixture on each of the 5 sardine fillets. Place the other 5 fillets on top of them. Cover with the other half of sauce. Place black olives and chopped preserved lemon on top. Bake for 10 minutes.

SOUP
◆◆ HARIRA

If you are the opposite of Talia and don't care for sardines but love soup, try this soup that we learned to make at the Maison Arabe. Moroccans sometimes eat it for breakfast, or at night with sweet pastries on the side.

½ pound lamb, cut into bite-size
    pieces
2 white onions, finely minced
½ pound dried lentils
½ cup canned chickpeas
1 celery rib, finely minced
6 tablespoons olive oil
a large pinch of salt
½ teaspoon powdered turmeric

1 teaspoon clarified butter
9 cups water
3 medium-size tomatoes
1 slice fresh ginger root, peeled and
    chopped
2 tablespoons tomato paste
4 turns of black pepper
¼ cup rice
3 tablespoons flour

Place the lamb, onions, lentils, chickpeas, celery, 3 tablespoons olive oil, salt, turmeric, clarified butter (called *smen* in Arabic or known as ghee in India; see Basic Recipes, p. 6, and India Night, p. 238) in a pot. Cook over medium heat for about 10 minutes.

Add the water. Cook over medium heat for an hour.

Take the tomatoes, burn the skin on a burner, and rub it off. Quarter the tomatoes and remove the seeds and gel (Ayada did this very efficiently with her fingers). Save yourself a lot of chopping and puree the tomatoes in a food processor with the ginger root. Mix in a bowl with the tomato paste, 3 tablespoons olive oil, and the black pepper. Add this mixture to the soup. Stir well and cook another 20 minutes. Add the rice. Cook 10 more minutes.

Take some liquid from the soup and mix it in a bowl with the flour until it is smooth and without lumps and put it back into the soup. Stir constantly while cooking, another 5 minutes.

MAIN COURSE
◆◆ LAMB AND CANDIED ORANGE TAGINE

Tagine is a Berber dish—both the pot and also the food cooked in it. The obvious should be stated: you have to have a tagine to make a tagine. A tagine is a casserole dish with a fitted cover with a tall chimney, available for purchase at many stores or online. Some are glazed pottery and some are unglazed. An unglazed tagine should be soaked for twenty-four hours before it is used for the first time. Unglazed tagines can only be used to cook one type of food because the clay absorbs the taste of the food. Tagines can be made with chicken, lamb, fish, and other ingredients, accompanied by a wide variety of sauces. But once lamb has been cooked in an unglazed tagine, the tagine cannot be used for fish. An unglazed tagine that has cooked beef cannot be used for chicken. So there is an obvious advantage to glazed tagines. Some tagines have a small hole at the top of the chimney, but a tagine with no hole is better because it becomes a sealed steam chamber. What makes the dish is the slow cooking process that takes place inside the tagine.

Meat tagines are usually made with something sweet, often dried fruit. In the following recipe, it is candied oranges, and Ayada insists that for the best results you should start the oranges the day before.

For three people, use two oranges. Three oranges would be good for up to five, which is about as much as can be cooked in a single large tagine. In restaurants, each serving is cooked in its own tagine.

2 yellow onions, minced
3 tablespoons peanut oil
1 tablespoon butter
½ teaspoon powdered turmeric
1 teaspoon cinnamon
3 turns of black pepper
½ teaspoon peeled and finely minced
    ginger root

3 slices leg of lamb, bone in (if you
    buy a leg or even a half leg from a
    good butcher and ask, he will slice
    it for you—¾-inch-thick slices
3 cups water
5 strands saffron
1 sweet orange
candied orange (see recipe below)
3 tablespoons sesame seeds

Put the onions in a tagine with the peanut oil and butter over low heat. Add turmeric, cinnamon, black pepper, and ginger. When oil is hot, add 1 slice per person of leg of lamb. Cook about 20 minutes. Add water and saffron. Let simmer in covered tagine for 1 hour. Periodically check to make sure water has not completely cooked away.

Cut top and bottom off an orange and peel with a knife to expose flesh. With a paring knife, cut about ¾ of the sections away from the membrane. Arrange them around the tagine decoratively. Pull the remaining orange flesh off the candied oranges, cut the peel into strips, and arrange them around the tagine like a sunburst. Sprinkle lightly with sesame seeds. Bring to the table with the cover on and dramatically unveil upon serving.

CANDIED ORANGES

2 oranges   4 cloves
2 cinnamon sticks   2 cups sugar

The day before dinner, scrape the oranges on a grater, just enough to remove the shiny outer skin and leave a rough orange underlayer. Do not expose the white underneath. Cut the oranges in quarters and boil them in ¾ quart of water for 20 minutes. Then discard the water and replace with an equal amount, adding the cinnamon sticks, cloves, and sugar. Continue boiling until the mixture begins to caramelize, then turn off the heat and let it macerate until the next day. On the next day, resume boiling until the water is gone and the oranges are in syrup.

DESERT
◆◆ FRUIT PASTILLA

Pastilla is the French translation of an Arab word for dishes wrapped in phyllo. It probably is not a good translation, since there is no *P* in the Arabic language, so the dish is sometimes called bistilla. This is a sophisticated urban Moroccan dish that would not be found in the countryside.

1 sheet phyllo dough
¼ cup peanut oil
1 pint whole milk
3 tablespoons sugar
3 tablespoons orange-blossom water
½ cup cornstarch
¼ cup sugar
1 cup heavy cream

IN SUMMER
6 strawberries, sliced
2 small plums, sliced
1 peach, sliced

IN WINTER
1 banana, sliced
6 strawberries, sliced

For each serving, cut 4 circles about 4 inches in diameter from the phyllo dough and fry them in hot oil for a few minutes until they turn color. Drain on paper towels.

Heat the milk, sugar, and orange-blossom water with the cornstarch. Keep stirring until the mixture becomes thick, then let it cool. Set aside a few slices of each fruit. Toss the rest of the sliced fruit in sugar melted in a little water in a skillet. Stir quickly in the hot syrup and immediately remove to cool.

Whip the cream until stiff with several drops orange-blossom water and ¼ cup sugar.

On each plate lay down a disk of phyllo dough. Cover it with the milk-cornstarch mixture. Lay down another disk. Spoon on some fruit with a little syrup. Lay down a third disk. Cover it with whipped cream and a few slices of the reserved uncooked fruit. Lay down the fourth disk. Cover it with whipped cream and put a slice of strawberry on top.

DRINKS
◆◆ MOROJITO

You would not expect to find a great bartender in a Muslim country, with the faithful told that they should not consume alcohol and the Maison Arabe being located near a minaret from which a loudspeaker blasts the call to worship five times a day. But genial Rashid Edhidi is the perfect bartender. A listener if you want to talk, an entertainer if you want to listen, he invents concoctions at a dizzying rate. And because there are so many nondrinkers, he invents alcohol-free drinks too. Talia loved them. Among his inventions is a drink of peach juice, mint syrup, coconut cream, and cucumber whipped up in a blender. Another is mango juice, grenadine syrup, bananas, and strawberries in a blender. But his signature drink, with or without alcohol, is something he calls a morojito.

1 large lime
1 quart pineapple juice
2 slices fresh ginger, chopped

1 handful fresh mint
1 tablespoon mint syrup

Cut the lime vertically into quarters and put them in a blender. Add the pineapple juice, ginger, mint, and mint syrup. Mix thoroughly in blender and then pour through a strainer.

Rashid's drinks are excellent for children and good Muslims, but I find them greatly enhanced by dark rum.

◆ SAFFRON TEA

Tea—most commonly flavored with saffron, mint, or lemon verbena—is the predominant drink of Morocco. It is the traditional welcome to a visitor or just a customer in a shop. Moroccans are obsessed with sugar and use copious amounts at any opportunity. They drink their tea like syrup. One local Berber in Marrakech said jokingly to me, "We serve tea to say 'welcome,' but if it doesn't have a lot of sugar in it, we are saying, 'Don't come back.'"

Wafaa suggested brewing the tea with no sugar and then letting guests add it according to their taste. But Aline Benayoun, a French Moroccan—French Moroccans are referred to as *pieds noir*, black feet, because of their European shoes—made an interesting point in her book *Casablanca Cuisine: French North African Cooking*. She said that one of the secrets of mint tea is to brew it with the sugar already added. This poses a problem for those who want no sugar, but I think it is true that the sugar draws out the mint, so I add about a tablespoon of sugar in the teapot.

In Morocco, as in most of the African continent, making and serving teas is an elaborate ritual. While food is the woman's domain, tea is made and served by the man of the household. To make it well is to be considered a master craftsman.

The usual tea is Chinese green tea called "gunpowder tea," which comes from Zheijiang Province on the coast of China, where it has been produced since the Middle Ages. The English named it gunpowder because the way the leaves were rolled into balls made it resemble gunpowder. The British introduced tea to North Africa when looking for new markets for their tea trade in the eighteenth century.

To make the tea the traditional way, you need a Moroccan metal teapot. If you don't have a metal pot that can go on a burner, then just pour hot water into a teapot to heat it up. Pour out the water and add tea and saffron (or tea and fresh mint for mint tea, or lemon verbena) and let it steep.

But the traditional process is to boil water in a kettle. Pour a small amount of hot water into a Moroccan teapot and swish it around to heat up the pot. Add loose green tea. Add one cup of boiling water to the teapot and mix well. Pour this first cup into a tea glass. This is considered the essence of the tea. Add one more cup of boiling water to the teapot. Swish it around and pour it into a second tea glass. This tea will be thrown away. It is made to cleanse the tea leaves and is considered bitter. Add saffron to the pot. It's true it's expensive, but you want enough strands so that you can taste it. Add 1 tablespoon sugar. Pour the first glass of tea back into the pot. Fill the teapot with boiling water. Put the pot on a burner over low heat until it comes to a boil. The tea is served in small ornate glasses. Before serving, pour tea into a glass, then back into the kettle two or three times to mix it well. When you serve it, raise the teapot as high as you can above the glasses. This will produce a foam in the glass, but it's also part of the flair of serving tea in Morocco.

SECOND NIGHT
◆ ZAALOUK SALAD

These salads are all very different in taste and texture, so we made small amounts of all three. This first one is good to make the day before and chill overnight.

4 medium-size tomatoes
1 small eggplant
2 garlic cloves, peeled
a large pinch of salt
1 tablespoon olive oil

1 teaspoon sweet paprika
2 teaspoons harissa
1 tablespoon cumin
5 turns of black pepper
a splash of wine vinegar

Burn the tomatoes on a burner and rub off the peel. Quarter them and discard the seeds and gel. Mince the tomato and set aside. Partially peel a small eggplant (there should be slightly more tomato than eggplant). Fatiha taught us to do this by cutting off strips of peel so the eggplant appears striped. Then dice it. Finely mince the garlic and mash it with the flat of your knife blade. Put it in a skillet with salt and olive oil. This is not an oily dish, so be careful not to add too much. Over medium heat, add the eggplant. After five minutes of cooking, add the minced tomato to the skillet with the paprika, harissa, cumin, and black pepper. Start mashing the eggplant. Fatiha taught us to do this with a wooden spatula, but at home I do it much more efficiently with a Mexican bean masher. (Why have only Mexicans figured out this tool?) Mash for a long time. When I made this with Ayada, hers was better than mine chiefly because she mashed it better. Mix and mash well. Add a splash of wine vinegar. Remove from heat. Chill.

◆ CABBAGE AND DRIED FRUIT SALAD

¼ head cabbage
5 dried apricots
4 dried dates
about 6 walnut halves

a pinch of salt
¼ cup olive oil
juice of ½ lemon

Slice cabbage as thinly as possible. Mince the apricots, dates, and walnuts. Mix with the cabbage, salt, a good drizzle of olive oil, and the lemon juice.

◆ ORANGE AND BLACK OLIVE SALAD

The secret of this salad is argan oil, an oil made from the pit of a tree fruit. It is produced only in Morocco, and only by women. It is available in the US at a few gourmet shops and online, for example at Kulustyan.com. If you do buy it online, make sure you buy the culinary variety and not cosmetic argan oil, which has become very stylish and expensive and will not harm you but has much less flavor. Good edible argan oil tastes like a nut oil, somewhat like walnut oil.

5 black olives	3 turns of black pepper
1 navel orange	¼ cup minced Italian parsley
a pinch of salt	3-4 tablespoons argan oil

Pit and chop the olives. Cut off the top and bottom of the orange and then peel it with a knife so that the flesh is exposed. With a paring knife, cut the segments away from the membrane and chop them. Put the olives and chopped orange in a small bowl. Add salt, pepper, and parsley. Toss the ingredients together and, just before serving, mix in a healthy drizzle of argan oil.

Argan fruit

MAIN COURSE
◆◆◆ PASTILLA OF PIGEON

This is the most elegant Moroccan dish we encountered. The blending of sweet and savory, the complex use of spices and flavors, all those things that characterize the best in Moroccan cooking are at their height in this dish. The key is using pigeon, and pigeon is not easily found. Don't kill one in the park the way Hemingway claimed he did in Paris in his lean years, because in most city parks the birds called pigeons are actually doves. Wafaa suggests chicken, but chicken meat is too white and bland for this dish. Some stores and butcher shops sell pigeon. Squab is an acceptable substitute. Quail works and isn't hard to find. You would generally cook one pigeon or squab per person, or two quail. Whatever bird you use must be cooked a very long time, a minimum of two to three hours, so that the meat shreds in your fingers. Poke it with a fork, and if it is ready the prongs will easily slip through the flesh.

3 tablespoons peanut oil
1 yellow onion, finely minced
1 tablespoon coriander leaf (cilantro), finely minced
1 tablespoon Italian parsley, finely minced
1 tablespoon plus 1 teaspoon clarified butter (smen or ghee, recipe on p. 238)
a pinch of salt
4 turns of black pepper
½ tablespoon plus 1 teaspoon powdered cinnamon
½ teaspoon fresh ginger root, finely minced ½ teaspoon powdered turmeric
½ teaspoon plus 1 tablespoon sugar
5 strands saffron
1 teaspoon ras el hanout
3 pigeons or squabs, or 6 quail
6 eggs
½ cup blanched almonds
1 tablespoon orange-blossom water
1 stick melted butter
3 sheets phyllo dough
4 tablespoons honey

Put the peanut oil in a pot over medium heat. Add the onion, coriander leaf, parsley, 1 tablespoon smen, salt, pepper, ½ tablespoon cinnamon, ginger, turmeric, ½ teaspoon sugar, saffron, and the ras el hanout (see Morocco Night, p. 108).

Add the birds and enough water to cover them. Cook with lid on for about 4 hours. Check periodically to turn the birds and make sure there is enough water. Add more water if needed.

When the meat is very tender to the prick of a fork, remove it from the pot. Pull off the skin, throw it out, and pull off the meat and shred it with your fingers.

Cook down the sauce in the pot so that it is fairly thick—not at all watery. Break into the pot 4 eggs and stir with a wooden spoon until they take on the texture of dry scrambled eggs. Put the egg mixture in a bowl and let it cool.

Place the blanched almonds under a broiler and watch closely. Remove as soon as they turn tan—which is only seconds before they turn black, so pay attention. Put them in a food processor and grind into a very coarse meal, not a powder or dough. Set aside a small amount to dust on the top. Add to the rest of the nuts 1 tablespoon sugar, 1 teaspoon ground cinnamon, orange-blossom water, and 1 teaspoon smen. Mix well.

Preheat oven to 350 degrees. Brush a baking sheet with melted butter. Lay down a sheet of phyllo dough. Brush it with melted butter. Place about a 2-inch-diameter pile of shredded pigeon in the center of the sheet and cover it with the egg filling. Place the almond mixture over that. Carefully fold over the phyllo so that the filling is wrapped. There should be only one thickness of phyllo, so cut away any excess. If a part starts to leak out, you can make patches and seal them with egg. You can brush with butter and add a second layer if necessary. Seal the dough with some beaten egg. Turn it over and brush with melted butter and then egg yolk. Bake for about 20 minutes until golden. After baking, heat the honey in a little water and brush on the top, then sprinkle some of the chopped almonds on top with a little cinnamon.

DRINK
◆ ALMOND MILK

This is a traditional drink. Because it is rich, Moroccans add water, but I prefer using 2 percent milk instead of whole milk.

½ cup blanched almonds
2 cups 2 percent milk

1 teaspoon orange-blossom water
3 tablespoons sugar

Grind the almonds into a fine powder in a food processor. Put the powder in a blender with the milk, orange-blossom water, and sugar.

DESSERT
◆ ALMOND GHRIBA

In Morocco, cookies are often served with tea. This recipe calls for mastic gum. Made from a tree resin with a pinelike flavor, this common ingredient in North African cooking can be found in pharmacies, health-food stores, or online. If you can't find the gum, the cookies will still be great without it.

1 pound blanched almonds
mastic gum
1½ cups confectioners' sugar
1 tablespoon powdered cinnamon
a pinch of salt
½ cup orange zest

3 tablespoons orange-blossom water
4 tablespoons butter, softened
2 tablespoons flour
2 teaspoons baking powder
4 eggs
2 tablespoons granulated sugar

Roast the almonds under a broiler and then grind them into a powder in a food processor along with a few flakes of mastic gum, if you can find it. Combine in a mixing bowl with the confectioners' sugar, cinnamon, salt, orange zest, orange-blossom water, butter, flour, and baking powder. Using a paddle, beat the mixture. In a separate bowl, whip 2 egg yolks and 2 whole eggs, saving the two whites for later, and add the granulated sugar. With your hands, mix the almond mixture with the egg mixture.

Cover dough and refrigerate for an hour.

Preheat oven to 350 degrees. With your hands, roll the dough into balls slightly smaller than a Ping-Pong ball, then roll the balls in confectioners' sugar.

Bake on a baking sheet for 15 minutes. Do not remove the cookies from the baking sheet until they are cool.

GREECE NIGHT

HINT: A NATION WITH SO MANY ISLANDS AND INLETS THAT WHILE
IT IS ONLY THE NINETY-SEVENTH-LARGEST COUNTRY IN THE WORLD,
IT HAS THE WORLD'S ELEVENTH-LONGEST COASTLINE.

I first went to Greece in 1973 when it was ruled by a grim group of colonels given to brutality, who had come to power a few years earlier with the backing of the US government. It had all the usual advantages of a military dictatorship. Prices were incredibly low and few other tourists were there to get in your way. In the Plaka, a picturesque Athens neighborhood, men sat at folding card tables drinking ouzo in little glasses with big bottles. For almost no money at all, you could pick a table and get a bottle and some little glasses. You could climb to the Acropolis and wander on your own through 2,500-year-old temples, something unthinkable in the restored and highly controlled site today. At the Herod Atticus Theater I saw the Greek National Theater perform Sophocles's *Electra* in the strong and guttural ancient Greek language. I still can almost hear the wild and angry Electra and a stern Clytemnestra, and it remains in my memory one of the most thrilling experiences I have ever had in theater.

The unloved colonels were forcibly removed the following year. When I next returned some seven or eight years later, the Acropolis was closed off, except to organized tour groups, because too many tourists, along with the pollution from a city now choking from too many cars, was damaging the ruins. In the Plaka the card tables were gone, replaced with table-clothed restaurant tables, one restaurant after another, and men grabbing the unending flow of tourists and persuading them in English to eat in their restaurant: "Come here. We have the shrimps." "Come here, we have what you want."

One young American tourist turned to one of these fast-talking hawkers and said—I will always remember this—"Do you make choron sauce?" The man did not hesitate an instant. "Sure we do. Come in."

I had actually heard of choron sauce, a kind of hollandaise with tomato, because back in those days I used to read Escoffier and thought knowing sauces was important, but I didn't think anybody would actually ask for it. And in Greece?

The food was simple. Spinach-and-goat-cheese pastries, lots of cucumber and tomatoes though no lettuce, yogurt, olives, all kinds of lamb dishes, grilled fish, and a lot of octopus, which in the islands they used to beat on the rocks to tenderize. The food—like the language at the Herod Atticus, like the landscape and many other aspects of the country—was European but with a Middle Eastern feel. You are not supposed to say this because the Greeks and the Turks are fierce adversaries, but a lot of Greek food is very similar to Turkish food. Often there are the same dishes but with completely different names. In Turkey a dish

Sole

The earliest Greek recipe for this type of dish comes from the fourth-century BC poet Archestratus who, while Greek, lived in the Greek colony of Gela on the island of Sicily. He wrote a book about food, *The Life of Luxury*, that occasionally reminds us that there used to be poetry and humor in recipe writing. He suggests this recipe for *kitharos*, a word that no scholar has been able to translate but is thought to refer to a flat fish like sole. He suggests

> . . . having pricked its body with a straight and newly sharpened knife. And anoint it with plenty of cheese and oil, for it takes pleasure in big spenders and is unchecked in extravagance.

This is how we made it:

3 small whole soles
a pinch of salt
½ cup olive oil

6 ounces feta cheese
3 tablespoons chives, chopped

Buy a sole or other flat fish whole. If you can find fish small enough, you can serve one per person. Have it gutted and skinned but keep the head and tail. (If you want to do it yourself, flat fish are easy to skin. Make a horizontal slit in the skin by the tail. Peel it down enough to where there is something to grab onto, and give a good yank.)

Preheat oven to 350 degrees. Lightly salt the fish, place it in a baking casserole, and generously pour olive oil on it. Bake for 15 minutes. Sprinkle with crumbled feta cheese and the chives. Bake another 5 minutes and serve.

DESSERT
◆◆ HONEY CAKE

You see this simple cake a lot in Greece, but this is a particularly good version of it.

¾ cup almonds, chopped
1 cup flour
1½ teaspoons baking powder
a pinch of salt
2 teaspoons cinnamon

¼ cup fresh orange zest
¾ cup butter
¾ cup sugar
3 eggs
¼ cup milk

Lightly toast the almonds in the oven or in a toaster oven. Mix in a bowl with the flour, baking powder, salt, cinnamon, and orange zest.

Preheat oven to 400 degrees. In a mixer with a paddle attachment, cream the butter and ¾ cup sugar, beat in the eggs one by one, and then add the milk. Mix in dry ingredients from the bowl.

Pour the batter into a 9-inch cake pan that has been brushed with butter and dusted with flour. Bake for 40 minutes. Let it cool.

SYRUP

1 cup sugar
¾ cup water

1 lemon
¼ cup orange-blossom water

Melt 1 cup sugar in a pot with the water. Add juice of 1 lemon and the orange-blossom water. Pour syrup over cake.

Lemons

DRINK
◆ ELLINIKÍ FANÁRI (GREEK LANTERN)

1 cup chopped parsley
1 tablespoon lime zest
1 cup fresh lime juice
1 cup cold water

½ cup sugar (or more depending on
    your taste)
club soda

Blend all ingredients except club soda in a blender or food processor. Pour it through a fine sieve. Chill. Pour into glasses of ice until ¾ full. Top the rest of the glass with soda. Stir gently.

CUBA NIGHT

HINT: THE LARGEST ISLAND IN ITS SEA.

To understand the role Cuba plays, why it has always been so fought over, why it has so much influence, why the subject keeps coming up, it is important to realize that in its world of tiny nations, Cuba is the Caribbean giant, far larger than any other island.

I have known Cuba through much of what will probably be remembered as the most extraordinary period in this island nation's history. I missed the no doubt exciting first two decades of the Cuban Revolution, but I have been going there ever since the early 1980s, when I was the Caribbean correspondent for the *Chicago Tribune*. With its own take on Karl Marx's idea of a "permanent revolution," the Cuban revolution has always been a work in progress. Not being a democracy and therefore not having voters to answer to, the government has been free to admit when it is wrong, reverse policies, and try new things. This can be seen in Cuban food.

When I first went to Cuba, the economy was based on trading sugar, oranges, and bananas at very favorable terms to the Soviet Union for oil. It was a political move, but also the Soviet bloc really did need the Cuban products. Much had been made of the fact that West Berliners had bananas, but they were scarce in East Berlin. People stood in long lines on the rare occasions that bananas became available in Central Europe.

In Cuba, the state ran everything. The state was good at education, spreading literacy, and had the best health care in the region, with the help of East German pharmaceuticals and medical training. Caribbeans from the other islands, including the US commonwealth of Puerto Rico, would go to Cuba for good-quality, inexpensive medical care. But the state was less good at markets and restaurants. As a visitor I found only a few places to eat, and for a number of years I knew more about Cuban food from eating in Miami than from eating in Cuba.

But one exception was the Bodeguita del Medio in the old section of Havana. It had been founded in 1942 by a country boy from Santa Clara, Angel Martinez, and he specialized in country food, mostly pork and fried bananas and black beans and rice. His contribution to Cuban dining was that he revived the mojito, a nineteenth-century Havana drink of uncertain origin. Ernest Hemingway, who lived in Cuba for twenty years, claimed that the Bodeguita was the best place for a mojito. It still is.

Hemingway was known for patronage of the Bodeguita and the Floridita, a more upscale eatery that specialized in lobsters. Back in the early 1980s, when there were still people working in both restaurants who remembered Hemingway, I was told at the Floridita that he came for sugarless daiquiris made with just lime juice and rum on ice, and that he rarely ate there. At the Bodeguita, Martinez was still there every day even though the restaurant was now state owned. He was elderly and nearly blind but a pleasant man to chat with, and when I asked him about Hemingway he said that he had not been a regular. "I think he came here three or four times. He went more to the Floridita. He came here, had a mojito, had a photo taken, and went to the Floridita to have more photos taken."

In the twenty-first century, Havana began to change. After decades of dreary state restaurants, today's Havana, like most other cities, offers a wide choice of restaurants. But the restaurants are not like those in other countries. The larger restaurants are usually state-owned establishments, but not at all dreary, since the government arrived at a formula to bring in European investors, mostly Spanish, with restaurant expertise.

But also the government started to allow small-scale private business. People were allowed to own their own restaurant as long as it operated out of their home (which of course is state owned). These little restaurants were called *paladares* from the Spanish word meaning palate or, colloquially, "pleasing to the palate." Such family-operated restaurants had already existed, but now they were legalized. The number of seats, non-family employees, and the types of food were all restricted by government.

In October 2010 the Cuban government liberalized the restaurant law, which has led to the opening of a fresh crop of far more sophisticated restaurants. Owners could now run larger establishments and even employ a large staff of non-family members. The paladar has gone from humble to upscale. Sometimes they seem to try too hard. One Miramar paladar, Cocina de Lilliam, garnishes a fish dish with a water glass with a live goldfish swimming in it, leaving the diner with both a moral and gastronomic conundrum. With this growth in restaurants, markets and even organic gardens started springing up around the capital city. Now there was more food, and I was getting more of a sense of what Cuban food is.

The food has a strong Spanish influence, but like Cuba's music and religion, it has pronounced African and Caribbean influences. Many Caribbeans, especially Haitians, migrated there to cut sugarcane, and Cuba had slave plantations far longer than anyone else in the Caribbean. Spain continued to bring Africans until 1860 and did not abolish slavery until 1886. I have met Cubans who knew their African-born grandparents.

APPETIZER
◆ TOSTONES

There are several islands in the Caribbean that specialize in the plantain dish tostones by one name or another, but what is uniquely Cuban is dipping them in *mojo de ajo*.

There are a lot of theories on how to peel a green plantain, which is a lot tougher than peeling a banana. This is the way I find easiest. Slice unpeeled green plantains into ¾-inch-thick disks. Place each disk flat on the cutting board with the peel around the side. Take a sharp knife and with the point make an incision only as deep as the peel. Stick the blade in the slot blunt side first and start turning the disk into the blade. Once about half the peel has been separated from the flesh, you can just pull the rest off with your fingers.

3 green plantains, sliced into ¾-inch   1 cup canola oil
    disks

Brown the plantain disks in very hot canola oil on both sides. Remove them to a paper towel and, after they cool, press them flat. In Cuba there is a special handheld aluminum press for just this purpose. A lot of people simply flatten them with a bottle. I, of course, used my Mexican bean masher. After they are flattened—just pushed down, not obliterated—refry them on both sides, cool them again on a paper towel, sprinkle them thoroughly with salt, and serve with mojo:

Peeling plantains

◆ MOJO DE AJO

Even if this dipping sauce was originally made with lime, which is often said, every time I taste a really good mojo in Havana, it is made with sour oranges. Sour oranges are important in Cuban cooking—a variety of orange with a green peel and orange flesh that, like a lemon or lime, is not in the least sweet (see Leafless Mexican Salad in Mexico Night, p. 72). Since sour oranges are hard to find, I use lemon juice with a very little fresh squeezed orange.

5 garlic cloves, peeled	juice of 1 sweet orange
1½ cups olive oil	a large pinch of salt
juice of 3 lemons	1 teaspoon dried oregano

Put the garlic in a food processor with the olive oil, fruit juice, salt, and oregano. Blend, then serve in a bowl.

SALAD
◆ ENSALADA DE QUIMBOMBÓ (OKRA SALAD)

The origins of okra are somewhat mysterious. Many historians think it originated in East Africa—Ethiopia, lower Egypt, or the Sudan. Others think it came from the Middle East. It is not certain how it ended up in West Africa, but from there it is assumed that the slave trade brought it to the Caribbean basin. The English word *okra* is from the Igbo people in Nigeria, and the Spanish name *Quimbombó* is Bantu from Central Africa.

There are three tricks to avoiding disaster with okra. One is that the farmer must harvest the buds individually as soon as they ripen. The other two are up to the cook: do not overcook them, and do not cut them before cooking, both of which will make them slimy.

1½ pounds okra buds	2 limes
2 tomatoes, quartered	a pinch of salt
1 red onion, sliced very thin	½ cup olive oil

Wash the okra and plunge it into boiling water. Remove when it becomes bright green but a fork easily sticks in it (about 5 minutes). Cut and discard the stems and place the okra on salad plates with the tomatoes and red onion slices. Mix the juice of the limes with the salt and olive oil, and sprinkle on top.

MAIN COURSE
◆ CARLOS'S PESCADO DE NARANJA

Once the law on restaurants was liberalized in the fall of 2010, Carlos Cristobal Marquez, a former personal chef to a Spanish investor, opened Paladar San Cristobal on the ground floor of his family home in downtown Havana. The house is one of those grand, crumbling buildings with ornate tile floors, potted palms, crystal chandeliers, high ceilings, and tangled makeshift wiring slung over ornate rococo masonry. The rooms have slid from elegant to kitschy, with old photos of everyone from Carmen Miranda to Fidel playing baseball. I went shopping and cooking with Carlos and he gave me this recipe, which I modified slightly. In his version, the fish is piled high with orange, but I preferred to use less orange and cook it down more into a sauce. Carlos, at least when he showed me, used red snapper, which can be caught right off Havana's seaside boulevard, the Malecón, but he also often used a white-fleshed, pink-skinned, yellow-finned fish with a triangular head and buck teeth that he called pezperro. Many fish in the Caribbean, including several in Cuba, have this name. Not having reefs nearby, I ended up using gray sole.

3 gray sole fillets	2 oranges
1 cup flour	a large pinch of salt
about 5 tablespoons butter	

Pezperro fish

Dredge fillets in flour and then sauté them in a skillet with butter. Set aside. Cut the peel off two oranges. This involves more then peeling off the rind; you have to cut off the white part and expose the orange flesh exactly the same way it was done on Morocco Night (see p. 115). Then, with a paring knife, cut the orange sections out of their membrane. You want to end up with about 1½ cups of orange sections. Toss them with 3 tablespoons melted butter in the skillet used to sauté the fish and a large pinch of salt. Use a wooden spoon to mash up the oranges until they cook down to a lumpy sauce. Serve on the fish.

◆ CONGRI

Like tostones, congri is a Cuban staple. It works well with canned black beans.

1/3 cup canned black beans
1 cup rice
8 small cubes minced pork belly (or uncured bacon)
4 garlic cloves, minced
1/4 yellow onion, minced

1/4 green bell pepper, minced
a pinch of salt
3 turns of black pepper
8 leaves fresh oregano
1 tablespoon ground cumin
a large pinch of chopped chives

Combine the black beans, the liquid from the can, and the rice in a pot. Add enough water to cover. Add the pork belly, garlic, onion, green pepper, a large pinch of salt, pepper, oregano, and cumin. Simmer until rice is done. Serve with fresh chopped chives sprinkled on top.

DESSERT
◆ PASTELITO DE GUAYABAS (GUAVA PASTRY)

This pastry is sold on the street in Havana, from carts in Parque Central and from carryout windows downtown. Our homemade version is a favorite of Talia's either for dessert or for breakfast, which is when Cubans often eat it.

1 batch puff pastry (see Basic Recipes, p. 22), or 1 frozen box
1 can guava paste

1 small container whipped cream cheese
1 whole egg
1 cup sugar

Preheat oven to 400 degrees. Cut out squares of puff pastry. Cover half of each with slices of guava paste (pastel de guayaba is sold anywhere that Cubans, Dominicans, or Puerto Ricans shop) and 2 tablespoons of cream cheese on top. Fold into triangles. Seal the edges with egg white and crimp them by pressing with the flat tip of a fork's prongs. Brush the tops with beaten egg yolk and sprinkle them with sugar. Bake 15 minutes at 400 degrees, then 20 minutes at 350 degrees.

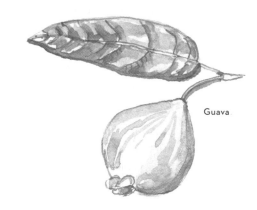

Guava

DRINK
◆◆ MOJITOS

Originally mojitos were made with guarapa, fresh-squeezed cane juice—which has led some historians to associate its origins with slavery, since slaves drank a lot of guarapa. But that was on sugar plantations in the Cuban countryside, and this appears to be a Havana drink. For children, you can make exactly the same drink, omitting the rum.

1 cup sugar
1/3 cup water
1/4 cup fresh spearmint leaves, chopped

12 limes
gold rum
1 bottle club soda
Angostura bitters

Melt the sugar with the water in a pot. Turn off the heat and add the chopped spearmint leaves. (You can substitute round-leaf mint, but the authentic mojito calls for spearmint.) Let cool. Squeeze the limes and add an equal amount of water to the lime juice. Put spearmint sprigs in glasses and crush with a wooden spoon. Add gold rum, ideally Havana Club, to the glass. Add ice, then fill 1/3 with the sugar spearmint syrup, 1/3 with the lime juice, and top off with club soda. Stir briskly. Put a dash of bitters on top.

NAPLES NIGHT

HINT: A CITY ON A BEAUTIFUL BAY THAT ONE DAY MAY EXPLODE AGAIN.

Art historian Bernard Berenson commented that Italy was saved by poverty, meaning there was so much charm and so many historic buildings in Italy because there was never the money to tear things down and rebuild them. Nowhere is this more true than in Naples, which does not seem substantially different from when I first saw it in the early 1970s.

It is still a tough and grubby seaport on one of the world's most beautiful bays, beautiful in part because of the elegant silhouette of Mount Vesuvius, an active volcano that has erupted a number of times, most famously when it buried the Roman city of Pompeii in 79 AD.

It is a city for true urbanites who love crowded, noisy, teeming ports. I plead guilty.

APPETIZER
◆◆ ARTICHOKES WITH ANCHOVY SAUCE

Artichokes of Mediterranean origin (see Brittany Night, p. 165) are small, much smaller than the ones that resulted when they immigrated to northern Europe. This dish was unavoidable, maybe even inevitable, since two of Talia's favorite foods are artichokes and anchovies. Actually, we all feel that way.

3 small artichokes, or 6 if they are the really little 2-inch kind
¼ cup olive oil
3 tablespoons white wine
a pinch of salt
3 turns of black pepper

½ cup chicken stock (see Basic Recipes, p. 24, or buy)
6 cured, salted (canned) anchovy fillets
4 garlic cloves, peeled and chopped
1 tablespoon Italian parsley, chopped

Slice off enough of the top quarter of the artichoke so that the tips are removed and there is a flat top. Trim the tough bottom off the stems if the stems are long. Cut the artichokes vertically into quarters, or halves if they are very small. Heat olive oil in a skillet and put artichoke pieces in the hot oil. Let them cook a few minutes on each side. Add white wine, salt, and black pepper, and cook until the extra liquid from the wine has cooked off. Add the chicken stock and cover the pan and cook over low heat for about 20 minutes or until the artichokes are tender to a fork. Remove the artichokes.

Add the anchovies and chopped garlic to the pan and cook until the anchovies melt into a sauce. Add parsley, and pour over artichokes.

MAIN COURSE
◆◆ PIZZA

You can't talk about Naples and not talk about pizza. The legend that pizza originated in Naples as mozzarella and sliced tomato on bread for children may not be exactly true. The word *pizza* seems to come from the word *pitta*, a flat bread. In the Middle Ages, throughout what is now southern Italy, baking food on flatbread, like focaccia, was common. The word *pizza* started showing up in the ninth century in towns near Naples, but not in Naples itself. No matter: Naples is clearly the birthplace of the modern pizza, which only dates back to the nineteenth century. The true pizza Napolitana is also a subject for argument, but it is a simple pizza with tomato, mozzarella, and oregano, perhaps with marinara—a sauce of tomato, garlic, and oregano that got its name from being used by ships at sea.

At the end of a broiling day in the mean city, Neapolitan families retreat to the broad curving boulevard of Via F. Caracciolo on the waterfront, where there is a row of outdoor pizzerias, some of which Neapolitans claim are the best in the city. You sit in the cooling breezes facing the Gulf of Naples—the bluish, geometric silhouette of the mountainous isle of Capri straight ahead, and Vesuvius, the dangerous beauty, on your left—and eat the definitive pizza while children play with the balloons and toys sold by vendors on the broad street.

There are three necessary features of a Neapolitan pizza.

First, the dough must be thin—okay, not as thin as it is in Rome, but much thinner than that of most American pizza. It must be baked in an extremely hot wood-burning oven. I assume that, like me, you don't have one, so . . . Preheat the oven to a temperature between 425 and 450, depending on how hot your oven gets. The dough should be slighty charred in a few places.

Second, the sauce must be very simple and pure, not oily, and must taste mostly of fresh tomatoes.

Third, the mozzarella cheese must have the distinct flavor of being made from buffalo milk. Americans get very confused about this because we have the habit of mislabeling the American bison a buffalo. A relative of cattle, the true buffalo, which today is found more in Asia than Europe—India has the largest population—is a big-horned animal with large pointed horizontal ears under the horns. Its milk is much creamier than cow's milk, though miraculously, while having twice the fat, it is lower in cholesterol, and some claim it is therefore healthier. It certainly makes richer cheese. The world's best mozzarella is made in small factories just south of Naples, but good buffalo mozzarella can be had for a price in much of the world, including the US. This cheese has nothing in common with the cheese that is melted on most American pizzas.

THE DOUGH

½ batch rising dough ball (see Basic Recipes, p. 23)

about ½ cup additional flour

Preheat oven to 450 degrees. For three 12-inch pizzas, you will only need a half-size rising dough ball, which has been rising in the refrigerator overnight. Flour the board and your hands thoroughly and pull off pieces of dough the size of a grapefruit. Flatten each piece into a disk. You can further thin it by holding it by an edge and moving your hold around the edge while dangling the disk to let gravity stretch it. Or practice being a real pizza maker and try spinning it. Be sure to let kids try this (you can clean up later). The disks need to be as thin as you can make them: remember, the crust thickens when it bakes. Push with your fingers from the center to further thin and to make a puffy ridge along the edge.

TALIA: *My pizzeria (Con un po' di fortuna—with a little luck)*

You want to make the pizza dough as thin as possible. First you have to get flour on your hands. Then you can pull and stretch the dough on the pizza pan. That's the safest way, but it won't get the dough all that thin. For better results, hold the pizza by the end with your hands apart so that it hangs down, and shake it gently in the air. If the dough tears you can always just roll it up into a ball and start over again. But the best way to get it thin (however, the most risky) is to softly toss it into the air like a Frisbee. Keep flipping it in a circular motion. Try to catch it gently. Don't throw it from your hand, and try not to let the dough land on the dog, or in a potted plant. But the dog usually loves it. And if it does, that's okay—just be sure you make some extra dough!

THE SAUCE

8 ripe medium-size tomatoes
2 garlic cloves, finely minced
a small pinch of salt
2 pinches of dried oregano

2 tablespoons olive oil
1½ pounds fresh buffalo mozzarella,
    sliced ¼ inch thick

Place the tomatoes on a lit burner and char all sides. After they cool, the skins will easily pull off. Quarter the tomatoes and with your fingers pull out all the seeds and gel. Chop up the quarters into 4 or 5 small pieces. Heat the olive oil in a skillet and sauté the minced garlic for a few minutes. Add the pinch of salt and oregano, the tomato pieces, and ¼ cup water. Over a fairly high heat mash the tomatoes with a potato masher. As soon as you have a lumpy sauce and not just pieces of tomato, turn off the heat.

Fill the center of the dough with tomato sauce. Place slices of mozzarella on top. The pizza should not be completely covered but spotted with pieces of cheese.

Bake for 25 minutes, longer if necessary to completely bake the dough. A little burning is good. Not all ovens cook at the same temperature and not all dials are accurate, so keep an eye on the pizzas as they bake.

◆ SARDINAS NAPOLITANASAS

As I said, Talia loves sardines. And this dish was too good to pass up, even if we weren't sardine fanatics. For this recipe, buy whole fresh sardines, gutted and scaled.

6 fresh sardines, gutted and scaled
¼ cup flour
¼ cup olive oil
5 garlic cloves, peeled and minced

½ cup white wine
½ cup white wine vinegar
¼ cup chopped fresh mint leaves

Dust the sardines in flour. Sauté them in a skillet with the olive oil and minced garlic. Place the sardines and garlic on a platter. Add the white wine and white wine vinegar to the skillet with oil. Cook until reduced by half. Pour this liquid over the sardines and sprinkle the mint leaves on top.

DESSERT
◆◆ ZABAGLIONE DI FRAGOLI

Originally, zabaglione was served with fresh figs, and if it's the fall and they are available, this is a wondrous treat. But if not, it is also good, some say better, with fresh berries. There are lots of arguments about where zabaglione comes from. It is a very old concoction. The use of marsala suggests Sicily, but it is sometimes made with other sweet wines, such as muscata, in other regions. Some argue it came from the north, perhaps Turin, but it has turned up all over Italy, Naples included. In France, it is called *sabayon*, but it is not French. It has also enjoyed popularity in South America. In the 1970s it was a fashionable dessert in many places including New York, but has since faded into relative obscurity. Let's bring it back.

8 egg yolks
¾ cup sugar

¾ cup marsala
16 strawberries

In the mixer, beat the egg yolks, sugar, and marsala in a metal mixing bowl with the whip attachment until the mixture has doubled in volume. Put the bowl in a pan of heated water—a bain-marie—and continue beating until it is frothy and a light lemon color. Pour over fresh strawberries.

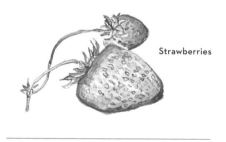

Strawberries

DRINK
◆ MINTED LEMONADE

Crush several sprigs of mint in a glass with a wooden spoon. Squeeze lemons and add an equal amount of water. Add sugar to taste and ice.

IRAN NIGHT

HINT: ONE OF THE OLDEST CIVILIZATIONS, IN 1935 IT CHANGED ITS NAME.

In 1935 the ancient nation of Persia was renamed Iran, which means "the land of the Aryans," but there were lots of debates at the time about what exactly defines an Aryan. In the Iranian sense it is a people who speak a Sanskrit-based language from which most European languages descend. By that definition, all Europeans except Finns, Basques, and Hungarians would be Aryans, which I don't think is what the Persians meant. As befitting such an ancient culture, Iran has a varied cuisine, differing considerably from one region to another.

The beans for the main course should be put in a bowl of cold water for soaking the night before.

SALAD
◆ SHIRAZI SALAD

Since trying this recipe for Iran Night, we have made it a family staple. It refutes the claim of Samuel Johnson, the celebrated eighteenth-century English writer, who once said, "A cucumber should be well-sliced, and dressed with pepper and vinegar, and then thrown out, as good for nothing."

2 tomatoes, finely chopped
1 cucumber, peeled and finely
   chopped
1 white onion, finely chopped

¼ cup olive oil
½ cup minced mint leaves
a turn of black pepper

Combine the chopped tomatoes, cucumber, and onion. Toss with the olive oil, mint leaves, salt, and pepper.

MAIN COURSE
◆ KHORESHT-E QORMEH SABZI (LAMB STEW)

1 cup red beans
½ cup olive oil
1 yellow onion, chopped
1½ pounds lamb, cubed
1 tablespoon turmeric powder
2 cups water
a pinch of salt

3 turns of black pepper
1 pound well-washed fresh spinach, chopped
½ cup coriander leaves (cilantro), chopped
⅓ cup Italian parsley, chopped
juice of 1 lime

Soak the beans overnight in a bowl of cold water. Sauté the onion in ¼ cup olive oil until it is translucent and a little browned. Add the cubed lamb and turmeric. After the meat is browned add the water, the drained soaked red beans, and the salt and pepper and slowly simmer for 90 minutes.

Lightly sauté in ¼ cup olive oil the spinach, coriander, and parsley. Add to the stew at the last minute with the juice of one lime. Stir gently and serve.

◆ POLOW

1 cup basmati rice
1 cup warm water

2 tablespoons salt
1 cup olive oil

Soak the rice in the warm water with the salt for 2 hours. Then boil until most of the water is absorbed. Add the olive oil. Simmer for 20 minutes.

DESSERT

◆ YAKT DAR BEHEST (ICE IN HEAVEN)

1 cup rice flour
1 cup cold milk
1 cup sugar

3 tablespoons rose water
½ cup pistachio nuts, shelled and
 crushed

Dissolve the rice flour in the cold milk. Simmer slowly on low heat, stirring constantly. When it becomes thick, add the sugar and rose water. Pour into serving cups and sprinkle with crushed pistachio nuts.

Rose and Pistachios

DRINKS

Three different types of drinks are common in Iran. First there is tea, *cha*. Until the fifteenth century, the Persians imported coffee from faraway places at great expense. But in the fifteenth century, they increasingly found tea easily available from the spice route to Asia known as the Silk Road. In the nineteenth century the region attempted, at first unsuccessfully, to grow its own tea. Eventually an area in the hills by the Caspian Sea proved suitable, producing a reddish-hued light black tea that Iranians drink constantly, often sipped with a sugar cube in their mouths.

There is also a popular drink called doogh.

◆ DOOGH

2 cups Greek-style yogurt
1 tablespoon honey
6 fresh mint leaves, plus extra for
    garnish

a pinch of salt
¼ teaspoon powdered cumin
1 quart club soda

Mix yogurt, honey, 6 mint leaves, salt, and cumin in a blender or food processor. Add the seltzer and gently mix well. Pour in tall glasses with ice. Garnish with fresh mint leaves.

◆ MINT SHARBAT

Sharbat are cool drinks made with a variety of herbs, spices, fruits, or seeds. The word *sharbat* is thought to be the origin of the French word *sorbet*.

1 medium-size cucumber, peeled
1 cup fresh mint leaves
½ cup sugar (more or less according
    to taste)

4 large lemons
a pinch of salt
½ cup water
club soda

Cut the cucumber vertically, and with a spoon scrape out and discard the seeds. Put all the ingredients except the soda in a blender or food processor with ½ cup water and mix until a smooth puree. Put ice cubes in glasses and fill halfway with mixture and the rest of the way with club soda. Stir gently.

EGYPT NIGHT

HINT: A LAND WITH THE ONLY BRIDGE FROM AFRICA TO ASIA.

The Sinai Peninsula is the only land connection between Africa and Asia, and because of this strategic position, like the rest of Egypt, it has known many outside rulers.

After the days of the pharaohs, the Greeks and Romans ruled Egypt for about nine centuries, then it was the Arabs for another nine centuries, the Turks for three centuries, the French ruled for three years, and the British took it in 1882 and controlled it until 1953 when Egypt regained independence. So there are many influences on Egyptian food and culture. This became clear to me as I crossed the barren, rocky Egyptian Sinai Desert on a camel led by a Bedouin tribesman who was obsessed with the cassettes he played of Jamaican reggae music. My camel was named Bob Marley.

While food products at one time came only from the Nile valley, Egypt's only fertile land, they now come from all over Africa, the Middle East, and the Mediterranean. Almost the entire population of eighty million people lives in the Nile valley, mostly in Cairo and Alexandria. But with its 386,660 square miles, this makes Egypt simultaneously one of the most densely and sparsely populated countries in the world.

Cairo is an intriguing city, with a skyline marked by modern buildings but also huge medieval mosques. The city has sprawled so far that the once-distant ancient pyramids are now in a Cairo suburb. There are rambling outdoor markets where most anything can be bargained for and little cafés where men sit and puff on long and ornate water pipes. But to me the most fascinating thing about Cairo is that every night, very late, sweepers come out with their handmade brooms and sweep away the sand blown in every day from the surrounding Sahara. Without the sweepers, Cairo, a city of about 7.7 million people, would eventually be buried in desert.

For this meal, start the dessert meringues the night before.

APPETIZER
◆ KUFTA

While fried fish croquettes are common throughout Africa, kufta, the Egyptian version, calls for fish from the Nile or for hamour, a spectacular big spotted red fish, somewhat endangered, from the Red Sea. Hamour is in the grouper family, and grouper would also work well with this recipe. But a milder, white-fleshed freshwater fish gives it a nice subtle quality. In Egypt, Nile perch might be used. You could use perch, pike, whitefish, or tilapia. This recipe will make enough kufta for an appetizer for six people.

3 medium-size potatoes, preferably the floury-textured types with thin skins
1 pound fish fillets
1 white onion, freshly chopped
2 garlic cloves, peeled and finely chopped
3 large sprigs Italian parsley, finely chopped
3 large sprigs coriander (cilantro), finely chopped
1 teaspoon powdered cinnamon
1 teaspoon coarse salt
3 turns of black pepper
1 cup flour
3 eggs
1 cup bread crumbs
1 cup peanut oil

Cook the potatoes whole for 40 minutes to an hour. In the last ten minutes add the fish fillets. Drain thoroughly and put in a mixing bowl and mash with the onion, garlic, parsley, coriander leaves, cinnamon, and salt and pepper.

When thoroughly mashed and blended, shape with your hands into oblong dumplings about 1½ inches in length. Flour the dumplings, dip them in a bowl of well-beaten eggs, and roll them in a dish of bread crumbs. Fry them in very hot peanut oil until golden.

MAIN COURSE
◆ CHICKEN AND FIGS

This recipe would work well in the fall with fresh figs, but it can also be made with dried figs.

3 lemons
3 tablespoons brown sugar
6 fresh or eight dried figs, sliced

1 preserved lemon (see Basic Recipes, p. 24), sliced
6 chicken thighs

Preheat oven to 400 degrees. Mix the juice from the lemons with an equal amount of water and the brown sugar. Arrange sliced figs and sliced preserved lemon on bottom of baking dish—enough to cover the bottom. Place the chicken thighs on top. Pour the sauce over it and bake 1 hour.

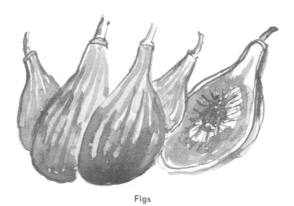

Figs

VEGETABLE
◆ BAMIA (OKRA)

Whether or not okra began in Egypt—as some historians say and others refute—it is common in Egyptian food today. See Cuba Night, p. 133, for more tips on okra.

½ pound young, small okra
¼ cup peanut oil
1 yellow onion, chopped

¾ cup beef stock (see Basic Recipes, p. 24, or buy premade)
½ lemon

Wash the okra. Sauté the onion in hot oil until it is wilted and translucent. Add the okra and stir for 3 minutes while sautéing. Then add stock and simmer for about 5 minutes more, or until the okra feels tender to a fork. Squeeze a little lemon on it.

DESSERT
◆ MERINGUES

It seems that the French, to their credit, wherever they went, no matter how briefly, left behind meringues. Egyptian meringues are made with brown sugar, which gives them a tawny color and a taste of molasses. I use turbinado sugar (see On Sugar and Spice, p. 15), which has a little less molasses, makes the meringues a lighter brown, and gives them a subtler flavor.

This dish needs to be started the night before.

3 egg whites, room temperature	1 cup heavy cream
3 cups turbinado sugar	1 cup blackberries

Preheat oven to 350 degrees.

Use one egg white per person. Put the egg whites in an electric mixer and beat them at high speed, slowly adding sugar. Keep beating until the egg whites are stiff enough to hold peaks. Hold a pastry bag wide and, with a spatula, spoon in the stiff egg whites. Fold over the top of the bag and hold the folds shut with one hand while squeezing and directing the nozzle with the other. (This is a great kids' project.) Starting at what will be the center and spiraling outward, make disks on a baking sheet with a diameter of 3 to 5 inches—whatever size you prefer, but remember that the meringues will expand while baking. Bake for 30 minutes, and then start turning the heat down, reducing it about 50 degrees every few hours until the oven is off. *Do not open the oven.* Leave overnight.

In the morning, take the meringues out of the oven. When ready for dessert, cover each disk with whipped cream and blackberries. For best results in whipping, keep the egg whites at room temperature but beat cream when it is very cold.

DRINKS
◆ CAIRO COOLER

I am not sure if there really is such a thing as a Cairo Cooler, but there certainly ought to be. Egypt is a warm Muslim country, so many people don't drink alcohol and there are a lot of cooling nonalcoholic beverages. Cairo has many juice bars. So why not a Cairo Cooler? There are a lot of recipes online with slight variations—this one is mine. Talia was passionate about this drink, without the rum, of course.

1 pint raspberries
juice of 3 limes
3 tablespoons sugar
10 fresh mint leaves

1 liter pineapple juice
2 bottles club soda
a few ounces gold rum (optional)

In a food processor, lightly puree the raspberries, lime juice, sugar, and mint leaves.
Add this mixture to a pitcher of pineapple juice. Put ice in a tall tumbler, fill ⅔ of the way with the juice, top with club soda, and gently stir. For grown-ups, a shot of gold rum at the bottom of the glass works well.

◆ CINNAMON WATER

If you are a stickler for authenticity, you might want to try a cinnamon drink.

3 cinnamon sticks
1 liter water

sugar according to taste

Simmer water with cinnamon sticks in it for 10 minutes, then cut off the heat and let it cool. Chill, add sugar to taste, and serve over ice.

ROMANIA NIGHT

HINT: THE FORGOTTEN LATIN COUNTRY.

A Balkan country speaking a Latin language, calling itself "Roman" but surrounded by Slavic countries, Romania is one of those quirks of history. With a past tied to the Austro-Hungarian and Turkish Ottoman empires, its food has some things in common with Hungary and some with Slavic countries, but little in common with its namesake, Rome, or Italy, or any other places with speakers of Latin languages. That is not to say that there is no good food there. In fact, to our utter surprise, Romania Night turned out to be one of our favorites.

APPETIZER
◆◆ FISH ROE SPREAD

Traditionally, this spread is made with the eggs of freshwater fish from the lower Danube such as carp or pike, but such roe is hard to find. We made ours with red lumpfish eggs, whose deep red color gave an attractive color to the spread.

½ cup red lumpfish eggs
about ½ cup bread crumbs
2 tablespoons whole milk

juice of 1 lemon
about ½ to 1 cup olive oil
about 15 small toast rounds

Place roe in a mixing bowl with the whip attachment. Add just enough bread crumbs to double the volume, plus the milk and lemon juice, and beat together. Then add the olive oil a drop at a time while continuing to beat, until the mixture is as stiff as a mayonnaise. Serve with small toast rounds.

MAIN COURSE
◆◆ SARMALE

This is Romanian stuffed cabbage. I have been eating stuffed cabbage all my life: it was a staple item growing up, and this is the best stuffed cabbage I have ever eaten. Of course, it also may help that it is the most *treyf* stuffed cabbage I have ever eaten.

This recipe will make between six and eight pieces.

¼ cup rice
1 pound ground pork
1 tablespoon salt
½ cup yellow onion, minced
1 tablespoon fresh thyme leaves
1 tablespoon fresh oregano leaves
½ head cabbage

1 pound sauerkraut
8 tablespoons butter
1 cup chopped yellow onion
2 cups tomato sauce #1 (see Basic Recipes, p. 25)
1 tablespoon hot paprika
6 strips thick-cut bacon

Cook the rice and add it to the ground pork. Add the salt, minced onion, thyme, and oregano. Form into oblong lumps about 2½ inches long.

Plunge a cabbage leaf into boiling water for 3 minutes, then plunge it into cold water, then wrap it around a lump of the meat mixture. Repeat, one at a time, wrapping each leaf immediately.

Preheat oven to 420 degrees. Soak the sauerkraut in cold water for 20 minutes and then wring the water out of it. Sauté the chopped onions in the melted butter. Add the tomato sauce, sauerkraut, and hot paprika.

Put half the sauce at the bottom of a baking dish. Fill the dish with the stuffed cabbage. Pour the remainder of the sauce on top. Cover with the strips of bacon and bake for 90 minutes.

Cabbage

DESSERT
◆◆◆ ALIVENCI

This dessert is both rich and very light and, even more miraculous, if you use nonfat pot cheese and nonfat sour cream, it does not have much fat and is still rich tasting.

2 tablespoons melted butter
about ½ cup flour
1 pound pot cheese
½ pound sour cream

¼ cup sugar
6 eggs, separated
about ½ cup confectioners' sugar

Preheat oven to 400 degrees. Brush melted butter on the bottom and sides of a 9-inch soufflé dish and then dust with flour, completely covering the interior. Gently tap the dish upside down so that any excess flour falls out.

Mix the pot cheese, sour cream, and sugar in a food processor. Beat in the egg yolks one at a time. Whip the egg whites to stiff peaks and carefully, with a rubber spatula, fold them into the cheese mixture. Pour into a soufflé dish. Bake for 30 minutes. Put confectioners' sugar in a screen strainer and hold it over the soufflé, tapping the side of the strainer until there is a white powder covering on top. Serve immediately.

ANDALUSIA NIGHT

HINT: WHERE TWO CONTINENTS MEET.

When I first visited Andalusia, General Francisco Franco was still in power, fascist slogans were written on the walls, feared police were strutting in the streets, crowds gave fascist salutes at political rallies, and I felt as though I had fallen back four decades in time to the 1930s. In the southern province of Andalusia, time went further back to the 1492 Reconquista, when the Spanish had just driven out almost eight hundred years of North African Muslim rule. Andalusia struck me as a Spanish-speaking Arab country. Its architecture was very similar to that of nearby Morocco just across the straits. The local Spanish had an Arabic sound, and the local dialect even more so. Even the food seemed North African. It was a poor region where bullfighting was invented, as was flamenco, almost an Arab blues, played among musicians in improvisational jam sessions traditionally held in caves. Four decades later, much of this is still true, but the region has advanced quite a few centuries.

Bisugo
(sea bream)

APPETIZER
◆ TAPAS

Tapas is really designed for bars, so that before dinner you can go on what the British call a "pub crawl," hopping from bar to bar, snacking and drinking before dinner. We had our tapas at home, a contradiction, but no more so than the American trend for "tapas restaurants," which also misses the point.

These little nibbles with drinks before a meal are generally much simpler in southern Spain than in the north.

3 red bell peppers	½ cup olive oil
5 garlic cloves, peeled and sliced	about 10 marinated anchovies
a pinch of salt	6 stalks green asparagus

Preheat oven to 350 degrees. Core and slice the peppers and mix with the garlic, salt, and olive oil. Bake until the pepper is limp. Serve with marinated anchovies, known in Spanish as *boquerones,* and with a few stalks of green asparagus steamed until they turn bright.

Almonds and garlic

SOUP
◆◆ AJOBLANCO

Andalusians, living in a warm, sunny climate, have a great tradition of cold soups, including gazpacho, an ancient food that originated in North Africa and that goes back well into the Middle Ages. Ajoblanco is closer to the original gazpacho than the more familiar tomato gazpacho: tomatoes did not appear in Andalusia until ships returned from the New World. Incidentally, Andalusians were often numerous in the crews and invading armies of these expeditions, which is why much of the Spanish architecture in Latin America is Andalusian.

Many Andalusians are poor, and ajoblanco is designed to use up old bread—white, crusty bread, like a French baguette—after it gets too stale. We are not big bread eaters, and faced with the possibility of buying bread a few days earlier to let it go stale, I decided it would be better to use bread crumbs, which worked well.

This recipe makes six generous servings, but it keeps well in the refrigerator.

1 cup bread crumbs
1 cup blanched almonds
6 garlic cloves, peeled
a generous pinch of salt, plus 2
  teaspoons

1 cup olive oil
5 tablespoons white sherry vinegar
4 cups water
9 muscatel or muscat grapes

Put the bread crumbs in a food processor with the almonds, garlic, and salt. Grind everything to a smooth paste and keep grinding as you add the olive oil—slowly, as if making mayonnaise. Add the white sherry vinegar and 2 teaspoons of salt. Keep turning the processor as you slowly add 2 cups of water. Pour into a bowl and stir in another 2 cups of water. Chill and stir before serving. The soup is traditionally served with a few muscatel grapes floating on top in each bowl if they are in season and available. We use seedless muscat grapes for their perfumey flavor and their handsome rust-and-topaz color. It is often suggested that the grapes be peeled, but peeling grapes strikes me as a foolish use of time—a lot of work just to remove an important part of the flavor and texture that make a grape a grape.

MAIN COURSE
◆ SEA BREAM AND JEREZ

Like neighboring Morocco, Andalusia has both a Mediterranean and an Atlantic coast. This dish comes from the Atlantic side, which is also where Jerez de la Frontera, an area famous for a particular style of fortified wine, is located. According to the story I have always heard and struggle to believe, Jerez wine is called sherry in English because when the British, who imported a lot of it, tried to say Jerez, pronounced *hay-rayth*, it came out *sherry*.

Sea bream is found on the European but not the American side of the Atlantic. There is also Pacific sea bream. The Spanish word for sea bream is *bisugo*, a word that in slang can refer to someone who is ridiculous: viewed from just the right angle, the sea bream does have a ridiculous smile. But gravitas seems like a lot to expect from a fish. If you can't find sea bream, look for some other small, white-fleshed fish, perhaps a small snapper or sea bass. The idea is to have each fish small enough for one serving. This recipe is for one fish—one serving—so increase the other ingredients depending on the number of servings.

1 sea bream
about ½ cup olive oil
2 generous pinches of salt
½ white onion, chopped
2 green bell peppers, cored and cut into strips

2 tomatoes, chopped
1 teaspoon fresh thyme
3 turns of black pepper
¾ cup dry sherry
¼ cup brandy

Preheat oven to 400 degrees.

Have the fish gutted and scaled but with the head and tail left on. Put it in an earthen baking dish. Drizzle with olive oil and sprinkle with salt and bake for 30 minutes.

Meanwhile, heat the olive oil in a skillet and sauté the onion, green peppers, and tomatoes over a low flame with the thyme, salt, and pepper. Add the sherry and let simmer until the sauce has somewhat reduced and the ingredients are well incorporated, about 30 minutes.

Remove the fish from the oven. Pour brandy on it and set it on fire. When the flames die, pour the sauce over the fish and serve it.

DESSERT
◆◆ FLAN DE NARANJA

This is another of Talia's all-time favorite desserts. This recipe serves four.

1 cup sugar
¼ cup water
1 orange, sliced

4 egg yolks
2 cups heavy cream
1 vanilla bean, split vertically

Preheat oven to 350 degrees. Heat ¾ cup of the sugar in water until it melts and turns amber. But at no point allow the temperature to get too hot, or the syrup will harden into something like a sucking candy. Place a thin slice of orange in each of 4 ramekins. Fill each ⅓ full with the sugar syrup.

Beat the egg yolks with the remaining ¼ cup of sugar. Heat the cream with the vanilla bean until the cream starts boiling. Remove the vanilla bean. Pour the cream on the beaten egg yolks. Scrape the seeds from the split vanilla-bean pod into the mixture and discard the husk. Put the mixture back in the pot and beat it with a whisk over moderate heat until it becomes thick. Remove from the heat and fill the ramekins with the cream.

Put water in a baking dish and put the ramekins in. The water should go ⅔ of the way up the sides of the ramekins. Bake for about 1 hour, then let cool and refrigerate. Before serving, pass a small knife around the edge of each ramekin and turn upside down on a dessert plate to unmold.

A Tip from TALIA

One of my favorite International Night desserts is our flan. However, there is something else really good you can do with the flan recipe if you have an ice cream maker: chop up some candied orange and throw it into the ice cream maker with the liquid unbaked custard, and you'll have vanilla-orange ice cream. And to add some extra pizzazz, throw in some chocolate chips!

DRINK
◆ SANGRIA

1 bottle red wine
¼ cup sweet sherry
¼ cup brandy
2 oranges

1 lemon, sliced
1 apple, diced
¼ cup sugar
1 bottle club soda

Pour the red wine into a large pitcher. Add the sherry, brandy, fresh-squeezed juice of 1 orange, 1 sliced orange, the lemon, and the apple. Add the sugar, stir well, and add a big splash of club soda.

For kids, use grape juice instead of wine and leave out the brandy, sherry, and sugar.

ALGERIA NIGHT

HINT: EIGHTY-FIVE PERCENT OF THE SECOND-LARGEST COUNTRY IN AFRICA HAS NO ONE LIVING IN IT.

Most of Algeria is taken up by the Sahara, a rivetingly beautiful sight, but without vegetation, it is mostly uninhabitable. I have flown over it for more than an hour and it looks like a yellow version of the sea, and like the sea it fills you with both awe and fear. Airplane seems the best mode of transportation for crossing it. But the other 15 percent of the country, the part with people living in it, has a fine cuisine, related to that of Tunisia and Morocco but with some distinct dishes and its own style.

SOUP
◆ FISH SOUP

Talia, the soup-a-phobe, conceded that this was one of the better soups she'd ever tasted.

1 yellow onion, thinly sliced and chopped
¼ cup olive oil
6 garlic cloves, peeled and sliced
2 tomatoes, chopped
2 celery ribs, chopped
½ bulb fennel, chopped
1 tablespoon harissa

1 medium-size thin-skinned potato, chopped (if the skin is thin, it doesn't need to be peeled)
2 pinches of salt
6 turns of black pepper
1 pound flounder fillet
a little more than 1 quart chicken stock (see Basic Recipes, p. 24, or buy)
14 strands saffron

Sauté the onion in olive oil in a large soup pot. Add the garlic, tomatoes, celery, fennel, harissa, potato, salt, and pepper. When all is thoroughly sautéed, add the flounder. Completely cover with chicken stock. Add 5 strands of saffron and simmer for 10 minutes. Put everything through the food processor, then return it to the pot and simmer for 15 minutes more. Serve with 2 or 3 strands of saffron in the center of each bowl.

BREAD
◆◆ MILAWI

I learned to make this bread in Tunisia and in Morocco, but it is eaten throughout North Africa. The recipe calls for semolina, introduced to Algeria by the Carthaginians, who were based in Tunisia. Semolina is especially important in North Africa, since couscous is made from it. Making milawi is a good kids' project.

3 cups finely ground semolina
3 cups water

a large pinch of salt
2 tablespoons olive oil

Mix the semolina with water and salt in a mixer with a paddle attachment. Keep mixing for about 5 minutes. It will become the texture of mashed potatoes at first, but after it becomes silky and a little shiny, mix in the olive oil. Then oil your hands and place the dough on an oiled surface, stretching it into thin, round disks. Cook in a hot cast-iron skillet, flipping to cook both sides.

MAIN COURSE
◆◆ CHAKCHOUKA

Sometimes spelled shakshouka, the name of this dish comes from a Berber word meaning "mixture"—the word has been adopted by modern Hebrew to mean "something that is very mixed up." Considering the name and the fact that the dish is popular in Morocco and Tunisia as well as Algeria, it is probably a food of the Berbers who wandered North Africa. It is a dish that finds fans wherever it goes. North African Jews brought it to Israel, where it has become extremely popular. I first encountered it at the home of Algerian friends in Paris, where it has a large French following. I thought it was a great dish and when I made it for Marian and Talia, they also loved it. Who wouldn't love chakchouka?

¼ cup olive oil
1 white onion, diced
1 red bell pepper, diced
1 green bell pepper, diced
3 tomatoes, chopped
6 garlic cloves, peeled and chopped
2 large pinches of salt

6 turns of black pepper
1 tablespoon dried cumin
½ cup harissa paste (see harissa in On Sugar and Spice, p. 11)
1 cup water
3 eggs

In a skillet, sauté thoroughly the onion, red pepper, green pepper, tomatoes, garlic, salt, pepper, and cumin. Add the harissa, then the water, and cook briskly for 2 minutes. Carefully break open the eggs on top and continue cooking until the whites are opaque. Sprinkle salt and black pepper on top. Carefully, so as not to break the eggs, scoop out and place on dinner plates with a large cooking spoon, or make the whole thing in individual ovenproof 6-inch casseroles.

DESSERT
◆ MAKROUD EL LOUSE

1 cup blanched almonds
1½ cups sugar
1–2 eggs

¼ cup flour
¼ cup orange-blossom water
¼ cup confectioners' sugar

Preheat oven to 350 degrees.

Powder the almonds, 1 cup of the sugar, and 1 egg in the food processor until the mixture has a doughlike consistency. If still powdery, add a second egg. Flour a table and place the dough on it with flour on top. With a rolling pin, roll the dough to ⅓ of an inch thick. Cut diagonally from two directions so that the dough is cut into 1-inch diamonds. Bake 20 minutes or until golden and puffed up but not hard. Cool.

Make a syrup by melting the remaining ½ cup of sugar in the orange-blossom water. Dip each diamond in the syrup. Sift powdered sugar on top.

DRINK
◆ ALGERIAN LEMONADE

3 cups fresh-squeezed lemon juice
3 cups water

sugar to taste
¼ cup orange-blossom water

Mix ingredients in a pitcher and chill, or pour over ice, or both.

Orange blossom

BRITTANY NIGHT

HINT: THOUGH NO LONGER A NATION, THIS PENINSULA IS STILL CONSIDERED ONE OF "THE SIX NATIONS" IN ITS LANGUAGE GROUP.

Once a kingdom, then a duchy, and since the late fifteenth century a region of France, Brittany is one of six remaining Celtic-speaking "nations." The Celts came from central Europe and were a dominant European culture during the Iron Age. By the third century they had spread west to the Atlantic, dominating the Iberian Peninsula, the British Isles, most of France, the lowlands, and Germany; they also spread eastward to the Black Sea and even to parts of Turkey. Today there are few traces left of these Iron Age leaders except on the far western coast of Europe. Brittany, Cornwall, the Isle of Man, Wales, Ireland, and Scotland are the only Celtic-speaking areas left, each with its own Celtic language. The Galicia section of Spain and northern Portugal also have some traces of Celtic culture, and some people with red and blond hair and blue eyes, but they do not speak a Celtic language. By the way, in case you are a basketball fan or from Boston, it is pronounced *keltic*, with a hard C.

There are five departments of Brittany, and, typical of the French—who have never liked this whole nation-within-a-nation concept—only four of them are in the official Brittany region. The fifth, despite the frequent protest of Bretons, is stuck in the Loire region. Like the Basque and Alsatian regions, Brittany has non-Latin roots and seems different from the rest of France. This made it a tremendous curiosity in earlier centuries, an exotic but not faraway spot for Parisians

to visit. The Bretons made souvenirs depicting Breton life to sell to them. Many French writers compared Bretons to people in France's far-flung empire—North Africans and Black Africans and Asians.

When I first went to Brittany, it reminded me of the New England that I'd come from— something about the white houses along a rough North Atlantic sea, even though the white houses were made of stone and not wood.

Gastronomically, although it has become very influenced by French cooking, the cuisine of Brittany has a number of characteristics in common with its Celtic neighbors'. Bretons make cider but not wine, though many today drink the excellent white wines of the nearby Loire. They are important salt producers, and Celts throughout Europe had a great salt-producing tradition. Salt is heavily used in Celtic food. So is butter, but unlike in the rest of France, it is almost always salted. Bretons are potato eaters and were the first to eat potatoes in France, which rejected this American root until the late eighteenth century. It was poverty that drove the Bretons, like the Irish, to grow potatoes, and at times to eat little else.

Another Celtic trait is the absence of ovens and the tradition of cooking breads, cakes, scones, and cookies on griddles. It was in Brittany that the most famous griddle cake, the crepe, originated.

Crepe batter should be made a day in advance.

APPETIZER
◆ ARTICHOKE

The artichoke is related to the sunflower, and if we would stop eating the buds off the bush we would see that they blossom into huge, beautiful purple flowers. They used to be Mediterranean plants, and according to legend were brought to the French court by Catherine de' Medici when she married Henry II in 1533 at age fourteen. Most of the stories of Catherine de' Medici introducing food to the French court are not true, and this one also seems unlikely, as fifteen hundred years earlier the Romans conquered Europe and planted artichokes in England—they probably showed up in France long before Catherine did. In any event, artichokes grow well in sandy soil, which Brittany has a lot of, so it became the leading non-Mediterranean zone for artichokes, and in fact they grow a lot bigger in Brittany than in their native regions.

3 artichokes
½ cup unsliced bacon, cubed
1 cup pork, cubed
1 white onion, sliced
3 carrots, sliced

3 sprigs fresh thyme
1 sprig fresh rosemary
½ bottle dry white wine
1 cup water

This is a recipe for 3 artichokes. Place a large sharp knife about ⅓ of the way down from the top of the bud and cut straight so that you have in one cut removed all the spiky tips. Cut off the stems—though you can leave a bit on the bottom, as they are often tender and tasty. Sauté the cubed bacon and pork with the onion, carrots, thyme, and rosemary. Place the trimmed artichokes in the pan and add the wine and water. Simmer with a lid on until the liquid has reduced to ⅓ of the original. Serve.

Artichoke

MAIN COURSE
◆◆ SEAFOOD CREPES

Originally all Breton crepes were made with buckwheat. Then white flour started creeping into recipes. A real Breton crepe is still made with buckwheat. Dessert crepes, which are a much later invention, are made with white flour. With a little instruction, crepe making is a great project for kids.

This batter should be made a day in advance.

THE CREPES

3 eggs

2 tablespoons butter, melted

1½ cups buckwheat flour

1½ cups milk

Beat the eggs with the melted butter, buckwheat flour, and milk. The batter should be thin but creamy. If too thick, add more milk. Refrigerate overnight.

The next day: Crepe griddles come with a little contraption resembling a windshield wiper for spreading the batter. Unless you make crepes very often, this equipment is not worth the space it will take up in your kitchen, but crepes should be very thin, which is why the batter needs to be thin. With a little practice, it is not difficult. Talia got pretty good at this.

TALIA: *The Crepe Maker*

Once you've melted some butter in a big pan, pour in a ladle full of the batter. Then, using the round bottom of your ladle, spread the batter in a circular motion until it's pretty thin. Once the center part is dry, it's ready to flip. You'll also see that the batter will darken slightly, and even get a little bubbly. Then you slide a spatula, a big one, under the crepe. Lift it and turn it on to the other side. To be honest, the bigger the crepe, the harder it is to flip it. I like making small crepes.

THE FILLING

1 tablespoon shallots, minced

1 leek, thinly sliced

4 mushrooms, sliced

½ tomato, finely diced

2 sprigs fresh thyme

a large pinch of salt

5 tablespoons butter

½ pound fillet of sole, cut into strips

½ pound bay scallops (these are the small ones)

½ bottle dry white wine

1 cup heavy cream

1 bunch fresh chives, chopped

3 small heads endive

2 tablespoons butter

Sauté the shallots, leek, mushrooms, tomato, thyme, and salt in about 2 tablespoons of butter. After everything is thoroughly sautéed, add the sole, scallops, and wine. Cook over medium heat for about 5 minutes. Lift out the fish and scallops, place some on each crepe, and wrap. Pour the heavy cream into the skillet with the liquid and cook vigorously until it has reduced its volume by about half. Add the remaining 3 tablespoons of butter and stir vigorously until completely incorporated in the sauce. Pour sauce over crepes. Sprinkle with chopped fresh chives.

Serve with endive that is sliced lengthwise and sautéed in butter. Endive is now a major product of Brittany, though before the twentieth century it was only a garden plant showing up in home cooking.

DESARTS
◆◆ GÂTEAU BRETONNE
(KOUIGN-AMANN, OR BRETON CAKE)

This is a favorite recipe of mine that I have been making since I was a pastry maker forty years ago. It is my version of Gâteau Bretonne, drawn from recipes for two butter cakes from Brittany that in their variations became similar. The Celtic name *kouign-amann* means "butter cake." The cake comes from the western end of the peninsula, the Finistère—the most traditional part, where people still speak the Breton language—and appears to have been first created, or at least first written about, in the mid-nineteenth century. The name *Gâteau Bretonne* first appeared about the same time in Paris. It is simply *kouign-amann* translated into French. Either way, what follows is different from the older Celtic recipes because it is baked in the oven in a cast-iron skillet and not on a griddle.

The secret of Celtic cooking is not just using a lot of butter but using a good amount of salt to bring out its taste.

1 pound flour
¾ pound salted butter
a large pinch of salt
⅓ pound sugar

a splash of vanilla extract
⅓ cup dark rum
9 egg yolks

Preheat oven to 400 degrees. In a mixer with dough hook, combine the flour with the butter. When it looks like cornmeal, add the salt, sugar, vanilla extract, dark rum, and 8 egg yolks beaten in one at a time.

Press the dough into a well-seasoned 10-inch cast-iron skillet (see Equipment, p. 17) and brush beaten egg yolk on top. With a fork, etch three wavy vertical lines in the top. Then etch three similar horizontal lines. Bake for 1 hour. Turn down temperature if the top starts getting too dark. After it cools, it is ready to serve straight from the cast-iron skillet.

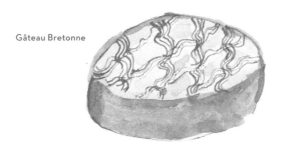
Gâteau Bretonne

◆ CREPES

Much as I love the cake, a lot of kids are crazy for dessert crepes. This is really a much less traditional Breton dessert than the cake, but it has become popular all over France. You make dessert crepes exactly the same way you make savory ones, except you use white flour instead of buckwheat. You can fill them with your favorite jams or fresh fruit or berries with a little sugar, or sliced peaches, pears, or apples sautéed in a little butter with as much sugar as you like, or you can buy hot fudge sauce and fill them with that. For the jam or chocolate variety, put confectioners' sugar in a sieve or sifter and sprinkle it lightly on the crepes. For fruit or chocolate crepes, you might want to add a large dollop of whipped cream on top.

DRINK

Sparkling dry fermented cider is Brittany's traditional drink, although a Sancerre from the nearby Loire would be very nice. Nonalcoholic sparkling cider is a good choice for children.

TANZANIA NIGHT

HINT: TWO COUNTRIES COMBINED AT ONE OF THE FIRST PLACES EVER INHABITED BY HUMANS AND ONE OF THE FIRST PLACES TO PRODUCE STEEL.

In East Africa, on the Indian Ocean, Tanzania and its name were created in 1964 by combining Tanganyika and Zanzibar. Here evidence of a human presence, or at least an earlier member of the Hominidae family, date back two million years. Two thousand years ago the Haya people living in this area built a type of blast furnace for turning iron and carbon into steel. In the nineteenth century, Zanzibar became an Arab-controlled slave center.

Famous for its wildlife, its art, and its music,

Tanzania is not famous for its cuisine. The usual dish is grilled meat, often with a curry sauce. There is a considerable Indian influence, and with mangoes, coconuts, ducks, and curry, we were able to put together a very good Tanzanian meal, including one of the best soups we've made. Even Talia loved this one. Perhaps that's because it is really more a vegetarian stew than a soup.

If you use dried beans, they must soak overnight.

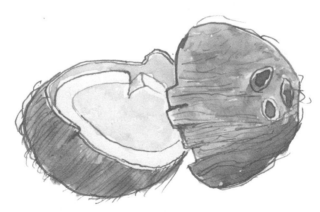

Coconut

SOUP
◆ COCONUT SOUP

2 cups dried red kidney beans
1 white onion, chopped
¼ cup peanut oil
2 tablespoons mild Madras curry
    powder
a large pinch of salt, plus 1½
    tablespoons
1 tablespoon cayenne pepper

6 turns of black pepper
3 tomatoes, finely chopped
1 coconut
6 cardamom seeds
2 cups coconut milk
2 cups chicken stock (see Basic
    Recipes, p. 24, or buy)
1 cup rice

Soak the kidney beans the night before.

In a large pot, sauté the onion in peanut oil. Add the curry powder (see Curry in On Sugar and Spice, p. 10), the pinch of salt, cayenne pepper, black pepper, and tomatoes. Add all the water from one fresh coconut (see A Slightly Nutty Way to Open a Coconut, p. 19), the cardamom seeds, the rest of the salt, the coconut milk, and the chicken stock. Cook until it comes to a boil, add the rice, and continue boiling for 10 minutes or until the rice is done. Serve with grated fresh coconut on top.

MAIN COURSE
◆ DUCK

This dish is served in the old capital of Dar es Salaam, which means "harbor of peace" in Arabic. To make it, you should find a young duck that is not too fat and weighs about six pounds cleaned.

1 6-pound duck
½ cup peanut oil
½ white onion, chopped
3 plum tomatoes, chopped
6 cardamom seeds
2 generous pinches of salt

1 tablespoon curry powder
½ tablespoon cayenne or other hot red pepper powder
2–3 cups chicken stock (see Basic Recipes, p. 24, or buy premade)

Cut the duck in quarters. Brown each piece on all sides in peanut oil. Add the onion, tomatoes, cardamom, salt, curry powder, and hot pepper. Add enough chicken stock to cover and simmer over low heat for 1 hour.

◆◆ UGALI

The duck dish is usually served with ugali. In fact, African cooks serve everything with ugali, but I don't for the same reason that they do—it really fills you up. It is the same idea as pap in South Africa or cou-cou in the Caribbean. Boil water, and slowly drop in white cornmeal through your fingers. There should be half as much cornmeal as water. Stir with a wooden spoon until it pulls away from the sides of the pan and there are no longer any lumps.

DESSERT
◆ MANGO CASHEW PUDDING

2 ripe mangoes, peeled and sliced
juice of 1 lemon
¼ cup sugar
¾ cup unsalted cashews

¾ cup brown sugar
½ cup butter
1 teaspoon salt
1 tablespoon powdered cinnamon

Preheat oven to 400 degrees. Fill the bottom of a baking dish with the sliced mango mixed with the lemon juice and sugar. Crush the cashews into powder with the brown sugar, butter, salt, and cinnamon. Spread this paste on top of the mangoes and bake for 30 minutes.

DRINK
◆ MANGO ORANGE JUICE

4 oranges
3 pints mango juice

¼ teaspoon sugar, or to taste
rum (optional)

Add the zest of one orange to the mango juice and the juice of four oranges. Add sugar to taste and pour over ice. A shot of rum makes it nice for the grown-ups.

QUEBEC NIGHT

HINT: A COUNTRY TO REMEMBER.

Je me souviens—"I remember"—is the slogan of Quebec, appearing on the province's license plates. I once spent a week in Montreal, talking to the leaders of the Parti Québécois, the political movement that advocates Quebec breaking away from Canada. This is not like the Basques or the Bretons leaving France. Quebec is one third of Canada. Yet both sides have discussed the issue for years, more or less civilly and without violence. Quebec, except for the tiny islands off the coast of Newfoundland of Saint-Pierre and Miquelon, which still belong to France, is the last of what once were many French-speaking areas of North America. To many Quebecers, Louisiana is the cautionary tale, where there is very little left of the French language and only a small amount of tradition, although the cuisine still inludes some very French elements: Quebec does not want to end up like Louisiana. Talking to leaders of the independence movement, I asked, Why *Je me souviens*—remember what? Where does it come from? I could find no one in the Parti Québécois who knew.

It is a bit mysterious, although the line by Eugène-Étienne Taché was carved under the coat of arms on the parliament building in Quebec City in 1883. The full stanza was "*Je me souviens / Que né sous le lys, / Je crois sous la rose*": "I remember that I was born under the lily"—the symbol of the French monarchy—"and grew under the rose"—the symbol of the British monarchy. And Quebecers who remember add the line "*mais toujours je me souviens mes origins française*": "but I will always remember my French origins."

Most Quebecers speak French as their first language and do remember, even if some get tired of what they see as a condescending attitude from France. They are Québécois, not French.

Quebec has Montreal, arguably North America's most charming city, and the grand old historic Quebec City, but a lot of it is backcountry where people speak a two-hundred-year-old French with trilled *r*'s and live a quiet rural life. There are towns along the Saint Lawrence River and the mouth of the Gaspé Peninsula where they still catch and salt cod, where water from the American heartlands rushes to a wild cold Atlantic, and where there is still one of the last wild Atlantic salmon runs in North America. You can see these fish putting their noses mightily into a swift current, filling you with admiration for their strength and their determination to get home.

My fondest memory from numerous trips to different parts of Quebec province was from 1973, when I sailed to Europe from Montreal on the *Alexander Pushkin*, a Soviet liner. These were the last days of transatlantic transportation, not cruise ships but ships for people wanting to get where they were going by means other than airplanes. It was a form of travel that would soon be killed off by the 1970s oil crisis. It was also the time of détente, a softening of relations between the Soviet Union and the West, that led to the Soviets putting three ships in service for transatlantic voyages, all three named after Russian writers.

When you left on a transatlantic voyage, there was a great commotion of friends and relatives waving good-bye from the dock. A brass band would be broadcast from the speakers and the lines cast off. You stood on an upper deck and you felt like an all-powerful giant up there with all the little people waving from the dock below. Then, in a few hours, you hit open ocean, and you felt alone and very small. But this shrinking took days from Montreal, because first you had to sail to the mouth of the Saint Lawrence one thousand miles away, past the thickly wooded banks of Quebec. Toward nightfall, small boats started to approach us as we passed by the town of Trois-Rivières. People were shouting in French, blasting handheld horns, holding up beer bottles and wine glasses. The faster boats zipped across our huge white bow, splashing wakes as big as their boats, but our stable ship, built for the open North Atlantic, didn't even feel it. The town had come out for a party to celebrate the passing of the big Russian ship. How could you not think that life was good in these little French towns along the Saint Lawrence?

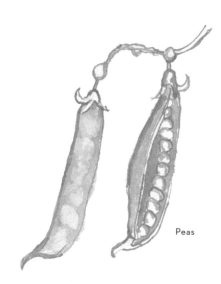

Peas

SOUP
◆ POTAGE SAINT-GERMAIN (PEA SOUP)

There is no way around this one. You can't have Quebec Night without it: Quebec is identified with this soup. The English people used to refer to French Quebecers, not always with kindness, as "pea soupers."

Having tried it both ways, I find this to be the rare dish that is best when you don't use fresh ingredients. Potage Saint-Germain is about dried peas. Quebec has a short growing season and a longer winter in which vegetables are hard to come by. But dried peas last, and then this is what you can do with them. In a Quebec winter, the herbs would be dried as well. But fresh is better.

To make this soup, you need to start soaking the peas the night before.

3 cups dried peas
3 cups chicken stock (see Basic
    Recipes, p. 24, or buy)
2 sprigs chervil
3 sprigs tarragon

3 inches of leek, soaked, washed, and
    sliced thinly
½ pound slab bacon, diced
3 tablespoons butter
2 tablespoons salt

Soak the dried peas overnight. The next day, simmer them in the chicken stock with the chervil, tarragon, and 2 inches of the leek. After cooking 30 minutes, purée the pea mixture in a food processor.

Put the diced bacon into a skillet with the butter. Add the remaining 1 inch of leek. After everything is browned—about 10 minutes—add the puréed peas and the salt and let simmer for 20 minutes. Stir well before serving.

MAIN COURSE
◆ DAUBE AU CIDRE

Living in a cold climate, Quebecers eat a lot of stews. In Quebec, cookbooks usually have a recipe for meat stewed in red wine. This kind of dish mostly comes from the center of France. But in Quebec—as in Normandy and Brittany, from where most Quebecer families come—no wine is produced. Instead, they make apple cider.

1 cup slab bacon, cubed
1½ pounds pork shoulder, cubed
½ cup flour
5 carrots, peeled and cut into 2-inch slices
16 pearl onions

10 small mushrooms or 5 larger mushrooms, halved
2 teaspoons salt
¼ cup red wine vinegar
1 bottle dry or brut cider (the corked, bubbly kind)

Toss the bacon in a skillet over medium heat, stirring occasionally for a few minutes until it is cooked. Dredge the pork shoulder thoroughly in flour and brown it in the bacon fat. Add the carrots, pearl onions, mushrooms, salt, and vinegar and cover with apple cider. Bring to a boil, then simmer for 2½ hours or until sauce becomes thick.

DESSERT
◆◆◆ GÂTEAU DE SIROP D'ERABLE (MAPLE SYRUP CAKE)

Having grown up in New England, I am passionate about maple syrup, a uniquely North American delicacy principally produced in New England and Quebec and, since there are some very precise temperature shifts required to produce it, much menaced by climate change.

If you love maple syrup, try this cake. Forget the grade A that Vermonters have so skillfully foisted off on New York gourmets and get some grade B. It is a little coarser, with a deeper maple flavor.

THE CAKE

2 cups flour
1 teaspoon baking soda
1 cup butter, cut into 1-inch cubes
1½ cups brown sugar

3 whole eggs
¾ cup maple syrup
a splash of vanilla extract

Preheat oven to 400 degrees. In a mixer with the paddle attachment, combine the flour, baking soda, and butter and paddle briskly. Keep paddling and add the brown sugar and then the eggs, one at a time. Continue beating until smooth. Slow the paddle to a gentle speed and add the maple syrup and vanilla extract and paddle until well mixed.

Pour the batter into a 9-inch springform pan that has been brushed with butter and dusted with flour. Bake until it rises, which should be about 20 minutes, then lower the temperature to 350 degrees and continue baking another 40 minutes. Cool before glazing.

THE GLAZE

14 ounces sweetened condensed milk
1 cup brown sugar
4 tablespoons butter

2 teaspoons salt
¼ cup maple syrup
a splash of vanilla extract

Melt together over medium heat the sweetened milk and brown sugar. Add the butter, salt, maple syrup, and vanilla extract. Keep stirring over moderate heat. When the glaze begins to bubble, turn off heat and cover the cake with it.

DRINK

Cider, dry or sweet, bubbly or flat. Nonalcoholic sparkling apple cider for the kids.

NORWAY NIGHT

HINT: A COUNTRY THAT NOW REWARDS PEACEMAKERS
BUT THAT USED TO CONQUER.

Norway is the home of both the Nobel Peace Prize and the Vikings. But after its Viking days it was more dominated than dominator, not obtaining its independence from Sweden until 1905. A holdover from the days before independence, the Nobel Prize, established by the Swedish chemist Alfred Nobel, is partly Norwegian and partly Swedish. Only the Peace Prize is awarded in Norway.

Anyone who has read *Growth of the Soil,* the 1917 novel about Norwegian farmers written by Norwegian Nobel Prize laureate Knut Hamsun, has a less than idyllic view of rural Norway. Coming from an impoverished working-class background and a great believer in the hard life away from civilization, Hamsun paints a grim picture of Norway. There were dairy products and some root vegetables and fruit in the summer along with fish, often preserved in salt, but that was about the extent of the national diet. For many centuries the Norwegian economy was dependent on its fisheries and particularly its trade in salted cod, and Norway remains a major producer of salmon and cod, both fresh and salted. An eighteenth-century poem by the Norwegian Peter Daas asks,

> If codfish forsake us, what then would
>   we hold?
> What carry to Bergen to barter for gold?

Faced with diminished cod stocks, Norwegians are still asking this question.

Norwegians have known hard times, but they also know that a good meal can be made from a few simple things.

Preparation of the lefse and the salt cod must begin the day before the dinner.

APPETIZER
◆◆ LEFSE AND SALMON

Raised on lox and bagels, of course we loved this dish. The lefse must be made the night before. This recipe serves about eight.

1 thin-skinned, medium-size potato, unpeeled
1/4 cup milk
1 1/4 cups flour

1 teaspoon salt
1/2 pound smoked salmon
1/2 cup sour cream

Grate the potato in a food processor with a grating attachment. Try to wring out as much liquid as possible. Add the milk. Knead in the flour and salt. Let the mixture rest in the refrigerator overnight.

The next day, roll it thin on a floured surface and cut into circles about 4 inches in diameter. Grill in a hot skillet until browned bumps form. Then flip and grill the other side. Serve with smoked salmon and sour cream on top.

MAIN COURSE
◆ BAKED SALT COD

This same recipe can be made with fresh cod, except you'd need to add a large pinch of salt.

1 pound salt cod
1 rutabaga, thinly sliced
1 leek, thinly sliced, washed, drained, and dried

2 cups light cream
3 tablespoons butter

Soak the salt cod overnight (see On Salt Cod, p. 19).

Put the rutabaga (the British call them Swede, but they are also Norwegian) and leek in a casserole dish with the soaked cod and add enough light cream to cover. Add the butter. Bake for 30 minutes. Place the cod and vegetables on a serving platter and reduce and thicken the sauce over high heat a little before pouring it over the fish.

DESSERT
◆ APPLE BLACKBERRY PIE

We loved this very simple and handsome pie.

1 batch short pastry (see Basic
  Recipes, p. 23)
8 or 9 apples, cored and peeled but
  still whole

1 jar blackberry preserves
1 cup fresh blackberries
¼ cup sugar

Preheat oven to 400 degrees. Cover the bottom and sides of a 9-inch springform pan with short pastry. Pack the apples tightly into the pan on top of the dough. If any break, just place the pieces in the right position. Fill the core holes and spaces with blackberry preserves and a few fresh blackberries. Cover with sugar. Bake 40 minutes, then reduce heat to 350 degrees and bake 30 more minutes.

Apple and blackberries

DRINK
◆ GLÖG

(See Sweden Night, p. 46.)

CORNWALL NIGHT

HINT: A LAND WHERE MANY SEAS MEET AND AN ANCIENT LANGUAGE IS SELDOM SPOKEN.

I was glad to see Talia's finger land right on the spot in Cornwall. It is not surprising that it's my favorite part of England: I am always drawn to extremes and this is the far western tip of the island, and I always love fishing ports. There are few places in the world where you can catch the variety of fish that live off Cornwall. That is because this Celtic tip of England sticks out into the North Atlantic at the spot where the English Channel, the Gulf Stream, and the Irish Sea meet. It is the Gulf Stream that gives Cornwall its own climate, warmer and with more subtropical species of vegetation than the rest of England.

Cornwall's fishing fleet, like those in much of the world, is greatly diminished. Most of the old fishing towns have turned to tourism. Penzance is now a resort. Beautiful Mousehole (pronounced *maw-zil*), a rough-hewn town on a steep slope cascading down to a harbor too narrow for modern vessels, lives on tourism too. Disgracefully, Land's End, the historic tip of England, has been turned into a seedy amusement park. But Newlyn remains a blue-collar, hardworking fishing port. It reminds me of Gloucester, Massachusetts, which was settled by fishermen from this West Country region, and has an area named Land's End and another named Penzance. It is not only that Gloucester, too, stands alone as a fishing town surrounded by towns that have turned to tourism, but like Newlyn it has a history of granite quarrying and has attracted great artists. In addition to its painting movement, Newlyn became famous for its art copper, which, not surprisingly, often depicted fish.

Cornwall, or Kernow in its language, is one of the "six Celtic nations." Cornish is a four-thousand-year-old language. And there are arguments about who the last native Cornish speaker was. One died in 1777 near Mousehole, but others say the last speaker did not die until 1891. But the language is not completely dead, as there has been a growing movement to revive it. Today less than 1 percent of the Cornish, the Kernowyon—some two thousand people—speak their Celtic language, Kernowek. That is the smallest percentage of Celtic speakers of any of the six. The language is closely related to Breton and Welsh, while Irish, Scottish, and Manx are distant cousins.

But there is a strong Celtic accent to Cornish cooking, including the use of salted butter and cooking on a griddle. We found appetizers so appealing that we made a meal of them. If we had picked a main course, it surely would have been fish. In Mousehole they make a pie with a cluster of whole fish staring up from the crust clustered in a circle, "starry gazey pie," but after some discussion we decided it was too weird for dinner.

APPETIZER
◆ SCROWLERS

The pilchard, the local sardine, has been a principal catch of the fleets in Newlyn and Cornwall since the early sixteenth century. With Celtic connections, the Cornish imported sea salt from Brittany and preserved sardines that they then shipped back to Europe. Margaret Perry, Newlyn's own local historian who lives in an apartment in an abandoned and remodeled pilchard plant, gave me this recipe for what is known there as scrowlers:

> Descale and clean the pilchards and split open. Season well. Grease the hot plate or griddle, cook the fish quickly, one side and then the other. Years ago, these were often cooked over an open fire, indoors. The smell was unbearable. Excellent barbecue food, though!

Even when you broil sardines, the smell lingers for a day. Worth it, though, we think. Here's how we adapted Margaret Perry's recipe.

6 whole fresh sardines, scaled and cleaned	a generous pinch of coarse salt
	1 tablespoon fresh thyme leaves

Our simple approach to scrowlers is to sprinkle scaled and cleaned whole sardines with coarse salt and fresh thyme and put them under the broiler for about 5 minutes.

SOUP
◆ NEWLYN CRAB SOUP

The tourism industry is generally bad for commercial fishing. It hikes up docking rates and most other prices. But it does tend to improve transportation. In 1859, a direct railroad line was completed between Penzance Harbor and London. Its purpose was to bring London vacationers to Penzance. But it also meant that Newlyn could be less dependent on producing preserved pilchards and start shipping fresh seafood to London. This gave birth to important trade in the local brown crab, sometimes called Newlyn crab, and Newlyn soon became famous for its crab soup.

This soup can be made with whatever crab is available, but the recipe makes an important distinction between the leg and claw meat and the meat inside the body, which the Cornish call "cream of crab." This meat is a little off-color but extremely flavorful, so use a crab large enough to have some good cream of crab and at least 1½ cups of other meat.

2 tablespoons salted butter
1 cup white onion, minced
a pinch of salt
1 teaspoon flour
1 teaspoon Madras curry powder (see
    curry in On Sugar and Spice, p. 11)

juice of ½ lemon
2 cups whole milk
1 large crab, or enough crabs to
    produce 2 cups of meat
3 pinches of minced parsley

Sauté the onion in the butter with the salt. Add the flour, curry powder, and lemon juice and stir with a wooden spoon until everything is mixed in. Then slowly add the milk and the cream of crab. Cook until slightly thickened. Add the rest of the crabmeat. Cook for 2 more minutes and serve with a pinch of minced parsley on top of each bowl.

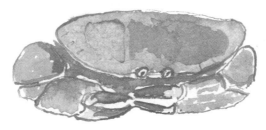

Newlyn crab

MAIN COURSE
◆◆ CORNISH PASTIES

Cornish pasties are considered by many to be *the* Cornish national dish. In July 2011 the European Commission gave it special name protection, the same way you can't call a wine Bordeaux if it is not from Bordeaux. The pastry was given a very specific definition, and without these attributes a pastry could not be called a Cornish pasty. The filling must include beef and rutabaga, which is called "turnip" in Cornwall. The texture must be chunky. It must be shaped like the letter D, and the dough must be crimped on the curved side. The Cornish pasty was lunch for miners who worked with tin and copper and had toxic heavy metals on their fingers. They would hold the pasty by the crimped edge and eat down to the edge that their fingers held, then throw that part away.

We did everything required to satisfy the name, but I am afraid we still don't have the right to call ours a Cornish pasty because a Cornish Pasty must be made in Cornwall. It can then be shipped anywhere for baking. I certainly don't want to be in violation of European law, so all I can say is that this is our pasty, and it bears a striking resemblance to something you might find in Cornwall.

To make the dough, you need suet. It is striking how often Cornish recipes call for suet because—dare I suggest this—I think it's very English, whereas Celts are big butter eaters. With only about a tenth of a percent of the population speaking the language, there are bound to be a few compromises. Intuition might tell you that butter makes a lighter crust: I remember once working for a French chef who was outraged by my suggestion of including any fat but butter in the dough. But in truth a touch of suet, lard, or even goose fat will make a crust lighter.

I used pork drippings because it was what I had. You can usually buy suet, but if not, get some beef-fat scraps from the butcher. Cook them down, strain the liquid through a cheesecloth, and let it cool and solidify. For a better-quality suet, melt it and strain it a second time. I grew up with my mother constantly doing this with chicken fat, which in Yiddish is called schmaltz. It's easy to do and stores well. The refrigerator of my childhood at any given moment had several jars of the stuff.

1 cup rutabaga, finely chopped
1/2 cup yellow onion, minced
1 pound sirloin, cut into small pieces
3 cups flour

1/2 cup suet
1/2 cup salted butter, cut into pieces
2 eggs

Preheat oven to 350 degrees. Prepare the filling: mix the rutabaga, onion, and sirloin.

For the dough, mix the flour and suet in a mixing bowl with the hook attachment. Mix in the butter pieces one at time until the mixture takes on a mealy texture. A little at a time, add water until it comes together as a dough. (You should add the water very slowly because you want no more water than is absolutely necessary.) Roll the dough out thin on a well-floured board and cut ovals about 6 inches long.

Place the filling on one half, careful to stay away from the edge. Then fold over the other side. Seal the edge by pressing with a fork, creating a crimped edge. Beat 2 eggs and brush on the pasties. Bake for 1 hour.

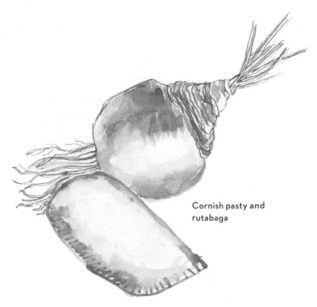

Cornish pasty and rutabaga

DESSERT
◆◆ LEMON PUDDING

This dessert comes from the village of Ley Mill in the woods of eastern Cornwall.

¼ cup bread crumbs	½ cup sugar
2 cups whole milk	3 eggs, separated
2 lemons	¼ cup heavy cream

Preheat oven to 400 degrees. Soak the bread crumbs in the milk for 30 minutes. Add the juice of 1 lemon, the zest from 2 lemons, the sugar, the egg yolks, and a splash of heavy cream. Beat well together. Whip stiff the egg whites and carefully fold them into the lemon mixture. Bake for 20 minutes, then another 30 minutes at 350 degrees or until no longer liquid.

DRINK
◆ KEMYSKANS HAF

Cornwall is known for a number of traditional alcohol drinks such as mead, a kind of wine made from honey, beer, and cider. It is also known for its apple juice and for Kemyskans Haf, which is Cornish for summer drink.

¼ cup fresh mint leaves	2½ cups ginger ale
2 tablespoons sugar	1½ cups apple juice
3 tablespoons hot water	lemon slices, ice cubes, to garnish
juice of 2 lemons	

Crush the mint slightly and place in a large pitcher. Dissolve the sugar in the hot water and add to the pitcher. Add lemon juice. Add the ginger ale and the apple juice then stir and crush a bit more with a wooden spoon. Add ice and lemon slices before serving.

SWEETS
◆◆ HEVVA CAKE

This is a very old confection, and while most recipes call for suet and baking in the oven, Hevva cakes bear a striking resemblance to Welsh cakes: I suspect that the original, like the original Welsh cake, was made only with butter and baked on a griddle. The original Celtic griddle was a stone put on the fire, but a metal griddle, the kind used for pancakes on a stovetop, works well.

The old Cornish fishery had luggers, two-masted fishing boats with gaff-rigged sails—square sails that gracefully straddled the masts and tilted aft. With their sails draped, they lay like marsh birds and gave charm to Cornish harbors, but they also maneuvered well for setting purse nets, nets that circled under a shoal of sardines and then scooped them up like a purse. A man called a huer stood on a cliff from a height where he could better spot the fish. When he spied a shoal he would shout, "Hevva!," from the Cornish word *hesva*, meaning shoal—a school of sardines or herring. After the luggers found the shoal, the huer returned home and baked these cakes so they would be done when the fishermen got in. Hevva cakes are often mistakenly called "heavy cake."

2 cups flour
8 tablespoons butter
¾ cup sugar
a large pinch of salt

¾ cup whole milk
1 cup dried currants
zest of 1 lemon

In a mixer with a paddle, beat together the flour, butter, sugar, and salt. Slowly add the milk, and more if needed to make the dough soft. Mix in the currants and the lemon zest. Roll the dough about ¼ inch thick and etch crossing diagonal lines on the top with a knife. (The pattern is supposed to look like a fishing net.) Cut into 3-inch squares. Put on the griddle over medium to low heat. The trick is to cook them all the way through without burning the bottoms. Keep the heat down and watch the tops. They will become shiny as the butter cooks up, then will return to a dry-looking matte appearance. At this point remove them so that they will still be soft and chewy.

HUNGARY NIGHT

HINT: THEY RULED AN EMPIRE, WERE FAMOUS FOR FOOD AND MUSIC,
BUT NO ONE UNDERSTOOD A WORD THEY SAID.

Hungary is a country that has been conquered by empires—the Celts, the Romans, the Turks—but that has also wielded tremendous power as the corulers of the Austro-Hungarian Empire, which extended from the Balkans through southern Poland. On the losing side of World War I, Hungary lost almost three fourths of its territory and all its ports, and it became a small, landlocked country.

The Hungarian language, Magyar, is one of only three European languages that is not part of the Indo-European language family and has almost nothing in common with any other languages.

The land of Liszt and Bartók and many of the great orchestra conductors of the twentieth century—Eugene Ormandy, George Szell, Antal Doráti, Fritz Reiner, and Georg Solti, to name just a few—Hungary has long been known for its music, especially its violinists and string quartets. It is also known as a land of food lovers. In the days of the Soviet Union, when the Communists demonstrated that the state could run science programs and health care but not restaurants, Hungary was the one place in the Soviet Bloc where you could find good food.

Hungarians like their food—their music too—rich and extravagant. In Budapest, even in Communist times there was a great love of pastry. The Turks had introduced coffeehouses, and the Hungarians made them into places to eat pastry. They remained at the heart of Budapest life.

Budapest is one of Europe's most beautiful cities, stretching from the foothills of the Carpathian Mountains in Buda across the wide Danube River to the urban flatlands of Pest, where the Great Hungarian Plains that once provided Europe's wheat begin. In Communist times the rooftop vistas across the Danube from Buda were unmarred by billboards or any advertising except an occasional red star.

Hungarians who became legendary had a cake named after them. Sometimes the cake, too, became legendary. In 1962 the pastry makers of the city honored the great nineteenth-century pastry maker József C. Dobos, who Hungarians claim was the inventor of butter cream, by parading through the streets of Budapest with a six-foot-diameter Dobos Torte, the seven-layer chocolate-butter-cream caramel-glazed cake that is his most famous creation.

Aside from the pastry houses, one of my favorite places in Budapest—I'm not sure if it still exists—was the Hungarian Pastry Museum. The museum displayed antique pastry-making tools, and there I learned all kinds of great trivia such as the fact that in 1900 there were sixty coffee and pastry establishments in Budapest, but by 1938 the number had grown to 299.

The Hungarian novelist George Konrád wrote of female café society in Budapest, "They vie with one another in secrets, memories, letters, and lies. With good taste they wage war, lady against lady. The decades go by, and still they sit in their hats and silk scarves and eat chocolate cake with whipped cream."

Eating light is almost anathema to Hungarians. My favorite story about Hungarians was told to me by my friend the photographer Sylvia Plachy, who was born in Budapest but was rushed across a field into exile by her parents after the 1956 uprising. Sylvia periodically goes back to visit friends, and after one visit she told me that all her friends in Budapest were on a health kick. They had gotten a food processor and were grating vegetables and putting them in whole-grain bread sandwiches. But first they would slather goose fat on the bread. "What's the goose fat for?" Sylvia asked. "You have to give it some flavor," she was told.

SALAD
◆ KALKÁPOSZTASALÁTA

This is about as light as a Hungarian dish gets.

½ head savoy cabbage, shredded to
⅓–½ inch pieces
2 cups crisp apples, peeled and
chopped
1 cup sour cream

1 cup mustard
1 tablespoon sugar
4 turns of black pepper
2 tablespoons fresh mint leaves,
chopped

Mix the cabbage with the apples. Mix in the sour cream, mustard, sugar, and pepper. Sprinkle the mint leaves on top.

MAIN COURSE
◆ LAMB PAPRIKÁS

There are many kinds of Hungarian paprikás—a stew made with paprika, a powder from red peppers. The paprika itself comes in five or six types in escalating degrees of heat. But in the US you are usually only offered the choice between sweet and hot. Paprikás can also be made with many different types of meat and a variety of sauces. I came up with this dish after looking at numerous recipes and experimenting. We loved the result.

1 cup bacon, chopped, cut from the
    slab
¼ cup olive oil
1 yellow onion, chopped
1½ pounds lamb shoulder, cubed
1 cup flour
2 tablespoons sweet Hungarian
    paprika
1 tablespoon hot Hungarian paprika

1 bottle dry white wine
1 teaspoon caraway seeds
8 pearl onions, peeled
3–4 cups beef stock (see Basic
    Recipes, p. 24, or buy)
3 tomatoes, chopped
1 pint sour cream
1 bunch Italian parsley

Render the bacon in a skillet with a little olive oil. Cook the onions in the fat until they wilt. Dust the cubed lamb shoulder with flour and then brown it in the fat. Add the sweet and hot paprika. Cover ¾ of the way with white wine. Add the caraway seeds and pearl onions. Bring to a vigorous boil, then reduce to a simmer. Add enough beef stock for the meat to be completely covered. Continue simmering for 1 hour, add the tomatoes, and continue simmering for another hour.

Add the sour cream, stir in well, and cook on high heat for about 4 minutes to thicken the sauce. Add dumplings (recipe below) and serve with minced Italian parsley sprinkled on top.

DUMPLINGS

2 eggs
1 cup flour

1 tablespoon minced parsley

Beat the eggs and add the flour and parsley—using just enough flour to make the mixture into a soft dough. Shape into small egg-shaped dumplings, about 1 inch long. Cook in slightly bubbling water for about 3 minutes.

DESSERT
◆◆◆ RIGÓ JANCSI

This is my prize recipe that I have been keeping secret. In the mid-1970s, I was the head chef of a new restaurant in Manhattan's Greenwich Village. One day the owner presented me with a small cube of chocolate on a plate. He was a nice fellow, and I thought he was bringing me a treat. But all he said was, "I want you to make this. It's called Rigó Jancsi."

He understood the nature of my dubious talent. If you give me a recipe, I will end up with something completely different. But if you give me the food, I can usually figure out how to copy it.

It was an extremely rich, dense chocolate mousse sandwiched between two thin layers of chocolate cake with a hard, dark chocolate glaze on top. The cake was easy. It took me just two tries, and only because I had to figure out it needed to be baked less. The chocolate on top did not take long either. But I worked on the filling for weeks, trying, throwing it out, trying again. Chocolate is fragile and demanding—also expensive. The owner wouldn't let me give up. Finally I got it. I gave up my cooking career not long after that, but I have been making this treat for my friends and family ever since. It is very rich and you can only eat a small piece, but don't worry about making too much because it seems to last forever. I sometimes think chocolate is a better preservative than salt. The little cubes are attractive because they are three different colors of chocolate.

Rigó Jancsi, at least according to Hungarian legend, is the name of a Gypsy violinist. There is a long-standing tradition in Budapest restaurants to let Gypsy violinists play for tips. Rigó Jancsi, with his violin and his striking dark looks, seduced an aristocrat's wife, a Princess Chimay, with his violin. One day, with the prince sitting next to her at the table, she slipped a diamond ring off her finger and handed it to Rigó, who put it on a finger of his bow hand without missing a stroke of a Brahms Hungarian dance. She left her husband and two sons and ran off with the Gypsy. What else could she do, now that she'd given him the ring in front of her husband? The story became famous in Budapest, and a pastry chef made this cake and named it after the Gypsy. There is more about this in my novel *Boogaloo on Second Avenue* and of course, like all good stories, it does not end well.

Start at least one day before serving.

THE CAKE

2 tablespoons melted butter
2 sticks butter
4 ounces unsweetened chocolate,
    melted

⅓ cup plus ¼ cup sugar
5 eggs, separated
a splash of vanilla extract
½ cup flour

Preheat oven to 350 degrees.

Cover an approximately 11 x 17-inch baking sheet with parchment paper. Brush it with melted butter and then dust it with flour, tapping the edge of the sheet to knock off any excess flour. Beat the butter in a mixer with a paddle attachment until it is creamy and then beat in the melted, unsweetened chocolate and ⅓ cup sugar. Continue beating as you add, one at a time, the egg yolks and then a splash of vanilla extract.

Whip the egg whites with the remaining ¼ cup sugar until they form stiff peaks. Carefully fold the egg whites into the chocolate mixture. Sift the flour into the mixture, folding in about a fourth at a time, moving a rubber spatula very gently to fold. Folding is not stirring, but involves a lifting and dropping motion as the bowl is slowly turned with the other hand.

Spread the mixture on the baking sheet. It should be about ¼ inch thick but does not have to be exactly even because it will spread out as it bakes, as long as you don't leave any holes. Bake for about 20 minutes, but watch carefully. It should have a shiny, moist surface when you take it out. If you overbake it, you'll dry it out.

Rigó Jancsi, violin,
champagne

THE FILLING

2 cups heavy cream
12 ounces semisweet chocolate

a splash of vanilla extract
¼ cup dark rum

Gently heat the cream and melt the chocolate in it. Add a splash of vanilla and the rum. Pour the mixture into a mixer with the whip attachment and whip it on high speed as it cools. This may take as long as 30 minutes. You can speed up the process by sticking the bowl in the freezer for a few minutes to chill, but while cold mixtures beat more quickly, warm mixtures turn out lighter. When the mixture becomes the color of light milk chocolate and the thickness of frosting, it is done.

Cut the cake into 2 equal pieces, and with a rubber spatula spread the filling on one half. Then place the other half over it and refrigerate overnight.

THE GLAZE

1 cup sugar
⅓ cup water

12 ounces semisweet chocolate

In a pot over medium heat, melt the sugar in the water. Add the chocolate. The quality of the chocolate does make a difference, so use something good. Mix well and spread on the top of the cake. Refrigerate at least 3 hours and then trim the cake to straight edges and cut into cubes. A serrated knife that has passed quickly through a burner flame works well for this.

DRINK

Cherry juice and club soda for the kids. For adults there are many pleasant Hungarian wines.

NEW ORLEANS NIGHT

HINT: A PORT THAT IS PARTLY BELOW SEA LEVEL.

Normally the first response to the idea of a port below sea level is, How do you keep the sea out of the town? The answer: with a system of earthen dams called levees. The old parts that made up the original city, such as the French Quarter, are safely above sea level, but many of the wards that were added on as the city expanded are as much as ten feet below sea level: without levees to keep the Mississippi River out, they would be dry land only part of the year. In 2005 Hurricane Katrina did not hit New Orleans, but it put so much water in the area that the levees could not hold the twenty-foot storm surges and 80 percent of the city was flooded.

The Midwest and South have a long history of not leaving the Mississippi untamed to do what it wants, and all along the river levees have turned into farmland what nature intended to be flood plains for spring rain and thawing snow. The artificially constricted river often rises too high to be held. In Louisiana, Cajun farmers are allowed to work land along the river with the understanding that the Army Corps of Engineers, at its discretion, can open sluices and flood the farms in order to save New Orleans from flooding. This happened in 2011, and the farmers accepted their sacrifice without complaint.

When Talia's finger landed on New Orleans we might have spun again because, after all, New Orleans is part of the United States, and therefore not international. But in many ways—especially eating—it is like another country. New Orleans, as the locals seem to love pointing out, has a variety of influences, including Spanish, Mexican, and African, but the dominant one is French. In my early twenties, I decided to learn about French cooking and I read every old French cookbook I could find. Then I went to France and discovered that such cooking no longer existed, especially not in Paris. But I found it in New Orleans. It is a kind of cooking that hasn't existed in France since the nineteenth, sometimes eighteenth century. In addition, it has African, Caribbean, Mexican, and Spanish accents. There is also the influence of a growing Vietnamese population, and many of the hundreds of construction workers who came to rebuild after Katrina were Mexican or Mexican-American from Texas. They brought their own food and wonderful food trucks that served menudo and other Mexican treats.

But the old New Orleans cooking dominates—with old-fashioned French sauces but also hot Mexican spices, an African taste for frying and thickening with okra, and Southern specialties like pecans thrown in. It is shamelessly rich food, without the modern quest for lightness, very full-flavored and irresistible.

APPETIZER
◆◆ FRIED OYSTERS AND SPICY MAYONNAISE

Biologically, all of the oysters on the Atlantic coast of North America are identical, from the Gulf of Mexico to Labrador, *Crassotrea virginica*. It is the conditions in which they grow that makes them different. The oysters raised in the warm waters of Louisiana grow very fast, and are plump with a mild flavor. That is why the people here do things that you would never do with pungent little northern oysters. For this dish, use the largest, most plump oysters you can find.

THE OYSTERS

12 large, plump oysters
1 cup flour
3 eggs, beaten

2 cups bread crumbs
1 cup lard or canola oil

Shuck the oysters, saving the liquor for the next course. Dredge them in flour, dip them in the beaten eggs, and roll them in bread crumbs. In New Orleans they fry oysters in lard, which is delicious. If you worry about your health, which is a reasonable concern, you might want to compromise and fry in very hot canola oil. But lard will taste better. (See On Fats and Oils, p. 6.) Remove the oysters to a paper towel when they first turn golden—do not overcook.

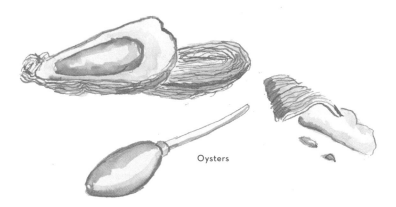

Oysters

THE MAYONNAISE

Canola oil is good for this recipe, because it does not compete with other flavors.

3 egg yolks
5 garlic cloves, peeled
1–2 cups canola oil

juice of ½ lemon
a pinch of salt
1 tablespoon cayenne pepper

Make a mayonnaise (see Basic Recipes, p. 21) with 3 egg yolks and 5 peeled garlic cloves ground well in the food processor. Add the canola oil slowly, drop by drop. When the mixture starts to stiffen, add the lemon juice and then resume pouring in the oil until it thickens. Before you are finished, add salt and cayenne pepper.

Dip the oysters in the mayonnaise to eat.

MAIN COURSE
◆◆ CRAB ÉTOUFFÉE

Étouffées are one of the basic New Orleans dishes. They start, as most New Orleans dishes do, with bell pepper, celery, and garlic, sometimes mockingly called the holy trinity of New Orleans cooking, and with a sauce made from a roux, which is an old-fashioned French way of cooking hardly ever seen in France anymore but essential in New Orleans.

½ green bell pepper, minced
½ celery rib, minced
5 garlic cloves, peeled and minced
½ yellow onion, minced
2 Dungeness crabs
2 cups canola or corn oil
1 cup flour

a pinch of salt
1 tablespoon cayenne pepper
4 tablespoons butter
2 cups chicken stock (see Basic
    Recipes, p. 24, or buy)
oyster liquor from appetizer
2 cups white rice

Put the minced bell pepper, celery, garlic, and onion in a bowl.

Crack open the Dungeness crabs and remove the meat from the body, legs, and claws. This should yield at least 3 cups of crabmeat.

Make the roux: Heat the oil until smoking in a cast-iron skillet and add the flour. Stir for 2 minutes and remove from heat. Add half of the minced vegetables and stir until the mixture becomes brown gravy. Add salt and cayenne pepper, and, putting the pan back over heat, continue stirring with a wooden spoon until it becomes thick and dark. Turn off heat.

Sauté the crabmeat in butter with the remaining mixed vegetables. Add the chicken stock and the oyster liquor from the appetizer. The roux will have now cooled into a paste. Add a big glop at a time to the crab and stock until you have a thick sauce. (You might not use all of the roux.) Serve over white rice.

VEGETABLE
◆ GRILLED SWISS CHARD

This is a great dish to make on an outdoor grill if you have one. Otherwise, a grilling pan on a stove works well.

1 bunch Swiss chard
1 cup olive oil
4 garlic cloves, peeled and minced
juice of ½ lemon

a large pinch of coarse salt
4 turns of black pepper
1 teaspoon cayenne pepper

Wash the chard and remove the leaves from the stems. Lightly oil the stems. Grill the stems until they are supple, with some blackened grill marks. Slice into bite-size pieces. Place the leaves on the grill and let them wilt and slightly char. Remove the stems and leaves to a bowl. Sauté the garlic in some of the olive oil and toss in with chard. Add the rest of the olive oil and the lemon juice, sea salt, black pepper, and cayenne pepper and toss.

DESSERT
◆◆ FRUIT BEIGNET

To be honest, we had planned to serve the beignet with the pralines, but it was just too much, so we made the beignet for breakfast the next morning. A beignet is a donut and it must always be served hot directly after cooking: personally, I think that cold donuts are inedible. When I am in New Orleans I always eat beignet for breakfast, though usually not fruit ones.

assorted pieces of fruit: apples,
 bananas, mango, strawberries,
 pears
2 eggs, separated
¾ cup sugar

1½ cups flour
¼ teaspoon baking soda
1½ cups whole milk
1-2 cups canola oil
½ cup powdered sugar

You could use almost any fruit for this. I sliced an apple and a Bartlett pear and dusted them with sugar. I also peeled and sliced a mango and a banana and removed the stems from small whole strawberries.

This operation is done best with an electric mixer with two bowls. Beat the yolks with paddle attachment for two minutes. Beat in ¼ cup of the sugar. Then beat in the flour, ¼ cup at a time, then the baking soda. Still beating, add the milk, ¼ cup at a time. Then beat in another ¼ cup sugar. Keep beating with the paddle on high speed until the mixture is smooth and has no lumps.

Now change bowls and replace the paddle with the whip. Add the remaining ¼ cup sugar to the egg whites and beat until they form soft peaks. Carefully fold the egg-white mixture into the yolk mixture.

Heat canola oil at least ½ inch deep in a skillet until it is very hot. (This—and working with hot oil in general—is not a job for children.) Using a long barbecue fork or tongs, dip a piece of fruit in the batter until it is thoroughly coated, then place it in the hot oil. You can do a few at a time. When they are golden, turn with a spatula. When both sides are golden, remove to paper towels. Place them on a platter and use a sifter to thoroughly dust them in powdered sugar.

DRINK
◆ HURRICANE PUNCH

New Orleans is one of the great homes of the cocktail. In the nineteenth century, when New England ice was cut into blocks in the winter, stored in ice houses, and shipped, one of the great destinations of the ice trade was the port of New Orleans for cocktails. The Sazerac (rye whiskey, herbsaint, Peychaud bitters, and a twist of lemon), the Hurricane (light rum, dark rum, passion fruit, orange juice, and grenadine), and Ramos Gin Fizz (gin, lemon juice, lime juice, orange flower water, a pinch of sugar, all frothed with beaten egg whites and milk) are all New Orleans cocktails.

Hurricane Punch is a popular nonalcoholic drink suggested for Mardi Gras when your friends are all getting too drunk but also a pleasant drink for kids.

2 cup water
2 cups pineapple juice
juice of six fresh limes
juice of 3 fresh oranges

juice of four fresh lemons
2 cups ginger ale
1 sliced navel orange for garnish

Combine water, pineapple juice, lime juice, orange juice, and lemon juice; chill. Add ginger ale before serving. Pour into cocktail or tall glasses and garnish with orange slices

SWEETS
◆◆ PRALINES

A little bit old French but a lot southern, pralines are one of the joys of New Orleans. Pecans are a species of hickory unique to North America and a treat I used to bring back for French people when I lived in Paris. There are various tales of the origin of New Orleans pralines, some of them going back to the seventeenth century, when the word referred to caramelized almonds in France. But of course in New Orleans, where they like neither simple nor light, they not only changed the nut but added butter and cream.

I don't know if people in New Orleans actually make pralines, since there are so many places to buy them, especially the old establishments in the French Quarter like Evan's Creole Candy Factory, which opened in 1900, or Laura's, which opened in 1913. But if you are not in New Orleans, pralines are not difficult to make.

This recipe is based on that of a very kind man who cooks in the French Quarter named Paul Prudhomme. You have to do this all quickly, so measure everything out before you start. This makes a dozen pralines.

½ cup butter
⅔ cup white sugar
⅔ cup light brown sugar
⅓ cup heavy cream

1 cup whole pecans
½ cup chopped pecans
⅔ cup whole milk
2 tablespoons vanilla extract

Butter a baking sheet.

Melt the butter in a pot and add both sugars. Stir over high heat with a long-handled wooden spoon until the sugar is melted. Add the cream and the pecans and keep stirring vigorously. After a few minutes add the milk, keep stirring, and after another several minutes add the vanilla. Keep stirring very quickly over high heat until the mixture is so thick that it seems more like dough than a sauce and has turned lighter in color, opaque, and has lost its sheen. Drop one spoonful on the baking sheet. If it is runny and shiny, it is not ready; continue stirring over heat. When it is ready, drop spoonfuls on the sheet and let them cool. They should be about 1½ to 2 inches in diameter.

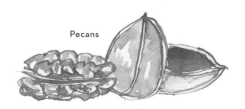
Pecans

SENEGAL NIGHT

HINT: A COUNTRY ON THE WESTERN TIP OF ITS CONTINENT.

Senegal is the westernmost point of Africa, which made it the shortest sailing distance to the European sugar colonies in the Caribbean. In Africa, sticking out is not always an advantage. The coast of Senegal and its ports became important centers for shipping slaves to the Americas. But in modern times, Senegal has been one of the more peaceful and democratic countries of Africa.

Senegal is the first place in Africa that I ever visited, so I was very excited to be there. My first morning, I walked out of my Dakar hotel and a man was staring at me. When I looked back at him, he seemed to become embarrassed and turned his gaze toward the ground. I thought that this man would like to talk with me, so I struck up a conversation with him. We talked about his life, his wife, his many children, the various jobs he worked to feed them. We talked about food. He told me of a Senegalese chicken dish called yassa. He was from a rice-growing area called Casamance, but he lived in Dakar. He asked me where I was from, how many children I had, and how long I was staying in Dakar. Most of the time he seemed a little awkward and kept looking at the ground, but we talked on, my first African conversation. He spoke French well. But after a while he simply stared down and didn't bother looking up anymore until he finally said, "When you leave, can I have your shoes?"

One of my fondest memories of the country is fishing in its great curving tropical rivers. The Saloum in the north and the Casamance in the south are both important commercial arteries; the Saloum because it comes from the peanut-producing area and the Casamance because it is the rice-producing area. But they don't look like commercial thoroughfares. The only traffic is the occasional canoe, back then usually paddled but by now more often with an outboard engine.

Both of these rivers are saltwater for miles above their mouths and wind into a series of quiet deep bends called bolongs, where eagles perch on baobab trees—sturdy trees with trunks far too thick for their delicate spreading branches—and swoop over the river to grab small fish with their claws while pelicans dive to scoop up fish in their bills. Monkeys hang from branches and seem to laugh at you if you try fishing. Along the Casamance in the grassy-floored forests delicate blue night heron watch you without moving while parrots scream from tree branches. Huge fromager trees, with their dramatic deep-creviced trunks so mysterious that they are the homes of spirits in many African religions, grow by the marshes and provide light-weight wood for the canoes. On the drier shores of the Saloum, flamingoes and huge gray goliath heron wade. The stretches of salt water are tidal and in low tide black oyster can be plucked from the mangrove roots of the bolongs. They are always cooked. Everything is cooked. West Africans have learned that raw food is too dangerous.

The wide expanses of salt water in the center of the river are brimming with sea life. Dolphins cruise by. Many of the locals fish with hand lines weighted with rocks. On a good afternoon they can feed their family and have something to sell. There are sixty-pound fish called carangue and 120-pound red fish in the carp family and thirty-pound barracuda that fight harder than the larger fish. I cannot understand how they catch these fish with a hand line because even with a rod and reel I found the barracuda very hard to play. They have delicate jaws and it is easy to yank the hook out of their mouth. Once they are caught you have something similar to a mackerel to eat, a dark, oily fish. If you slit them behind the gills to bleed them as soon as they are caught, they are better. But the prize fish is the capitaine, which runs about forty pounds and has succulent white flesh resembling that of striped bass. Wherever the French go, they call their favorite local fish capitaine. There are capitaine fish, of no relation to each other, all over the world. When the British find a fish that they like, they call it cod, like the black cod of the Pacific Northwest and the blue cod of Australia, neither of which are cod any more than the capitaine has anything to do with captains.

I wanted to have fish for Senegal Night, but I couldn't have everything and I wanted accara and I wanted yassa. Maybe next time. You can always substitute. Take some striped bass and call it capitaine and prepare it like yassa as they do in the Casamance. A few hours of marinating is sufficient, and you can skip the grilling stage and otherwise follow the yassa recipe. However, in Senegal, the reverse of most Western countries, fish is ordinary and chicken is special.

Both the accara and the yassa need to be started the day before.

APPETIZERS
 ACCARA

Black-eyed peas, the basic bean of Africa and consequently of the American South, are a lot of work. You have to begin the day before.

1 pound black-eyed peas
1/2 cup yellow onion, chopped
2 tablespoons salt

1/2 teaspoon baking soda
1–2 cups peanut oil

The day before, soak the black-eyed peas in warm water for 10 minutes and then start rubbing them. You are trying to remove the transparent skin that also has the black eye on it so that you're left with plain white beans. When you rub them, some skins will come off and float to the surface, but some won't, so you have to periodically sift through the beans and pick out loose skins.

The next day, check for a few missed skins, floating or in with the beans. Drain out the water and rinse. Add the onion, salt, and baking soda. Puree all of it into a batter in the food processor. You may need to add a little water to make it batterlike and not doughlike, but don't let it get too runny.

Heat the peanut oil very hot in a skillet and drop the batter in the oil one spoonful at a time. Use a spatula to flatten each one. Brown the bottom, flip, and brown the other side. Drain on paper towels. Eat with kaani.

Black-eyed peas

TALIA: *Black-Eyed Peas*

Squish! Squash! That's what you do when you skin black-eyed peas. First you take a bowl full of warm water and then pour a bunch of black-eyed peas into it. Wait about ten minutes, then plunge your hands into the water and grab a big handful of peas and squish them with your hands. It's so much fun, and once you have squashed a bunch of them the peels should come to the surface of the water and you slowly pick them out. You will have to do this several times. After a while you will have to take the remaining ones one by one and put them in between two of your fingers and SQUEEZE! What's interesting is that the black dots on the black-eyed peas that make them look like "black eyes" are part of the skin, so when all the skins come to the surface not only do the peas look like a white, ordinary bean: seeing the "eyes" come up to the surface, you might have no choice but to laugh for a quick second.

◆ KAANI

The Senegalese way of saying that you have to take the bad with the good is "If you want to eat accara, you have to have kaani." This is supposed to be a painfully hot sauce. A little spice is good with the accara, but you can adjust to your tolerance level.

1 yellow onion, chopped
5 garlic cloves, peeled and chopped
a pinch of salt

¼ cup peanut oil
2 tomatoes, chopped
½ Scotch bonnet pepper

Sauté the onion, garlic, and salt in the peanut oil. Add the tomatoes and the Scotch bonnet pepper. (You can make it less spicy by stirring the pepper around and removing it, or more spicy by leaving it in, or even more spicy by mincing it and mixing it in.)

MAIN COURSE
◆ YASSA

This very simple and extremely flavorful food is the most famous dish in Senegal. Marinate it the night before.

one chicken, quartered
a pinch of salt
4 turns of black pepper
juice of 8 limes

½ cup plus 1 cup yellow onion, chopped
chicken stock (see Basic Recipes, p. 24, or buy it)
¼ cup peanut oil

Rub the chicken pieces with salt and pepper. Put them in an earthenware casserole with enough fresh lime juice to cover the chicken ⅔ of the way. Add the ½ cup of chopped onion and the chicken stock. Marinate overnight in refrigerator.

Set aside marinade in refrigerator. Grill chicken. The ideal is a charcoal grill, but a grill pan on high heat works well, cooking about 10 minutes on each side. While the chicken is grilling, sauté the remaining 1 cup of onions in peanut oil. Add ½ cup more chicken stock. The sauce should thicken and the onions caramelize a bit by the time the chicken is grilled on both sides. Then add the chicken and marinade and cook until the sauce is reduced and a bit thickened. Serve with rice.

DESSERT
◆◆◆ SOMBI SOUFFLÉ

A Senegalese chef from the Casamance, Pierre Thiam, makes a rice dessert called sombi, which is typical of his rice-producing region. The dish involves rice, coconut, lime juice, a few slices of fresh mango, and toasted coconut on top. A great combination, except that Talia, Marian, and I agreed—apologies to the Casamance—that we did not want a rice dessert. After all that really good accara and the rice with the yassa, the meal called for something lighter. So, like a French colonialist, I took the Senegalese idea and made it a French soufflé—politically incorrect but gastronomically perfect.

3 tablespoons butter
3 tablespoons flour
2 cups coconut milk
1 split vanilla bean
4 eggs, separated

2½ cups sugar
2–3 mangoes, coarsely chopped
juice of 1 lime
2½ cups grated coconut
3 tablespoons melted butter

Preheat oven to 350 degrees. Melt 3 tablespoons butter in a skillet and stir in the flour until it begins to thicken. Add the coconut milk and the vanilla bean. Slowly bring to a boil, reduce heat, and continue stirring with a wooden spoon until the mixture thickens.

Beat the egg yolks with 1 cup sugar. Add the hot coconut milk and vanilla. With a fork and spoon, scrape all the seeds out of the vanilla bean and discard the husk. Transfer to a food processor, add the mangoes, and pulse quickly but do not completely purée. Add 1 cup sugar, the lime juice, and 1½ cups of fresh grated coconut. Mix well.

Beat the egg whites with ½ cup sugar until it forms stiff peaks. Fold carefully into the coconut-mango mixture.

Spread 1 cup of grated coconut on a baking sheet and broil for a few minutes until the coconut turns a little brown.

Brush the melted butter onto the bottom and sides of a soufflé dish. Then dust with sugar, tapping the dish to knock off excess. Gently pour in the coconut-mango mixture, which should be slightly over the top of the dish. (You can extend a soufflé dish to make it really high by fashioning an aluminum-foil collar.) Run your index finger around the edge of the batter to define an edge: such tactile chores are usually appreciated by kids, who instinctively want to cook with their hands.

Sprinkle the toasted coconut on top of the soufflé and bake the soufflé for 40 minutes. The volume should increase by at least a third before you remove it from the oven. Remove the collar if you made one, and serve immediately.

DRINK
◆◆ TAMARIND JUICE

Sometimes you can buy tamarind juice, which is commonly available in Africa, but it is not that difficult to make if you can find a pound of tamarind pods.

Peel the pods, remove the netting of veins, and put the fruit in a pot with a quart of water. Add ½ cup of sugar. Simmer over low heat for 10 minutes. Cut off the heat and let sit for an hour. Mash up the fruit with a wooden spoon and pour through a strainer. Chill it and serve.

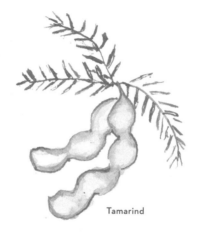

Tamarind

AQUITAINE NIGHT

HINT: AN ATLANTIC REGION BY THE MOUNTAINS.

We were both very happy when Talia's finger landed on the Atlantic coast of France just above Spain. On a map of France, the word *Aquitaine* was clearly spelled out vertically, but Aquitaine is more commonly referred to in France as the *sud-ouest,* the southwest of France.

Although Aquitaine was a kingdom in the Middle Ages, it is made up of several peoples, each of which have their own culture and therefore their own food traditions. There is the wine-producing region of Bordeaux, with its port city built on the wine trade. There is the Dordogne, where ducks and all their parts are nearly an obsession, and there are numerous groups along the Pyrenean border with Spain, including the Basques.

The Basques are an ancient people who speak the oldest living language in Europe. No one knows how old their language or culture are, but when the ancient Romans first encountered the Basques more than 2,200 years ago, they found that they were already an ancient people. Their language in no way resembles any other. "Yes" is *bai,* "no" is *ez,* and "thank you" is *eskerrik asko.* The Basque lands, as currently defined, are divided into seven provinces, four in Spain and three in the French region of Aquitaine. I have been going there every year, sometimes several times a year, for more than thirty years. When I met Marian I took her to Basque country and it was in a famous mountain pass above the village of Arnegui that I proposed to her. Talia, at her young age, has been there at least eight times.

When we are there we often eat in the little restaurants near the ancient fishing port of Saint-Jean-de-Luz—Donibane Lohitzune in Basque—where tuna, sardines, and anchovies are landed. There the restaurants frequently serve one of my favorite foods in the world as an appetizer, the fresh oysters from the Arcachon, a beautiful bay where two rivers meet the sea near the Bordeaux wine country. They also serve one of Marian's favorites, *bulot,* a one-inch meaty shellfish in the welk family. And they frequently serve Talia's favorite food, fresh grilled sardines. So all three of us are very happy.

TALIA: *Sardines in Saint-Jean-de-Luz*

There is something fresh and different and, well, sweet about Saint-Jean-de-Luz that you won't find anywhere else. Walking down the streets, hearing the language, it's all special, but one of the best things is the food. Basques are masters in the art of food.

One of the great foods you can find in Saint-Jean-de-Luz is fresh grilled sardines. Not the canned variety: the delicious, real, fresh fish. You might think, What's so unusual about sardines? It's the taste, which bears no resemblance to the taste of canned sardines. The texture is smooth, and the flavor slightly bitter for a quick second, before it dissolves into a calming, mild deliciousness. The Basques usually prepare grilled sardines with small bits of tomato and garlic, making them even more flavorful.

When you order this dish at a restaurant, the fish will most likely arrive whole. To remove the head, tail, and bones, make a cut to the fish right in front of the tail and slide the knife up the body, stopping right before you get to the head. Simply lift the knife, remove the fillet, and set it to the side of the plate. Then place the knife under the spine of the fish, grab the tail, and lightly pull up. The spine, tail, and head will quickly come up, leaving you with another fillet. Take the spine, tail, and head and put them to the side of your plate. Eat the fillets. Continue doing this to every sardine until you have finished your meal.

APPETIZER
◆ GRILLED SARDINES

Here in New York City, bulots and oysters from the Arcachon are hard to find, but there are excellent fresh sardines flown in from Portugal. Sardines do not grace the Atlantic shores of North America, so they have to be flown in, but they are fished in California. Either way, sardines are a plentiful and well-fished catch and an extremely healthy one, rich in omega-3 and fatty acids that benefit growing children. Also, because they are fairly low in the food chain, they contain far fewer pollutants, which tend to be concentrated in larger fish.

This is how we cooked them, in the style of Saint-Jean-de-Luz. If you want to be authentic you should use Basque salt, excellent coarse salt from the Salinas Añana in Vizcaya, or if you wanted to be more authentically Aquitaine rather than authentically Basque, there is also very high quality coarse white salt from Ile-de-Re a few miles north of the Aquitaine border.

9 fresh whole sardines	½ cup parsley, finely chopped
coarse salt	½ tomato, finely minced
½ cup olive oil	2 garlic cloves, finely minced

Have the sardines gutted and scaled at the fish store but make sure that the heads and tails are left on. No decapitated or maimed fish for this dish. Throw some coarse salt on the fish. Place the sardines in a pan under a broiler for about 10 minutes, until the fish skin begins to bubble up. Heat some olive oil in a skillet and add the chopped parsley, tomato, and garlic. Cook briefly, until the garlic is yellow and the parsley bright green. Place the sardines on serving plates and pour the sauce over it.

MAIN COURSE
◆◆ STEAK BORDELAISE

For the main course we chose something from Bordeaux, steak Bordelaise with marrow, the ultimate dish for this red-wine country. The sauce is my own variation on the somewhat more complicated classical French cuisine version.

3 grass-fed, dry-aged shell, entrecote,
   or strip steaks
2 tablespoons butter
1 teaspoon flour

½ cup glace de viande
½ bottle red Bordeaux
2 marrowbones
½ pound French green beans

Grill the steaks however you like them. I like them very rare; Talia likes them medium rare. Well-done is one of the great gastronomic misnomers. Leave it with at least a little color.

For the sauce, start with a beef stock, which you can buy or make (see Basic Recipes, p. 24). Then glace de viande has to be made. Sometimes it can be bought. It is simply a concentration of beef stock made by cooking out the water. A gallon of beef stock will make about two cups of glace de viande. It should be dark and thick.

You start by making a roux. But be careful: too much roux turns a great sauce into bad gravy. Melt one pat of butter in the skillet. Add no more than a healthy pinch of flour—about a teaspoon—and stir until blended. Add the glace de viande and the wine. It does not have to be great Bordeaux, it does not even have to be Bordeaux, but it does have to be a big-bodied red, such as a cabernet sauvignon. There is a myth that you can use any kind of wine for cooking. But food is only as good as its ingredients. It would be a waste to use a really great grand cru, but don't get too cheap.

Cook the sauce over high heat until it has reduced to about a quarter of its original volume and has become dark and thick. While it is cooking, take the beef marrowbones, two good center bones cut from legs away from the joints, so that the marrow will push out with your finger in a straight tube. Slice two such tubes into ⅓-inch-thick disks. Place on the sauce shortly before it is finished, just long enough to heat the marrow.

Pour the sauce over the steaks. Serve with the skinny green beans that are called "French beans" although they are as French as Le Jazz: American beans brought to Europe and named French beans by Americans when they were brought back to the US a few generations later.

DESSERT
◆◆ GÂTEAU BASQUE

This is almost a sacred cake in our household. We usually have one or two in the freezer from Basque country. We have friends there who are gâteau Basque bakers in the Nivelle valley. But we also make it ourselves.

Not far from Saint-Jean-de-Luz is a curving river called the Nivelle. The Nivelle valley has rugged velvet-green mountains with fluffy clouds riding their tops, and a series of very similar villages with red-trimmed white Basque houses and a court for playing jai alai—any of a number of racquet sports that were invented in this valley and have become the Basque national sport.

This valley is also where gâteau Basque was invented. No one is sure exactly when, but it probably began as a bread with cherries in the middle. The town of Itxassou, as lovely a village as Europe has to offer, is famous for its black cherries, known in Basque as *xapata*.

There are two kinds of Basque cake: cherry filled and custard filled. We make cherry filled, but that is because we have a supply of black-cherry preserves from Itxassou. Other black-cherry preserves might work as long as they are made with whole black cherries. Otherwise the custard filling is also very pleasant.

The best gâteau Basque is made by our friends the Pereuils in the village of Saint-Pée-sur-Nivelle, where jai alai was invented. Though we are friends and have been dinner guests in their home on numerous occasions, they will not show the recipe to me or anyone outside their family. The recipe dates back five generations to the mid-nineteenth century, and their cake differs from modern confections. But not having that recipe I have devised my own, which makes a cake resembling those found in modern Basque pastry shops.

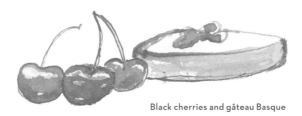

Black cherries and gâteau Basque

3½ cups flour
1 stick plus 6 tablespoons salted
    butter, cut into cubes
2 teaspoons baking powder
2 cups sugar

2 drops vanilla extract
2 drops almond extract
¼ cup dark rum
5 egg yolks
1 jar black-cherry preserves

Put the flour in a mixer with a hook attachment and beat in the butter. When there are no lumps and the flour is the consistency of a coarse meal, add the baking powder and sugar. While beating add the vanilla and almond extracts and the rum. Beat in 4 egg yolks, one at a time. When the dough becomes an even, homogenous ball, let it sit for 1 hour.

Preheat oven to 400 degrees. Press about two thirds of the dough into a 9-inch springform pan. Build up the sides and place the black-cherry preserves in the well. Cover with the rest of the dough. This should also be a thick layer. Brush the last egg yolk, beaten, on top. I like to put aside a little dough, roll it out to about a ⅓-inch thickness, and cut a Basque symbol with a cookie cutter. You probably don't have a cookie cutter that makes a Basque symbol, but anyone with a little drawing skill could hand-cut one with a knife. Place the symbol in the center of the brushed cake, but don't brush it, so that the symbol bakes to a lighter color than the rest of the cake. Bake for one hour.

Basque symbol

If you can't find a satisfactory black-cherry preserve, make pastry cream. This is a French invention, whereas the xapata cherries are Basque, which is why I suspect that the original recipe called for cherries. But the cream also makes a good filling.

PASTRY CREAM

4 egg yolks
½ cup sugar
3 tablespoons flour

1½ cups heavy cream
1 vanilla bean

Beat the egg yolks with the sugar. While continuing to beat, add the flour. Pour the cream into a medium-size saucepan and bring to a boil with the vanilla bean. When heated to the point when the cream starts to mount the sides of the pot, quickly pour it into the mixing bowl with the yolks. With a spoon, rub the vanilla bean against the side of the bowl to remove seeds; discard the pod. Beat all the ingredients together and then place the mixture back in the saucepan over moderate heat and beat vigorously until it becomes very thick. It is important to keep the cream moving in the pot so that it does not curdle on the bottom while heating. When the liquid has thickened, remove from heat and let cool.

DRINKS

The steak dish is the kind of food that stands up to a big, great red wine, so this would be a chance to splurge on a good Bordeaux. For kids, there is an organic grape juice from local grapes that is actually made in Bordeaux and exported to the US. If you can't find it, try to find another good-quality red grape juice as opposed to the purple Concord grape juice I used to drink as a kid. Not only is it funny tasting, but it's too rich to drink with a meal. My grandmother always used to dilute it with water, which didn't help. So see if you can find better grape juice alternatives, or look for the juice from Bordeaux.

KOREA NIGHT

HINT: A NATION WITH TWO POINTS OF VIEW.

The first international news event that I can recall was the Korean War ending in 1953. Korea had been occupied by Japan since 1910, but after the Japanese were defeated in World War II, Korea became the spoils of war, with the northern half controlled by the Soviet Union and the southern half by the US. The Korean War only intensified the division, and Korea remains two countries with people of the same ethnicity and culture and a seemingly insoluble political division.

Of the many Asian groups that have settled in North and South America and Europe, Koreans have had one of the smallest culinary impacts. Compared to Indian, Thai, Chinese, Japanese, and Vietnamese, the food of Korea has enjoyed little popularity. In my neighborhood in New York the Korean people who own the small grocery store, as many Koreans do throughout New York, started selling their homemade kimchi, Korean fermented cabbage and hot pepper. Since there were few Koreans in the neighborhood, few bought it.

I think the reason for this lack of interest in Korean food is that it is less about the individual dishes than it is the way a meal is constructed. A Korean meal is put together very much the way a Chinese meal is, but the Chinese have individual dishes that have attracted attention even though few Westerners ever eat a Chinese-style meal. Korean dishes do not seem to work well outside of the context of the Korean meal. At least they have no dish that has caught on the way lo mein, sushi, curry, pad thai, or spring rolls have. Perhaps something will someday. In the meantime, you can still enjoy an excellent Korean meal.

Koreans have a very healthy diet, high in protein and low in fat. They use sesame seeds, which are thought to be extremely healthy, a great deal. (See On Sugar and Spice, p. 15.)

We put this meal together with the guidance of some recipes from my friend Mih-Ho Cha. All of the dishes in this meal except the dessert are served at once, so be prepared with some attractive and varied serving dishes and bowls.

Before you start, spread three cups of sesame seeds on a sheet and broil until they turn golden but before they turn black. A toaster oven toasting half at a time works well for this, because it is easy to monitor the toasting.

MAIN COURSE
◆ BULGOGI

1 pound beef sirloin
½ cup soy sauce
5 tablespoons sugar
4 garlic cloves, peeled and minced
a generous pinch of salt

5 tablespoons mirin
2 tablespoons toasted sesame oil
2 tablespoons toasted sesame seeds
1 cup green onion, chopped
5 leaves of lettuce

Slice the sirloin as thin as you can. Put it in a marinade of the soy sauce, sugar, garlic, salt, mirin (see On Sugar and Spice, p. 12), sesame oil, toasted sesame seeds, and green onion. Marinate for at least 5 hours.

Cook the beef and marinade in a skillet for a few minutes over moderate heat. Wrap the meat in little packets of lettuce. Cook down the sauce to half of the volume and pour over the lettuce packets.

◆ SPINACH NAMUL

This was our favorite.

2 tablespoons soy sauce
1 teaspoon sugar
1 garlic clove, peeled and finely
   minced
1 tablespoon fresh ginger root, minced

1 tablespoon toasted sesame seeds
a generous pinch of salt
½ cup green onions, chopped
1 pound well-washed spinach

Make a dressing of the soy sauce, sugar, garlic, ginger, toasted sesame seeds, salt, and green onions.

Using a strainer, plunge the spinach into boiling water. Remove immediately and quickly place under running cold water. Wring it dry and fluff it out with your fingers. Mix it with the dressing.

◆ KOREAN FISH

You could make this with most any fish that has the skin on. A good crispy skin is important to Korean cooking. I chose salmon simply because it has my favorite fish skin and crisps nicely.

1 pound salmon with skin, cut in strips
¼ cup soy sauce
2 tablespoons honey
1 tablespoon toasted sesame oil
1 teaspoon mirin
a pinch of salt

4 turns of black pepper
2 teaspoons cayenne pepper
1 garlic clove, peeled and minced
1 tablespoon fresh ginger root, minced
1 green onion, chopped

Broil the salmon skin side up so that it bubbles and crisps.

Combine the soy sauce, honey, sesame oil, mirin, salt, black pepper, cayenne pepper, garlic, ginger, and green onion. Pour this sauce over the broiled fish.

◆ PA JUN

This popular dish, a kind of pancake, must be fairly modern; either that or the recipe has changed, since wheat flour was seldom available until after the Korean War.

2 eggs
1 cup flour
1 cup water

5 green onions, split and cut into
1-inch squares
2 tablespoons salt
½ cup untoasted sesame oil

Beat the eggs. Add the flour, water, green onions, and salt. Mix well and let sit for 10 minutes, making a runny batter. Heat the sesame oil in a large skillet. Pour the batter into the hot oil. This will fill the pan. When brown on one side, flip and brown the other. You can also split the batter and make 2 smaller pancakes, which would be easier to flip. Cut in wedges on serving plate.

DESSERT
◆ FRUIT

I asked every Korean I know: "What is a good Korean dessert?" Everyone had the same answer: "Fresh fruit, peeled and sliced." Even the great August Escoffier, who defined classical French cooking in the early twentieth century, said that a great meal should end with fruit. In fact, we all loved this plate of fruit because it was full of beautiful colors and offered the perfect complement to the other dishes. We made Korean Night in the winter, which was perfect, because winter fruits go particularly well.

Peel and slice an Asian pear—which not by chance is sometimes called a Korean pear—and three persimmons. Peel and section an orange (see instructions in Cuba Night for Carlos's Pescado de Naranja, p. 134). Arrange fruits decoratively on a platter.

SWEETS
◆ KANG JUNG

1 cup light brown sugar
5 tablespoons honey

¾ cup water
2 cups toasted sesame seeds

Over moderate heat melt the light brown sugar and honey in the water. Add the toasted sesame seeds. Pour on a buttered baking sheet. With a spatula, shape the mixture into a ½-inch-thick square. When slightly cool, cut into rectangles.

DRINK
◆ SUJEONGGWA

This must be made at least 24 hours in advance.

8 cups water
½ cup fresh ginger, peeled and sliced
6 cinnamon sticks
1 cup sugar

6 dried persimmons (they can be
  found in specialty shops or online)
¼ cup pine nuts

    Put water, ginger, and cinnamon in a pot and boil for 20 minutes, then simmer another 30 minutes. Add sugar and dissolve by stirring. Then let the mixture cool. Remove stems from dried persimmons, wash, and add to mixture.

    Store in the refrigerator in a covered pitcher or jar for a day. Serve over ice, with a few pine nuts sprinkled on top of each glass. The persimmon will be soft and also good for eating. Arrange fruits decoratively on a platter.

Persimmons

HAITI NIGHT

HINT: THE FIRST BLACK REPUBLIC.

Sometimes you suffer for being first. In the eighteenth century, the richest European colony in the world was the French colony of Saint-Domingue, which is now Haiti. It produced sugar and coffee in an economy entirely based on slave labor. Between 1680 and 1776, eight million Africans were brought as slaves to Haiti. And yet in 1776 there were fewer than three hundred thousand Africans left in the colony. The French had determined that caring for slaves made less economic sense than working them to death and buying new ones. By 1791, when the revolution broke out, the white population was only about thirty thousand. The worst nightmare of every slave

Banana bush

owner in the Americas unfolded in Haiti. The African slaves rose up and by force of numbers and determination overwhelmed the owners. A brutal war with shifting fortunes continued for more than a decade. Napoleon sent an army to retake the island, and in 1802 and 1803 the level of brutality and cruelty on both sides was horrifying. But in the end the former slaves, from the ashes of a society of astounding cruelty, attempted to build a republic. It was the first black republic in the world, but it was not cheered by any democracy. It terrified the established Western world. Everyone boycotted the new Republic of Haiti, including the Vatican. Europeans began looking into European-grown beet sugar as a replacement for the cane sugar of their Caribbean slave colonies. And so Haiti was on its own. It created its own society with its own customs. A religion, Vodoun, that mixed Roman Catholicism with several African religions took root and in two generations became well established. Haiti also developed its own language, Haitian Creole, which combined several African languages with French and a touch of Spanish and English.

Haiti became an impoverished country but a unique society. I have spent a great deal of time there, beginning in my days as the Caribbean correspondent for the *Chicago Tribune* from the mid-1980s to mid-1990s. Anyone who spends a lot of time in Haiti will be shaped by the experience. In Haiti I saw human beings at their most noble—their most poetic, most romantic, bravest, kindest. But I also saw humanity at its worst—astounding cruelty and violence. With all of this, Haiti remains permanently on my mind and in my heart.

What is the one taste that instantly brings back all of these memories the minute it lands on my tongue? It is peanut butter. Haitians make, bottle, and sell a homemade peanut butter with hot Scotch bonnet peppers in it, *mambo piment*. It is the best peanut butter I have ever tasted.

Haiti's Barbancourt, double distilled and dark, is simply the best rum in the world. And amazingly, through coups d'état, revolutions, massacres, and strikes, the quality of the rum never waivers. There is a small mushroom I have never seen anywhere else called djon djon, which, appropriately, turns rice black. And there are the dishes in this truly Haitian dinner. Truly Haitian, except that in Haiti, it would probably be eaten midday, which is when Haitians eat their big meal. A light supper, perhaps just a bowl of soup, would be evening fare.

Blanc manger must be made a day in advance, and pikliz must be made at least two days in advance.

PICKLE
◆ PIKLIZ

This condiment is a standard accompaniment for most Haitian dishes and goes well with the ones in this meal.

½ head cabbage, sliced very thin
3 carrots, grated
1 white onion, sliced thin
2 shallots, sliced thin
10 peas

6 green beans, trimmed and cut into
    narrow vertical strips
½ to 1 Scotch bonnet pepper
about 2 cups white vinegar

Mix all the vegetables well and put into a 2-pint pickling jar with 2 seeded quarters of a Scotch bonnet pepper—or, depending on how hot you like it, 3 or all 4 quarters, but in separate pieces. We used a moderate 2 quarters: all 4 would be fire. Tighten lid and keep at least 2 days before serving. Pikliz will keep for many months, even more than a year, if the lid is tight.

APPETIZER
◆ GRILLED OCTOPUS

This dish actually should be made with conch, which the Haitians call *lambi*. Conch, though, is hard to get, not only where I live but everywhere. In Haiti, fishermen have become so accustomed to taking young, undersize conch that they no longer even remember what a full-size adult looks like. The mature conch has a broad lip that extends far beyond the coiled body. Look at the piles of shells bleached white and pink in the Haitian sun that accumulate where fishermen work, and you will not find one fully mature shell.

In Haiti and much of the Caribbean, conches are important. Slaves used the shells as horns to signal an uprising, and in Haiti they are still often blown at political demonstrations. The conch shell is the symbol of rebellion and of freedom. The meat is thought to be an aphrodisiac. On the outskirts of Port-au-Prince, fishermen grill conch on their boats and prepare them just as in the recipe below, rowing up to late-night waterside "dance clubs" and selling the grilled conch off the boats to men at the clubs. In rural Haiti, the shells are often used to mark graves.

Aside from availability, there is another reason for eating octopus instead of conch. Throughout the wider Caribbean region, people are focused on eating the predators of octopus, larger fish such as grouper, and the prey of octopus, shellfish such as conch and crabs. But they seldom eat the octopus. This means that with ever fewer enemies, the octopus are becoming increasingly numerous and are competing with humans for conch and crab, further diminishing those populations.

Octopus is arguably better food than conch. Stories of how it is tough and must be beaten to break down the fiber and make it edible are not true. However, this is true of conch. So why isn't more octopus eaten? Simply because fishermen hate them. Octopus are hard to kill and they do not lie peacefully on the deck of a fishing boat or even in a tank. They wander. They like to get into things. They crawl into bags and gear. They hang from the ceiling of the pilothouse. They crawl into the engine hatch. They are a nuisance, but a tasty nuisance.

If you follow this simple recipe, the octopus will not be tough. Have the fish store remove the organ sack and the ink sack, cut off the beak in the center, and cut out the eyes.

1 medium-size octopus, about 6 to 8
    pounds uncleaned
juice of 6 limes
3 tablespoons peanut oil
a pinch of salt

3 turns of black pepper
1 garlic clove, peeled and minced
3 thin slices of white onion, rings
    separated and cut in half
1 Scotch bonnet pepper, minced

Plunge the octopus into boiling water and keep it there for 10 seconds. Let it cool down and then do the same thing again. See Talia's sidebar for more on this process. Then let it simmer in water just below bubbling for 1 hour.

Cut the octopus into bite-size pieces and mix the pieces with the lime juice, peanut oil, salt and black pepper, garlic, onion slices, and Scotch bonnet pepper. Serve chilled.

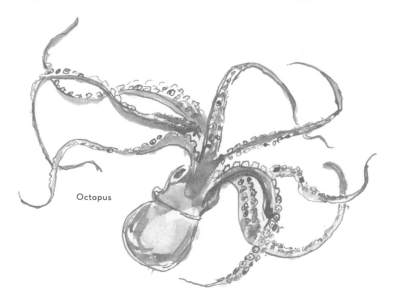

Octopus

TALIA: *Preparing Octopus*

Octopus feels exactly like rubber. Weird. It reminded me of the times I went swimming with dolphins. They feel like rubber as well.

This octopus dish was thoroughly delicious. However, for it to be edible you have to make the octopus tender. You simply boil a pot of hot water and place the octopus inside, then you take the octopus out, cool it, poke it, and see if it's tender enough to stick a fork through its body. The routine goes like this: boil then cool, boil then cool.

MAIN COURSE
◆ GRIYO DE PORC

Until the 1980s, pork was the common meat of Haiti. The so called "Creole pig" was small and black and lived off the land, foraging for food. Haitian peasants could let them grow and only slaughter them when they needed the money, so they were a kind of living savings account that required little investment. Then it was discovered in 1978 that some of these Creole pigs carried Asian Swine Flu, a highly contagious disease dangerous to livestock. There have been similar outbreaks in other Caribbean countries. When Cuba experienced such an outbreak, the infected pigs were quarantined and the pig population was saved. But in Haiti, the US Agency for International Development, USAID, decided that the Haitian outbreak was a threat to livestock in the Caribbean and the US—and undertook a program to kill 380,000 Creole pigs and replace them with big fat American pigs. The problem was that these larger pigs truly earned the name pig: they ate an enormous amount of food. To Americans, they were a superior animal because they converted food into meat at a far better rate than the meager Creole pig. But that assumes you can afford to keep a piggier pig. In the Haitian rumor mill, the incident is often cited as a plot by the Americans to destroy the Haitian peasant, but in international-development circles it is often cited as an example of why aid to poor countries often fails: a lack of knowledge about local conditions.

In Creole (which, by the way, in Creole is written *Kreyol*), there are at least three spellings for *griyo* or *griot*, an African word for an elderly wise man. I have always thought this dish got its name either because the meat was cooked until it became wise or because it was so cooked that it looked elderly, but I am not sure.

1 pound pork shoulder, cubed	3 garlic cloves, peeled and minced
juice of 2 sour oranges, or juice of 3 limes and ½ sweet orange (see Mexico Night, p. 72)	½ cup peanut oil
	a large pinch of salt
3 slices of white onion, rings separated	3 turns of black pepper
	4 sprigs of fresh thyme

Place the cubed pork shoulder in a bowl with the citrus juice. Add the onion, garlic, peanut oil, salt, black pepper, and thyme. Marinate meat for at least 5 hours.

Roast the meat in the marinade for 2 hours at about 350 degrees. Remove meat from juice and fry in hot peanut oil while cooking down the roast juices in a skillet. Pour the sauce over the meat.

◆ BANANE PESE

This is the exact same recipe as the tostones from Cuba Night, p. 132, except with a different sauce:

SAUCE TI MALICE

Literally, the sauce name means "a touch of evil." How evil is up to you. In Haiti, some restaurants make the sauce especially mild for *blans*, a Haitian word that comes from the French word for whites but in Haiti means anyone who is not Haitian. I liked this sauce hotter and would specify, *"pa twò blans"*—not too much for white people. They always understood.

¼ cup white onion, chopped
juice of 4 limes
¼ cup peanut oil
1 garlic clove, peeled and minced

a pinch of salt
½ to 2 Scotch bonnet peppers, minced

Place the chopped onion in a bowl with the lime juice and marinate 30 minutes. Remove the onions and sauté them in peanut oil with the garlic, salt, and amount of Scotch bonnet that suits your taste. Mix with the lime juice and cool to room temperature.

VEGETABLE
◆ GREEN BEANS AND CARROTS

For a heavier vegetable dish, Haitians often like gratiné, which is an old French dish in which vegetables are baked in a sauce with cheese. But for a lighter dish with a big meal, green beans and carrots is a standard.

½ pound green beans, cut into half-inch pieces
½ pound carrots, cut into half-inch sticks

¾ cup shallots, thinly sliced
3 garlic cloves, peeled and thinly sliced
3 tablespoons butter
a pinch of salt

Steam the green beans and carrots for only two minutes. Sauté shallots and garlic in butter and salt. Then add and sauté beans and carrots.

DESSERT
◆◆ BLANC MANGER MAMICHE

The most common dessert for poor Haitians, which really is most Haitians, is *pan patat*, a sweet-potato pudding similar to the dessert for Mexico Night, p. 76. But for more affluent Haitians, a lighter, more delicate dessert is blanc manger. This dessert, a tropical version of an old French recipe, turns up in eighteenth- and nineteenth-century writing and is found most anywhere in Latin America where the French ever ruled, including Mexico and the Dominican Republic. But nowhere has it remained as popular as in Haiti.

This recipe was given to me by my Haitian friend Ginette Dreyfus Diederich, who comes from an old Haitian family. Mamiche was her mother, and this classic Haitian dessert recipe has been in her family for generations. The dish should be made the day before.

½ cup whole milk
½ cup evaporated milk
¾ cup canned coconut milk
¾ cup sweetened condensed milk

a splash of vanilla extract
1 packet gelatin powder
½ cup fresh grated coconut

Mix the milk and evaporated milk and bring to a boil. Mix the canned coconut milk and the sweetened condensed milk and add to the hot mixture away from the heat. Add the vanilla.

Dissolve the packet of gelatin in a few ounces of hot water. Stir until completely liquid. Add a spoonful of the warm milk mixture, stir, and then blend the entire gelatin mixture into the heated milk mixture. Pour into individual dessert cups. Toast the grated coconut under a broiler until slightly brown and sprinkle on top. Refrigerate overnight.

DRINK
◆ PLANTER'S PUNCH

You wouldn't think Haitians would have anything named after the planter class, but they do drink planter's punch, though more often they serve it to foreigners. It can be made with any juices and spices available. A shot of golden rum added to it is key for adults, but even without that it is a great fruit drink.

We used 1/3 orange juice, 1/3 guava juice, 1/3 pineapple juice, and grated nutmeg on top.

However, one time on the island of Dominica, a beautiful little island where there's nothing for tourists to do, with not even much in the way of beaches, I spent a day on a farm with a Lebanese farmer and businessman named Khalil Azar, experimenting with his homegrown produce. We tried a planter's punch with equal parts lime, passion fruit, and guava, which rated high, but the ultimate punch was a mixture of grapefruit, lime, pineapple, and tangerine juice with the local unbottled rum mixed with honey and some cardamom. We might have considered nutmeg, but he didn't grow it.

NEWFOUNDLAND NIGHT

HINT: WHERE NORTH AMERICA IS CLOSEST TO EUROPE.

The English, via John Cabot, traveled the shortest route possible in finding America. Even before Cabot's 1497 voyage, there were rumors around Bristol of men reaching a land beyond the sea. Cabot, born Giovanni Caboto in Genoa, was an experienced navigator jealous of that other explorer from his hometown who had gotten a commission from the Spanish and landed in the Caribbean, enshrining the name Columbus. In the English he found his sponsor, and he left from Bristol in May 1497 with an eighteen-man crew. No instrument had yet been invented for measuring longitude, but latitude was easily verified: he knew how to go east and west but could get lost on north to south. The standard navigating technique, called *easting* or *westing*, was to fix latitude and then try to stick with it. Cabot left Bristol, sailed around Ireland, and tried to stay on a westerly course. It took him only thirty-five days of sailing to reach land. There is some argument about whether he landed in Labrador or Newfoundland. Some have even suggested he reached the Cape Breton Islands of Nova Scotia, but this would have been off course. (The reason they are called Cape Breton is that sailors from Brittany, somewhat south of Bristol, westing to America in later years, landed there.)

On his return to Europe, the news spread quickly that he had landed in a place rich in cod. Famously, Raimundo di Soncino, Milan's envoy to London, reported that the cod were so thick that Cabot's men simply scooped them up in baskets. Though this dubious technique was never adopted, Newfoundland lived on fishing cod ever after, or at least until 1994.

When I worked on commercial fishing boats as a teenager in New England, I was impressed and charmed by the fishermen I worked with from Newfoundland and Labrador. They were burly Irishmen (the Newfoundland accent is a modified Irish brogue), tough, good-humored men with remarkable maritime skills. However, not one of them knew how to swim. You don't swim in Newfoundland. Even in the summer the sea is so cold that, were you to fall overboard, you could survive only a few minutes.

This was a sobering thought years later when I hand-lined for cod on a Newfoundland cod skiff where there was only a foot-high rail to lean over when I dropped my line. The inshore Newfoundland cod hand liners were among the most skilled fishermen I have ever seen. It was as though they were physically connected to the line they held in their hands and could grope the bottom for fish. When a cod bit, they could twirl their thumbs to bring up the catch as fast and smoothly as with a reel.

In the 1970s, after Canada, like most countries in the world, claimed exclusive rights to fishing within two hundred miles of its coastline, the government invested in a huge fleet of trawlers to fish the descendants of the cod that Cabot's men had seen. While the trawlers were catching enormous quantities, the inshore fishermen were complaining of fewer and fewer fish being landed on their small skiffs. They claimed that the big ships at sea were scooping up all the cod. Few listened, and then in 1994 there were so few cod left that the government declared a moratorium on cod fishing off New-foundland. The five-hundred-year Newfound-land bonanza was over.

When I arrived to research my book *Cod* in 1995, the fishery had been shut down and the fishermen I went out with were allowed to fish only because they were tagging their catch and releasing them to help scientists understand what was happening. Sticking tags into the backs of fish was a new skill and not easy. We killed one fish by accident because we stuck it too many times trying to insert the tag. We cooked it and ate it. Fresh-killed cod, its white flakes falling off, is a rare treat.

When I returned ten years later to research *The Last Fish Tale*, everyone I knew had either moved to Alberta or British Columbia to work the tar sands or had rerigged a boat for crabbing. Unused cod skiffs could be found rotting in the marshes. Crab was now the Newfoundland catch, and no one was certain whether these creatures had moved in because the cod, which ate them, had vanished, or if they had always been there but no one had cared when there was cod to catch. But now crab had replaced cod. The cod men were crabbers; the fish plants were crab plants. Newfoundland was trying to replace its fishing industry with a tourist indus-try, selling tourists souvenirs of the cod that was no longer there. The restaurants did not serve the local crab but brought in cod. Tourists, after all, went to Newfoundland to eat cod, not crab. The shops sold tourists cod hats, cod T-shirts, cod-shaped chocolates, cod ornaments, cod business-card holders. But the cod were gone.

So for Newfoundland Night, our menu had to be crab and cod. But first a word on molas-ses buns.

BREAD
◆ MOLASSES BUNS

I had to make buns because they are historic in Newfoundland and Labrador. In earlier times, they were what men took with them in the frozen wilds. When I was researching my biography of Clarence Birdseye, he wrote in his letters from Labrador about taking buns with him on dogsledding trips in the early twentieth century. He even wrote a recipe for pork buns. There are numerous old recipes for buns around, some of them one or two centuries old. The following is a recipe for molasses buns. But I have to warn you that though they are quite good, and get better as they age—at their best when two or three weeks old—they are the most filling food I have ever experienced. One small bun and you will have little appetite for dinner. So make them on Newfoundland Night and keep them in the refrigerator for someday when you are going fishing, hiking, skiing, snowshoeing . . .

The recipe calls for scrunchions, a Newfoundland staple. Scrunchions are small chunks of fatback pork, fried until crisp. Remember to save the liquefied fat from making them to use in the buns. If you can't find fatback, use slab bacon and cut it up into small rectangles.

1 teaspoon baking soda
¼ cup hot water
1 cup molasses
¼ cup scrunchions
1 cup melted pork fat
½ cup raisins

1 teaspoon powdered cinnamon
1 teaspoon ground cloves
1 teaspoon ground allspice
½ cup sugar
about 1 cup flour

Preheat oven to 250 degrees. In a big bowl, mix the baking soda and hot water. Add the molasses and beat until foam forms. Add the scrunchions, melted pork fat (from making the scrunchions), raisins, cinnamon, cloves, allspice, and sugar. After everything is well mixed, add flour ¼ cup at a time until the mixture becomes a thick dough that you can shape in your hand. Form into balls the size of a small snowball, place them on a well-greased baking dish in a roasting pan of water—a bain-marie—and bake for 4 hours. Cool and keep covered in the refrigerator.

APPETIZER
◆◆ CRAB CAKES

At this point, nothing could be more Newfie than crab cakes, but our recipe for them was developed when Talia and I were on a book tour for *The World Without Fish* in Portland, Oregon. My friends at the Oregon Culinary Institute invited us to give a talk to their staff, and then we all ended up making crab cakes together. Talia and I have been making them ever since. This recipe makes nine small crab cakes.

2 cups crabmeat
2 eggs, beaten
2 green onions, chopped
1 sprig of fresh oregano
1 sprig of fresh thyme

a generous pinch of salt
½ teaspoon hot paprika
½ cup bread crumbs
½ cup canola oil

Put the crabmeat in a bowl with the beaten eggs. Add the green onions, oregano, thyme, salt, paprika, and bread crumbs. Mix well. Form the mixture into patties about 2½ inches in diameter. Fry in hot canola oil until golden on both sides and drain on paper towels.

TALIA: *On Crab Cakes*

When you fry crab cakes you want them to be a nice golden color. Not dark brown or black! This means you have to use your hands to make the cakes thin, not thick, so they will cook with very little frying. When you put them in the hot oil and they start sizzling, it only takes a minute or two on a side (so no snoozing at the pan), then flip them over for another minute or two.

If they're not done, you can always flip them back again. If they're overdone, dark brown or black, feed them to the cat!

◆◆ TARTAR SAUCE

Marian and I thought this sauce was great, but Talia said that she preferred Hellmann's. You can't always win.

3 egg yolks	a pinch of salt
juice of ½ lemon	1–1½ cups canola oil
2 tablespoons Dijon mustard	2 tablespoons sweet pickle relish

See Basic Recipes, p. 21, for mayonnaise. Make this one with egg yolks, lemon juice, Dijon mustard, a pinch of salt, and (slowly added) canola oil. After removing from the food processor, stir in the sweet pickle relish.

MAIN COURSE
◆ STELLA'S COD

The usual way to cook cod in Newfoundland is to boil it and serve it with scrunchions. How often can you eat scrunchions? Quite often, according to some Newfies. In 1996, after the cod fishery had been closed for two years, some cod came on the market from the research fishery, as it did from time to time. Stella's, a cozy little restaurant in St. John's, had it on the menu for the first time in months. It was as good a cod as I had ever eaten—except maybe the one we boiled after we accidentally killed it while trying to tag it at sea—and the chef there, Mary Thornhill, gave me the recipe. I've been using it ever since. It is based on the same idea as fish and chips in that the batter seals in the cod, but this is a lighter batter. Mary does not use scrunchions or fatback of any kind. She thinks it's unhealthy. Can you imagine that?

2 cups flour
5 turns of black pepper
3 tablespoons sweet paprika
3 eggs
about 1 cup milk

about 1¼ pounds cod fillet
¼ cup canola oil
1 bunch Italian parsley, minced
½ pound green beans

On a plate, mix the flour, black pepper, and paprika.

Beat the eggs with the milk in a bowl.

Cut the cod into 3 pieces. Roll the pieces in the flour mixture, dip them in the eggs, and fry them in hot canola oil until golden on all sides. Sprinkle with parsley. Serve with green beans that have been steamed for 3 minutes.

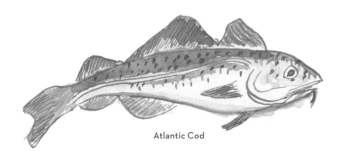

Atlantic Cod

DESSERT
◆ APPLE CRUMBLE

First, make the custard sauce, called crème Anglaise by the French:

THE CUSTARD SAUCE

4 egg yolks
1 cup sugar

1 vanilla bean
1 pint of light cream

Beat the egg yolks with the sugar. Split the vanilla bean lengthwise and place it in a pot with the light cream. Bring to a boil and pour into the bowl with the egg yolks and sugar. Scrape the vanilla bean with a fork and spoon and discard the husks. Mix well, then pour back into the pot and beat briskly over medium heat until the liquid thickens. Keep the mixture moving so that it doesn't curdle on the bottom, and as soon as it thickens, pour it into another bowl and refrigerate. This sauce can be made in advance and keeps well for a number of days. It should be poured cold on the hot crumble.

THE CAKE

3 apples, unpeeled but sliced
1 cup sugar
3 tablespoons powdered cinnamon
juice of 1/2 lemon
1 stick butter

1 cup brown sugar
a generous pinch of salt
3 tablespoons white sugar
1/2 cup oatmeal
1/4 cup flour

Preheat oven to 400 degrees. Mix the apple slices with the sugar, cinnamon, and lemon juice. Put in a small deep casserole or soufflé dish.

In a mixer, cream the butter with the paddle attachment. Add the brown sugar, salt, white sugar, oatmeal, and flour. Mix the ingredients together and then press the dough on top of the apples, completely covering them. Bake for 1 hour.

Serve hot out of the oven with a pour of the cold sauce. Just one pour. Don't drown it.

INDIA NIGHT

HINT: THE MOST POPULOUS DEMOCRACY IN THE WORLD.

To get a sense of how crowded life in India can be, consider the fact that while it is the seventh-largest country in the world in area, it is the second-largest country in the world in population, behind only China.

The Indian love of spices and of bright colors is interconnected. The Indian kitchen is aglow with the colors of spices such as turmeric, a root that is dried and powdered and gives food, tabletops, cooks' fingers, clothing—everything it touches—a brilliant, deep yellow-orange color that has become pervasive in Indian life. Turmeric has a special role in the Hindu religion: it is thought to bring good fortune, and it's forbidden in the homes of mourners. Brides paint their faces with it. It is also used as a medicine, steeped in milk to relieve coughs and colds. Some spices, such a cardamom and cinnamon, are native to the south of India, while others, such as coriander and cumin, were brought in through trade with the Mediterranean region. Cloves came from Indonesia, and hot chili peppers, a recent but now entrenched arrival, were brought in the fifteenth century by the Portuguese, who discovered them in the Americas and spread them around the world.

India Night was one of our favorites. Many of the recipes, though considerably altered, were inspired by Julie Sahni's masterful book *Classic Indian Cooking.*

Following tradition, we used no silverware for this meal. Indian food is all finger food. Sauced foods are eaten by scooping up rice in your hand first or scooping with bread, which is what we did. The bread—naan—needs to be started the day before.

APPETIZER
◆◆ PIAZ PAKODE

3 tablespoons peanut oil
1 cup chickpea flour
2 tablespoons ground cumin
a large pinch of salt

1 teaspoon cayenne pepper
1 cup warm water, or more
6 thin slices from a big yellow onion
½ cup canola oil

Add the peanut oil to the chickpea flour. Mix by scooping up a small amount of flour and rubbing it between the fingers of your two flattened hands. Continue doing this until all the flour is permeated with the oil. Then add the cumin, salt, and cayenne pepper. Add warm water and mix until it becomes the consistency of pancake batter. Let sit unrefrigerated for half an hour.

Heat the oil until very hot. Dip onion slices in the batter. It doesn't matter if they fall apart a bit—just grab each slice in one hand and plunge it into the batter, then place in the pan, being careful not to let your fingers touch the hot oil. Cook until crisp and solid, then flip with a spatula and cook the other side. Remove when darkened and a bit crisp. Place on paper towel to cool, and after 2 minutes serve on a platter.

BREAD
◆◆◆ NAAN

In India this is a restaurant bread; it is generally not made at home. Home cooking books do not talk about naan. But it is a great bread for sopping up Indian food and was the only eating utensil for our meal. It is a good parent-kid project. Talia made the breads and I cooked them and together we turned out a stack quickly. You only need one a person, and the rising dough ball (Basic Recipes, p. 23) will make about eight, so you might want to halve the recipe for the dough ball, which needs to have been made the day before so that it can be left to rise in the refrigerator.

Thoroughly dust your hands and the work surface with flour. Pull off a ball of dough about the size of a medium apple. With your fingers, flatten the dough into a disk. You can hold it up by the edge and, by turning it, let gravity stretch it further. Try to get it about ¼ inch thick.

Heat up a large cast-iron skillet. When hot, put about 2 tablespoons ghee in and then drop in a dough disk. Cover the skillet with a lid, but check it every minute or so. When the bread is no longer gooey and has darkened spots on the bottom side, flip it. Keep the lid on and check as needed, though after a few you will have a sense of the timing. Cast iron gathers heat, so you will have to reduce the heat after a while. Add new ghee with each bread.

This bread hardens if you keep it, but can be restored by a spin in the microwave.

GHEE

This is the primary cooking fat of Indian cuisine; it's also used in a number of other countries, including Morocco and Sri Lanka. Ghee is butter with all the milk liquid and solids removed so that only pure butterfat is left. Ghee acts more like oil than butter, lasting for long periods and heating to high temperatures without burning. It is also used as a folk medicine: it's supposed to reduce stress and help the brain to operate. It doesn't do much for the heart, though, being loaded with saturated fats. If kept more than ten years but no more than a hundred, it is called kumbhaghrta, but if it's more than a century old, it is called mahaghrta. Of course, no one cooks with these tonics, but the cooking variety of ghee does last long enough so that in the first and second century AD, before there was any refrigeration, ghee was shipped from India to Rome, where it was used as a luxury cooking oil for the wealthy. Romans were the first foodies.

Ghee can be bought at Indian or Asian stores or it can be made. Cut up a pound of butter and melt it over low heat. When completely melted, foam will form. Let it crackle and sizzle as the liquid is cooked off. Once it stops crackling, turn up heat and stir until the solid residue turns brown. Turn off heat and let it cool so the residue sinks to the bottom, and skim off the amber oil.

MAIN COURSE
◆◆ ROGAN JOSH

The name is Persian and refers to cooking in hot oil, so it is supposed that the dish originated in Persia, now Iran. But rogan josh has long been identified with the northern Indian state of Kashmir, where it is a leading dish. There are many variations, with little in common other than the red color and the use of lamb.

1 yellow onion, chopped
1/4 cup fresh ginger root, peeled and chopped
2 tablespoons coriander powder
2 tablespoons cayenne pepper
1 cup plain Greek-style yogurt
1 cup sour cream
a large pinch of salt

1 pound of leg of lamb meat, cubed
5 garlic cloves, sliced
4 tablespoons ghee
1 cup heavy cream
2 tablespoons black cumin seeds
1 tablespoon powdered cardamom
2 tablespoons garam masala (see On Sugar and Spice, p. 11)

In a food processor, combine onion, ginger, coriander, cayenne pepper, yogurt, sour cream, and salt. Puree.

Toss the cubed lamb meat thoroughly in the pureed mixture. Let it sit at least 30 minutes, then simmer in a skillet for 20 minutes.

Meanwhile, sauté the garlic in ghee until lightly browned. Add to simmering skillet. Add the heavy cream, black cumin seeds, and cardamom. Simmer 20 more minutes and add garam masala.

This dish keeps well for a few days in the refrigerator, and may even improve.

VEGETABLES
◆ KARI

1/4 cup ghee
1 teaspoon turmeric
a large pinch of salt
1 long green Indian pepper (or half a serrano pepper), sliced

1 teaspoon black mustard seeds
1/2 pound thin "French" green beans
1 cup grated coconut
1/4 cup coriander (cilantro) leaves, minced

Heat ghee in skillet with the turmeric, salt, Indian pepper, and black mustard seeds. Add the green beans. Sauté until bright green, only a few minutes. Add the grated coconut. Toss in the coriander leaves. Turn off heat, toss well in pan, and serve.

◆ HARE GOBHI KI SABZI

2 bunches broccoli, broken into florets
    with stems
8 garlic cloves, peeled and sliced

¼ cup ghee
1 tablespoon turmeric
a large pinch of salt

Peel the skin off the broccoli stems with a paring knife. Sauté the garlic in ghee until lightly browned. Add more ghee, the turmeric, and salt. Add broccoli and cook, uncovered, until the broccoli is bright green.

Broccoli

DESSERT

◆ NARIAL BARFI

1 coconut

2 cups sugar

2 tablespoons cardamom powder

2 tablespoons powdered cinnamon

Open a fresh coconut (see A Slightly Nutty Way to Open a Coconut, p. 19). Grate the meat and pour a cup of coconut water in a pan. If you don't have that much, add water. Add the sugar and cook over high heat, stirring gently with a long wooden spoon until the sugar melts and it becomes a clear syrup. Add the grated coconut—it should be about 3 cups—and the cardamom and cinnamon. Stir vigorously over high heat with the long-handled wooden spoon for at least 7 minutes, until mixture is opaque and whitish. Pile it into a well-greased baking sheet and flatten with a spatula to about 1 inch in height. Let cool. Lift from the sheet with a spatula and cut into squares.

DRINKS

Half mango juice and half pear juice. Add a generous pinch of cardamom powder and cinnamon and grate in some nutmeg. Shake well. Pour over ice.

Chai tea, which is made of spices and steeped in milk, is an ideal end to this meal.

FRENCH GUIANA NIGHT

HINT: THEY CALLED IT THE GREEN HELL.

L'Enfer vert, the green hell. Hell for Europeans, anyway. The first European known to visit was Christopher Columbus, who named it the Land of Pariahs. In 1608 Tuscans tried to establish an Italian colony to exploit the riches of the rain forest, but the plans were canceled when the nobleman whose idea it was suddenly died. During that century three different attempts by the French to settle there failed. The French eventually did establish a colony with a small population clinging to the coastline. The Dutch and the British did the same, creating French, Dutch, and British Guiana. But the dense rain forest beyond the narrow coastline, the green hell, is still impenetrable, the vegetation so thick that navigating treacherous rivers by canoe is the only way to enter. The Europeans tried their usual Caribbean program, importing slaves to work plantations, but the Africans ran off to the interior, where they tried to reestablish an African way of life.

Finally the French accepted that it was hell and in 1851 started sending political prisoners there, ostensibly to serve out sentences, but of the seventy thousand men and women sent to the penal colony between 1851 and 1947, only eighteen thousand survived their sentences. Many tried to escape, but few could survive the rain forest. Even today it is said that an outsider can survive alone in the interior for at most three days. The penal colony eventually became a human rights scandal, and in 1947 the French

were forced to shut it down, too.

One time when I was there, the French Foreign Legion, in an intensive jungle-survival training program, sent soldiers up the Maroni River and dropped them off with orders to chop down trees and float back to the coast. Eventually they had to be rescued, because the tropical hardwood trees would not float.

My own very small contribution to this tradition of disaster is that I was sent there twice, once by the *New York Times* to cover a guerrilla war in neighboring Suriname, the former Dutch Guiana, and once by *National Geographic*. Neither story was ever published.

When I went for the *Times*, I followed a guerrilla army. Their leader would come to a village, find an attractive teenage girl, disappear into a hut, and leave the rest of us to make camp. The only evidence of combat was that they once managed to shoot down an army helicopter. It is probably still there, so overgrown that it is no longer visible, swallowed up by the green hell. From a small plane at two hundred feet, the green canopy looks solid except for the occasional café au lait ribbon of a narrow winding river.

Eventually, the guerrilla fighters tired of their news coverage and abandoned me, laptop computer and all, on a rock in the Maroni River. Fortunately, a canoe came along and I was taken by an armed man to a village several miles up the river where I was led to a long-haired, sunburned, nearly naked white man who had that Conradian quality of having been "out too long." When I explained my predicament he smiled and said, "Relax, *vous êtes en France*"—you are in France—and handed me a card identifying himself as a French government official. In 1946 French Guiana and the islands of Guadeloupe and Martinique all became départements of France with the same legal status as the départements of Aquitaine or Provence.

Most of the people in the interior were descendants of slaves, known as "bush negroes," who had escaped centuries earlier into the rain forest and reinvented Africa with their own languages and religions. There was also a variety of indigenous people, small in stature, steeped in traditions, living in thatch-roofed homes on stilts.

Traveling up the Maroni is the reverse of modern air travel. Instead of removing your shoes, buckling the safety belt, and surrendering all vestiges of both free will and responsibility, once you enter the Maroni, your survival depends on the decisions you make. So the first thing I did when I returned for more than a month-long journey was to hire a good guide, good boatmen, and a solid pirogue. I hired a French guide who seemed to speak every known language except English, including about a dozen languages of the Maroni. The two tall, muscular, and graceful boatmen were Ndjuka, a tribe of "bush negroes" known for their boating skills and well-made dugouts. They came with a twenty-foot-long narrow pirogue, a single hollowed-out log from an angelique tree with sides built up with ebony boards, plus a Yamaha 40 outboard motor.

As the days went by, clothing seemed increasingly irrelevant. The shoes were the first things to go. I was either stepping into the river or the bank, where I would sink a foot into mud and have to retrieve my shoe. We could never penetrate more than a dozen yards from the riverbank anyway. The shirt also seemed unnecessary. The bush villages where we stayed were small communities of fewer than thirty people in wooden huts, each marked with different carvings to signify different tribal groups with slightly different languages. They lived on the river, *libi,* which in their languages came from the word *liba,* which means life. They fished in it, traveled in it, washed in it, and the children played in it, developing their boating skills in yard-long dugout canoes. They would find coves in the river where piranhas congregated so they could plunge sticks into the water and watch the fish snap them in two.

As in African societies which they had imitated, it was important to them to act out large displays of friendship to anyone encountered. Without this demonstration, you would arouse tremendous suspicion.

"*Fa weki!*" I would shout, my arms wide open, my face smiling.

The smile and gesture would be returned, larger than I could ever do. "*Yu de?*"

"*Me de,*" I answered.

The conversation was repeated ten times in every village—How are you?—And you?—I'm fine.

At the center of every village was a steel skillet more than a yard in diameter over a wooden fire. This was for making couac. First they would soak bitter cassava root, the kind laced with a natural poison, for a few days. Then they would grate and hang it in a hemp press to squeeze out the poison. Then they would dry it into a flour, which they would put in the skillet and gently stir for a full day over a low fire until it was reduced to little dry beige grains. Couac travels on the river and keeps for months and we ate it with every meal, absorbing the juices of whatever fish or game we cooked.

After dinner I would choose two trees to which I could attach my hammock. With all the snakes, lizards, and mouse-size insects—large enough to be spotted crossing a trail from twenty feet away—suspended from a tree was the only place you wanted to spend the night. There is a trick to sleeping in a hammock (a word that originated in indigenous languages from this region): if you lie diagonally rather than front to back, you will have a flat bed and sleep well. Because they are situated on the equator, the Guianas have almost equal hours of daylight and darkness—very long, dark nights during which the forest roars with birds, mammals, and insects making so much noise that it seems like one continuous scream. Since we camped by the riverbank, there was a break in the canopy through which you could see up to a night sky so bejeweled with stars it looked like mica schist reflecting sunlight. In bed with a bottle of rum and a Cuban cigar (I provisioned well), I would gaze up at this wonder and feel content.

There would be couac for breakfast, sometimes with fish if anyone had caught one. We would shove off in the first light of day. The river was the color of satin-finished pewter, and trees on the opposite bank formed black hulks above the thick white mist on the river. Sometimes we would drag lines and pick up a fish for lunch or we would trade with villagers. We had rum, which was of great value as an offering to the spirits at the little stone and wood altars

called obiasanis that had a place in every village. Once, a man of the Boni tribe supplied us with a skinned iguana. Like most exotic animals, it had that predictable resemblance to chicken. And of course we ate it with couac.

Some days the river was calm; some days we had white-water rapids to negotiate. The Ndjukas did this with remarkable skill and calm. A tall, muscular Ndjuka called Lange, for the length of his body, stood in the bow with a long pole made from the hard flexible wood of the takari tree. He twirled it like a majorette, putting his entire body into pushing off of rocks on one side or the other and plunging it straight to the bottom to measure depth. He called out his soundings to the man at the motor, who hoisted the outboard when the water was getting shallow. "*Gadogi danki*"—well done, thank you. We constantly cheered. *Danki, danki*.

The Ndjukas went fishing and hunting at night, and one evening I asked to go with them, which they politely agreed to even though it was easy to see they weren't happy. They loaded a tiny two-man pirogue with fishing tackle and ammunition. These little dugouts shifted with every movement of one's body. I knew I could not handle the large wooden-stocked antique rifle that fired with a kick like the right hook of a heavyweight champion. How could anyone absorb that recoil and not capsize our unstable craft? It seemed hard enough to be the one swinging a lantern to find the reflection of eyes in the bush. When I tried to land a small fish on a hand line and nearly capsized the three of us, they silently rowed back to camp and dropped me off—the rejected hunter.

They shot agouti, small, cute rodents that were gamey in stews, but the flavor was moderated by lots of couac. They also shot tapir, a delicious animal that tasted like pork, cooked in a rich stew with couac. One tapir was big enough to last for days. It is an endangered species but we ate a lot of endangered species, because to people who live in the rain forest, they themselves are the species that is in danger. They also laughed at the notion of deforestation; the idea of not enough trees seemed absurd.

The riverbanks were dazzling in their beauty. Fuchsia water hyacinth bloomed on the surface of the river; the trees on the bank were flecked with yellow and blue from flitting butterflies. The bright yellow leaves of the black ebony trees, known locally as *gringon fou*, a wild fantasy tree, glowed in the distance.

But if you pulled over to the beautiful shore, you entered a world of frightening hostility. After sinking in mud, you were attacked by stinging flies, and butterfly-like creatures dropped stinging darts on you; the grass had razor-sharp edges that cut your legs, and if you lost your balance and grabbed a branch, more likely than not it would have sharp thorns or thistles or would be covered with some type of aggressive insect.

As Talia's index finger landed squarely on the Guianas, right on the Maroni River, I started thinking of all this and much more. What to cook for French Guiana night? I wasn't going to shoot an agouti or skin an iguana, and I'm not sure I can remember how to make couac, which seemed to take a day of cooking. But there was the coastal food that I often dreamed of while in the interior on an all-game diet. It is a style of cooking that French Guiana, Martinique, and Guadeloupe have in common, a cuisine rooted in that of the unwilling immigrants, the Africans and Asian Indians who were brought to all three places for labor.

The accras de morue needs to be started several days before.

APPETIZERS
◆◆ ACCRAS DE MORUE

It is a curious thing in the Caribbean that there is great passion for foods once associated with slavery. Salt cod, because it was high in protein, sold cheaply, and was loaded with salt for surviving tropical heat, was a basic slave food and yet remains popular throughout the Caribbean. Remember the accara of Senegal? The African word is used for these salt cod beignets, though in French Guiana they are balls, not pancakes as in Africa. Variations on these are made almost everywhere in the Caribbean, but only in Puerto Rico, where they are called bacalaitos, are they flat like the African accra.

Pepper sauce goes well with this. Throughout the Caribbean, homemade hot sauce is sold. I used one I bought in Guadeloupe more than ten years ago. It is so hot I will probably never use it up because the tiniest drop goes very far. If you can't find Caribbean-made pepper sauce, make ti malice (see Haiti Night, p. 226). Of course, in Guiana the leading hot pepper is the red one that we call cayenne, named after its capital. Do not under any circumstance use Tabasco sauce, which is a Louisiana product with a vinegar base and completely wrong for Caribbean food.

This is a three-step recipe. It will make between eight and ten balls, to be served with drinks.

½ pound dry salt cod	2 tablespoons fresh chives, chopped
1 tablespoon butter	about 3 cups flour
1 tablespoons flour	2–3 eggs, beaten
1 cup whole milk	about 3 cups bread crumbs
1 egg yolk	½ cup canola oil

Several days before the dinner, soak the salt cod (see On Salt Cod, p. 19), either changing the water regularly or soaking it under running water, for between 24 and 36 hours. You can taste little pieces to check on the desalination. The fish should remain as salty as you can bear. If it gets too soaked, you can add salt later, but it would be a pity to.

The day before the dinner, melt the butter in a large skillet. Stir in the flour with a wooden spoon until it becomes a smooth paste. Add the milk a little at a time and keep stirring with the wooden spoon over moderate heat as it turns into a thick, creamy sauce. When all the milk is in and it is quite thick and with no lumps, cut the salt cod into pieces and put them in the skillet with enough heat so that the sauce will cook the cod. As it cooks, you can mash the fish apart with an old-fashioned potato masher until there are no big pieces and you're left with just a thick sauce. Add the egg yolk and keep stirring rapidly until the yellow color is gone. Then turn off the heat. Add the chives and mix well. Put in a container and store overnight in the refrigerator.

The next day, with the help of a spoon, fashion balls the size of small apricots from the refrigerated fish paste. Dust them in flour, dip them in beaten eggs, roll them in bread crumbs.

Heat an inch of oil very hot in a skillet or pot. Fry the balls, remove to a paper towel, and serve immediately.

◆ BLAFF D'OURSINS

I love Caribbean food, but this is one of my favorite dishes in all of the Caribbean. It is an illustration of how perfection can be achieved through simplicity. There are many blaffs, notably fish or shrimp, but a blaff of sea urchin is the best.

½ cup rice
¾ cup water
another pot with 3 cups water
⅓ cup chopped white onion
3 garlic cloves, peeled and sliced
2 sprigs fresh thyme

a large pinch of salt
12 sea urchins
1 Scotch bonnet pepper, sliced
1 green onion, chopped
fresh-squeezed lime juice

Cook the rice in the water. In another small pot bring 3 cups of water to a boil. Throw in the onion, garlic, thyme, and salt. Reduce heat and simmer for 5 minutes.

Pour this broth into small bowls or broad, large teacups. Scoop the meat from a sea urchin (the store will usually open them for you) and add it to the broth along with a slice of Scotch bonnet pepper. Remove the pepper after a minute or leave it for the diner, depending on how much heat is wanted. Sprinkle green onion on top and squeeze lime juice into the bowl according to taste. Serve while still hot.

Sea urchin

MAIN COURSE
◆ COLOMBO DE PORC

Colombo is the word in Creole, the French-African language of the Caribbean, for curry, which was brought to the Caribbean by indentured laborers from India. After African slavery was abolished, Indians were brought in on a contract that was essentially limited contract slavery. Colombo is often served with rice, but I prefer using root vegetables such as cassava in the curry for a starch. Root vegetables, known in the English-speaking Caribbean as "ground provisions," are the base of all cooking in the interior of Guiana, on the coast, and in the rest of the Caribbean as well.

Cassava, from which couac is made, is particularly important, even as a political metaphor. Most of the food of the Caribbean, including papaya, mangoes, pineapple, sugarcane, coconut, breadfruit, and salt cod were brought in from other places, most of it for cheap food to keep slaves working in the fields. But cassava, which means "native," is native to the Caribbean. Cassava was a basic food of both the Caribs, who moved north from the Guianas, and the Arawaks, whom they invaded on the northern islands. In fact, when the Caribs attacked Columbus and his men with poison arrows, the poison they used was extracted from cassava root. In the interior, before eating the shredded roots they squeeze the poison out of them in straw slings that are hanging from every carved wooden bush hut. The word is *cassava* in English, *manyók* in Creole, *manioc* in French, and, in Spanish, *yucca*. Political leaders from Aristide in Haiti to Castro in Cuba often use the image of the cassava in their political discourse. Most of the cassava sold in markets—and all of it in the US—is a poison-free variety, so you will need another source for your arrowheads.

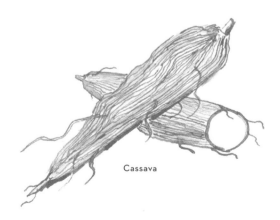

Cassava

I used a colombo I found in the open market in Pointe-à-Pitre, Guadeloupe, which is one of the best and most colorful markets in the Caribbean. It was a little dull in color, so I added additional turmeric, and also lacking in heat, so I add more cayenne pepper (see On Sugar and Spice, p. 10).

½ cup coconut oil
1 pound pork shoulder, cubed
about 6 inches peeled cassava, cut into round disks
1 unpeeled white yam, cut into disks that are then halved
2 turmeric roots, sliced
1 red bell pepper, cored and cut into strips
1 green bell pepper, cored and cut into strips
½ white onion, chopped
12 ounces coconut milk
¼ cup heavy cream
4 tablespoons colombo (curry powder)
1 teaspoon powdered turmeric
6 cardamom seeds
1 teaspoon cayenne pepper

Put the coconut oil in a skillet over medium heat. Add the pork shoulder and brown on all sides. Add the cassava, white yam, and turmeric roots. Cook for about 30 minutes over moderate heat. Add the red and green bell pepper and white onion. Cook another 5 minutes, stirring so that all the peppers and onions get cooked. Add the coconut milk, heavy cream, colombo, turmeric, cardamom seeds, and cayenne pepper.

Reduce and thicken on high heat for about 5 minutes while stirring so that nothing burns on the bottom.

DESERT
◆◆ COCONUT CAKE

There are no coconut palms in the interior, but the coast is packed with them. A coconut is a seed. It falls to the ground, takes root, splits, and a shoot comes up the middle. Left unattended, they spread like weeds. I visited the island where the wrongfully accused Captain Alfred Dreyfus was sent in 1895 and chained to a bed in a twelve-square-yard stone house with iron bars. No one ever goes to this island, and there is not even a boat landing, but I talked a gendarme with a rubber Zodiac into dropping me off on the rocks and returning for me in an hour. As he pulled away, I heard him shout over his engine, "*Au revoir, Dreyfus II,*" which under the circumstance did not strike me as particularly funny. The island had become overrun with coconuts. Even Dreyfus's prison, which had lost its roof, had coconut palms growing in it along with some new coconuts with shoots. A palm puts out a lot of coconuts. I started anxiously looking out the rusted iron bars, imagining a life alone, existing on coconuts, and was very happy when I could hear the mischievous gendarme return.

This cake, my own invention based on a number of Caribbean traditions, is a favorite of ours, a celebration of coconut. It must be made with fresh coconut (see A Slightly Nutty Way to Open a Coconut, p. 19). The recipe is actually a variation on pound cake, calling for 1 pound each of flour, sugar, and butter. It is better to make it the day before so that it can cool overnight.

THE CAKE

1½ cups grated fresh coconut
1 pound flour
1 pound sugar
1 pound butter
2½ tablespoons baking powder
a large pinch of salt
a splash of of vanilla extract

1 tablespoon powdered cardamom
1 tablespoon powdered cinnamon
1 tablespoon powdered cloves
1 cup coconut water from the fresh
   coconut
1½ cups milk
2 whole eggs, beaten

Preheat oven to 400 degrees. In a mixer with a paddle attachment, combine the grated coconut, flour, sugar, and butter. While beating, add the baking powder, salt, vanilla extract, and the powdered cardamom, cinnamon, and cloves. Then, while still mixing, add the coconut water. After it's mixed in, add, a little at a time, the milk and eggs. When it is a fully incorporated batter, pour into a buttered and floured 9-inch springform pan. Bake for about 40 minutes or until the cake becomes solid and pulls away from the edges of the springform. Let cool, if you can, overnight.

THE SYRUP

¼ cup water
¼ cup dark rum

1 cup sugar
3 cups grated fresh coconut

Over moderate heat, melt the sugar in the water and dark rum. Stir until it becomes a clear syrup, but don't let it bubble. Pour the syrup over the cake. Cover the top with grated fresh coconut.

DRINK
◆ TI PUNCH

On our journey up the Maroni, we loaded a few bottles of cane syrup, a basket of fresh limes, and a case of white "agricole" rum made directly from fermented cane juice. These are the essential ingredients for the true Caribbean rum punch affectionately known in Creole as "ti punch." This drink wards off tropical heat, fear, and anxiety with a pleasant cloud of indifference. We left so early that by ten o'clock, when the sun had turned white-hot, we had already been traveling for four hours and the guide would smile and announce, "Uh, *c'est l'heure du premier punch*," and I would concur and fix everyone their first punch of the day.

Punch comes from the Hindi word *pac*, which means five. In British-controlled India, the five ingredients of punch were tea, lemon, cinnamon, sugar, and alcohol. In the French Caribbean, the list has been pared down to three ingredients: lime, cane syrup, and rum. The syrup is bottled and sold but can be made by melting three parts sugar to one part water over moderate heat. The rum is traditionally white agricole rum.

I used to know a veterinarian-turned-philosopher in Martinique, now long gone, Robert Rose-Rosette, who wrote whole treatises on the significance of punch. He described a good punch as "voluptuous" and insisted that it must be made by the drinker at the table. "No two people make punch the same," he would say. "You can sit together and enjoy your differences." After having a few ti punches with Dr. Rose-Rosette, I was convinced that he was right.

Just bring glasses, cut-up limes, sugar syrup, and spoons to the table. This is not a fruit drink and should only have a taste of lime, but everyone is welcome to their own formula.

For kids, a good replacement for the third ingredient is either club soda or water. They too can decide on their own formula.

GERMANY NIGHT

HINT: AN OLD LAND THAT FOR MUCH OF ITS HISTORY HAS NOT BEEN A SINGLE COUNTRY.

One of my favorite lines of German poetry comes from the nineteenth-century poet Heinrich Heine:

Denk ich an Deutschland in der Nacht
Dann bin ich um den Schlaf gebracht

When I think of Germany in the night I am robbed of my sleep.

Like all good lines of poetry, it means several things. He meant, first of all, that away in exile he missed his homeland so much that he couldn't sleep. He meant that Germany so set his mind turning with thoughts and ideas that he couldn't sleep. But he also meant that Germany so filled him with apprehension that he couldn't sleep. While writing about Germany over the years I have felt so electrified with ideas that I couldn't sleep. But at other times I have felt so disturbed that it affected my sleep. Most German writers have expressed this same appreciation, fascination, and apprehension for their native land. Germans spent most of the nineteenth century struggling to fuse together a single nation of German-speaking people. And yet Germans often admitted a fear of this nation that was struggling to be born. Heine said that it would produce "a crash such as never before has been heard in the world's history." In 1871, led by the Prussians, a German empire was formed that included most of the German-speaking lands except the most powerful German state, Austria. Eighteen years later, in 1889, Friedrich Nietzsche predicted that Germany would provoke "a crisis like no other before on earth."

It wasn't until the twentieth century, in 1933, that the predicted crash, the crisis like no other, finally happened. Adolf Hitler came to power and for the next twelve years showed the world such mad horror that when it was over, even some Germans questioned if there should ever again be a Germany. Germany was divided among the victorious allies into American, French, British, and Russian zones. After the French, British, and American zones were allowed to merge into a single German state in May 1949, the Soviets, in October, formed their zone into a second Germany. This was a completely unnatural division, since culturally there had never been eastern and western halves to Germany. If anything, the various German states were more divided by religion, culture, and even accents between north and south. But East Germany and West Germany lived on until 1990, when east and west were again united.

Throughout many years of writing about Germany, about its struggle to live with its history, about its east-west division, about its culture, its wine, and its food, I have often thought that if Heine's crash had never happened, if Hitler had never come to power, Germany would simply be thought of as a culture that produced great music, great art, great filmmakers—such as Fritz Lang, who influenced Alfred Hitchcock and who so brilliantly captured that dread of Germany in *M*—brilliant scientists such as Koch and Einstein, good food and unique and rare wines, and great writers in a fascinating language of thrilling creative possibilities.

History stalks Germany. I most felt this in the years East Berlin was divided from the West. There, a half century after World War II, the German legislature still stood, a charred ruin burned down in 1933, four weeks after Hitler came to power, the fire he was to use as a pretext for the suspension of civil liberties. Spellbound, I would wander through the Mitte, what had been downtown Berlin, where the buildings still had the lines of bullet holes from automatic rifle fire and holes blown out from bombs and artillery. You could almost hear voices from the past.

But I also went to see Hans With's sausage factory outside of Frankfurt where they still made the original frankfurter and got angry at the mention of the phrase *hot dog*. The real frankfurter was all pork with a smooth texture from Germany's first fine grinding machines, and shaped like—well, like a hot dog. I visited a laboratory in Berlin where they studied beer quality and used a stopwatch to time what they called "head retention"—the amount of time a glass of beer would hold its foam. I had dinner with the German Wine Queen and her parents at their farm, where they made wonderful crisp frankenwein and their own sausages. Germany has always offered such moments too.

The main course, sauerbraten, must be started two days before the meal.

APPETIZER

◆ SPÄTZLE

There is a restaurant we go to in Manhattan whose spätzle is one of Talia's favorite dishes, so when her finger landed on Germany—in fact somewhere in Bavaria, in the heart of spätzle country—we immediately knew what the first course would be. Some historians believe that these little noodles originated in Bavaria, where the name means "little sparrow."

To make spätzle, you need a spätzle maker. It is a small gadget that fits in a drawer, costs less than twenty dollars, and is easily available in kitchen shops or online. I have tried to improvise with a colander and a wooden spoon, but this is a study in how to make a simple task difficult. Also, the spätzle maker is a great tool for kids. Talia loves being the *spätzlemacher* and I suspect other kids will too.

3 eggs	2 cups flour
1½ cups milk	10 chanterelle mushrooms
1 teaspoon grated nutmeg	4 tablespoons butter
2 large pinches of salt	1 bunch fresh dill, chopped
4 turns of black pepper	

In a mixer with a paddle, beat the eggs and add the milk, nutmeg, salt, and pepper. Beat in the flour a little at a time until the mixture becomes a thick batter, not a dough, very sticky but still pourable. A visual assessment is more important than a measurement. If too thick, more like a dough than a batter, beat in more milk.

Rub the top side of the spätzle maker and the inside of the chute with cooking oil. Boil water in a large pot with another large pinch of salt, and when it reaches a vigorous boil, rest the spätzle maker on the top of the pot. Pour batter into the sliding shoot and move it back and forth so that the spätzles fall into the boiling water. When they float on the top they are done, which only takes a few minutes.

Sauté the chanterelles (or another wild woodland mushroom) in a skillet with butter and another large pinch of salt. Thoroughly drain the spätzle, then toss in the butter and mushrooms and serve with fresh chopped dill sprinkled on top.

SALAD

◆ RED CABBAGE AND KALE

These are two of Germany's favorite traditional vegetables.

½ cup bacon, chopped
1 cup chopped kale
2 cups red cabbage, sliced very thinly

¼ cup cider vinegar
1 teaspoon caraway seeds

Fry about ½ cup chopped bacon in a skillet over medium heat until it begins to crisp and there is liquid fat in the skillet. Add the kale and cabbage and keep tossing until the leaves become limp. Add the cider vinegar and caraway seeds. Mix well and let cool before serving.

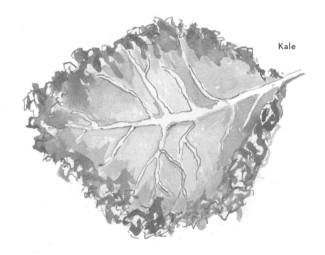

Kale

MAIN COURSE
◆◆ SAUERBRATEN

Meat in Germany, whether sausage, stew, or cutlet, generally comes from a pig. In the old East Germany, pork so dominated that I knew Jews who had a recipe for marinating it in lemon juice so that it would turn white like chicken. They called it "kosherizing the pork."

Sauerbraten is one of the few famous German meat dishes that is not made from a pig. This recipe must be started two nights before serving.

1¼ pounds top round, sometimes called a London broil
1 slice plus 4 slices fresh ginger root
2 cups unfiltered cider vinegar
2 cups water
½ yellow onion, sliced
¼ cup sugar
6 black peppercorns
6 cardamom seeds
10 whole cloves
2 bay leaves
1 teaspoon cinnamon
1 teaspoon mace
2 teaspoons cayenne
2 teaspoons coriander seeds
2 carrots, split and sliced into 2-inch pieces
1 parsnip, split and sliced into 2-inch pieces
6 brussels sprouts
2 tablespoons flour

Rub the top round with a slice of fresh ginger root. Place in a deep bowl. Put the other 4 thin slices of ginger root in a pot with the vinegar, water, onion, sugar, peppercorns, cardamom seeds, cloves, bay leaves, cinnamon, mace, cayenne, and coriander seeds. Bring to a boil. Pour over meat in the bowl. If the meat is completely covered, no turning is needed. Cover bowl with plastic wrap and keep in the refrigerator for 48 hours.

After 2 days, heat olive oil in a Dutch oven and brown the meat on both sides with the carrots, parsnip, and brussels sprouts. When everything is browned, remove and set aside the vegetables and add 2 cups of the marinade, making sure to include some of the spices and sliced onions. Simmer over low heat, covered, for 2 hours. Return the vegetables to the pot and continue simmering for another 10 minutes. Remove the meat and vegetables. Add the flour, stirring over high heat until well incorporated. Strain the remainder of the marinade, add the liquid to the pot, and stir over high heat until it has been reduced to a thickened gravy. Slice the meat thinly across the grain. Serve meat slices and vegetables with gravy.

DESSERT
◆◆◆ APFEL STRUDEL

I remember my grandmother stretching leaves of strudel dough over the backs of her small hands on a metal table. It was a very long process, especially when you consider that it takes at least ten leaves to make a strudel. Fortunately, you can get satisfactory results with frozen phyllo dough, easily available in grocery stores. I have to admit that apple strudel is my absolute favorite pastry. My second choice would be poppy-seed strudel, also a German dessert.

Talia is to my knowledge the fourth generation in my family to make strudel, though the line probably extends even further back.

TALIA: On Strudel

Strudel is such a funny word. It's fun to say and fun to make. You can invent your own recipe or follow these instructions for what my dad and I found to be a delicious apple strudel. To make apple strudel, you'll need a box of phyllo pastry dough. The paper-thin slices of dough inside are very fragile, so be careful not to let them break. After about ten minutes in the open air the dough will start to become dry and hard to work with, so try to work fast, but don't become sloppy in the process. Lay two leaves of phyllo dough flat and then take some apple filling and place it in a thickish long pile on top. Then take two more leaves of dough and place them on top of the apple filling, tucking the ends underneath the bottom leaves. This is a lot of fun to do! The very first one I tried to make broke in my hands. My dad and I just started laughing. Then the cat came in and ate the pieces of dough that had fallen on the floor. We laughed and joked around with her, then I washed my hands and got back to work. My next try was more successful. After you seal up the first layers, take some melted butter and a brush and paint the dough with the butter. After the dough is completely covered, take another layer of dough and place it on the top, tuck in the ends, and start painting the butter on this piece of dough. After repeating this same process with approximately ten layers you stop and place the final layer on. The strudel was delicious! I hope to make it again soon.

So do we all. Actually, although the word *strudel* is German—it means a whirlwind—it probably didn't originate in Germany. Phyllo dough—though *phyllo* is a Greek word—is Turkish in origin. Since the Turks occupied Hungary from 1541 until 1718, most Turkish things that entered Western European culture, such as phyllo dough and coffeehouses, came in through Turkey. The original strudel was probably Hungarian and filled with sour cherries, though Hungarian strudel, *rétes*, is often filled with poppy seeds, cheese, or apples. Through the Austro-Hungarian Empire, strudel spread to the Balkans and Austria, and from Austria to Germany.

6 apples (we used Cortlands), peeled, sliced off the core, and chopped in half
¼ cup walnuts, finely chopped
1½ cups sugar
2 tablespoons cinnamon

about 14 sheets of phyllo dough
10 tablespoons butter, melted
1 egg yolk
a dash of milk
whipped cream

Preheat oven to 350 degrees. Mix the apple slices, walnuts, 1 cup sugar, and the cinnamon. Place 2 sheets of phyllo dough on a baking sheet and pile the filling in a column in the center. Fold over the double sheets to cover the filling. Brush the top of the dough with melted butter and gently roll over the strudel, being careful not to tear the pastry. Brush with butter again. Cover with a sheet of dough and tuck the sides under. Brush with butter, turn the brush again, cover with another sheet of dough, and repeat the process with at least 6 more sheets of dough. With the last one, instead of brushing it with butter, brush it with an egg yolk beaten with a dash of milk and sprinkle sugar on top. Bake for about 1 hour, until golden brown. Serve with big clouds of whipped cream.

DRINKS

Buy some elderberry syrup and mix with club soda at a ratio of three to one for a wonderful drink that goes well with these dishes.

Even more wonderful for adults is a good German wine. German wine is in the odd position of being both underrated and very expensive. The high prices are due to the small production and intense labor aimed at a small market of people in the know. Germany has some of the most northern vineyards in the world: they struggle for enough sunlight, and this has resulted in a unique, sweeter style of wine. The vines are usually grown on sloping riverbanks—such as the Rhine and Mosel—for the added sun reflected off the river. Germany got a bad reputation for wine after World War II when ruthless producers started adding sugar to imitate the natural sweetness of the wine, which further led to the false adage that white wine must be dry to be good. Wines are rated by the sugar content of the grape juice, and in grapes sugar is produced from sunlight, so in these northern vineyards, the goal is to produce as much sugar as possible. Furthermore, the prized grape is Riesling, a very acidic grape with a delicate flavor that is best appreciated with a touch of sweetness. It is a cold-resistant but unproductive grape: some vines yield only two bunches. More can be produced through pruning, but this lowers the quality of flavor. The more sugar, the longer it has grown, the fewer grapes, and the more expensive and valued. *Kabinet* has the least sugar, but if the grapes aren't harvested they will shrivel a little and develop more sugar, though less juice, used for a wine called *spätlese*, which means "later." If you let the grapes hang longer on the vine, risking freezing, you'll get *auslese*, or in a good year a few of the best grapes are selected for *beerenauslese*, and in a great year, maybe one in every fifty grapes may be selected for a *trokenbeerenauslese*, a wine astonishing in its complexity, intensity, and price.

But German wine does not go with most food. It is good with hams and sausages or before or after meals. I was once invited to dinner by one of the finest wine producers in Germany, an ancient schloss in the Rheingau, and my host served California reds with the main course. However, the dishes in our German international night actually do go well with German wine. Marian and I had a *spätlese* from the Mosel.

MONGOLIA NIGHT

HINT: THE WORLD'S MOST SPARSELY POPULATED NATION WAS ONCE
THE CENTER OF THE WORLD'S LARGEST EMPIRE.

Crossing Mongolia by train, I complained in my notebook that hours could pass without my seeing any sign of a human being. Visiting the humble little republic between the powerful nations of China and Russia, it is difficult to appreciate that Mongolia was once a world power. Its leader Genghis Khan, the thirteenth-century Mongolian general, took by military force more territory than any other conqueror in history. At his height he controlled a swath of land from Asia to Europe, from the Pacific coast of China westward to the Caspian Sea, including parts of present-day Afghanistan and Iran. Mongolian soldiers were illiterate but tremendously skilled horsemen and treated the people they defeated with less cruelty than most European armies of the time. Yet they were always referred to as "the Mongol hordes."

Marco Polo never met Genghis Khan, who died before he was born, but he did know the Mongols when they still had considerable power, a people of a distinct race with a non-Chinese indigenous language. I took Marco Polo's book with me when I visited Mongolia in the 1990s shortly after it broke from the collapsed Soviet Union and became an independent country. There was a notable similarity between what I was reading and what I was seeing. On the rare occasions when I came across people, they were living in the round tents called gers that Marco Polo described, always with horses tethered outside. In the morning there were fires burning by the tents for cooking.

Almost all of the people I encountered were either standing next to their horse or on horseback. Even the train signalmen were on horseback. A third of the population is still nomadic, wandering the more fertile steppes, the prairie grassland of the north. They herd sheep from their horses. In the south lies the arid Gobi Desert. It took Marco Polo a month to cross the Gobi at its narrowest point, though I crossed it by train in a few hours. Very little of the country is suitable for agriculture.

"There is nothing to eat," Marco Polo wrote in his journal, and food is still scarce. There is no fresh fruit, and meals consist mainly of mutton, horse meat, and camel meat. As I traveled farther south and the grass got thinner and the soil rockier, there were fewer horses and more furry two-humped camels.

The one place that had something close to crowds of people was the capital, Ulan Batar, where more than a million people, almost half the population of Mongolia, live. The city dates back to the seventeenth century though it had the look of a Soviet city, like one of the huge metropololises of eastern Russia. It still had hammers and sickles displayed on factories and housing projects.

To me, the most interesting thing about the capital was the clothes that people wore. Women wore long silk coats with sashes in bright colors and the men wore incredible hats—one that looked Alpinish and another that resembled the dome of a temple, with red velvet visors with yellow piping and a deep blue silk dome with a gold braided ornamental knot tied on the top.

You may notice that there is little about food in this description of Mongolia other than Marco Polo's observation that there wasn't any. This is not exactly the case. I found a great variety of meat-stuffed dumplings. You might worry about the meat, but everything was nicely seasoned. The closest thing to a vegetable was the ubiquitous green onion.

Of all the international nights, Mongolia Night took the most digging and pondering to come up with a meal for which I would not have to ask my family's forgiveness. To eat truly Mongolian, we would have had to sit with the horses by the fire outside the ger and heat up stones to put in a pot with chunks of meat and then take the closed pot or aluminum can back into the ger to cook. Horhog is sheep cooked with hot stones; boodog is a similar dish made with a goat. After cooking, the stones are sometimes licked for good health. The cuisine seems better suited for camping than the New York apartment where we live.

Miraculously, the meal we came up with was a favorite with Marian, Talia, and me, but yes, I did play a little loose with authenticity. That is probably the key to a good Mongolia Night.

MAIN COURSE
◆ MONGOLIAN HOT POT

The hot pot probably did start in Mongolia sitting around those fires by the ger. Even before Genghis Khan it had spread to northern China, where today a great number of ethnic Mongolians still live, and from there throughout China, where it is called a Mongolian hot pot. Usually a sunken metal bowl heated from below by charcoal or gas replaces the traditional lazy Susan in the center of the table. The Mongolian hot pot has taken on different characteristics in different Chinese provinces. In the city of Zigong, in Sichuan Province, where I was researching my book *Salt*, a team of Chinese historians I had come to know invited me to a Sichuan-style Mongolian hot pot. Great handfuls of toxic red peppers were thrown into the broth so that my eyes teared, I was having trouble breathing, and I felt intense pain all over my mouth. The learned locals seemed to be having a wonderful evening, apparently unaffected by the most pungent dish I have ever endured. There are several variations of Mongolian hot pot throughout Asia. In Japan, there is sukiyaki and shabu shabu. In Thailand, there is Thai suki; in Vietnam, lau mam, which involves salt-cured fish; and in Singapore it is called stea, "steamboat."

Our hot pot has Mongolian, Chinese, and Japanese elements to it, but part of the fun of a hot pot is that you can add anything that will taste good poached in stock. Further straying from authenticity, I used an electric fondue pot, which is not very Mongolian but does the job well.

THE BROTH

An authentic Mongolian hot pot would start with a mutton stock, but I used a beef stock (see Basic Recipes, p. 24). To this I added chopped green onions, a few cloves of garlic, half a cup of soy sauce for every liter of stock, and a few slices of fresh ginger. Heat this broth and put out the ingredients below. The idea is to drop your choice of ingredients into the broth and fish out with a fork or chopsticks whatever you put in.

thinly sliced beef: Tell the butcher you
   are making carpaccio. Bring it to
   the table frozen. A frozen slice will
   be cooked in one minute.
bok choy
carrot sticks
strips of different-colored bell peppers
thick onion rings

green beans
Chinese cellophane noodles
whole-wheat soba noodles
cubes of firm bean curd
shiitake mushrooms
enoki mushrooms
squid cut into rings
bansh (see below)

BANSH

Traditionally this dumpling is made with mutton, a mature sheep, but we made it with the more available lamb. This recipe makes about nine or ten dumplings.

½ pound ground lamb
2 large pinches of salt
2 tablespoons coriander powder
2 tablespoons onion, finely minced
2 tablespoons garlic, minced
2 tablespoons parsley, finely chopped

2 tablespoons fresh dill, finely
   chopped
3 turns of black pepper
2 cups flour
2 cups water

Mix the ground lamb with a large pinch of salt and the coriander, onion, garlic, parsley, dill, and black pepper. This is the filling.

In a mixer with a paddle, beat the flour, another large pinch of salt, and the water until the mixture becomes a silky, sticky dough. Beat well so it loses some stickiness and then work the dough on a well-floured table with well-floured fingers. Tear off a small amount of dough and press and stretch it into a fairly thin 4-inch circle. Place a small mound of filling in the center, stretch the ends of the dough over the top, and twist to make a pinwheel pattern. Mongolian cooks take great pride in this. The dumpling is now ready to be placed in the cooking broth. Leave it in about 10 minutes.

Bansh

DESERT
◆◆ UL BOOV

This means "shoe," which refers to the shape of the pastry. I saw some problems with this dish, but it was the only Mongolian dessert I could come up with. Mongolians carve patterns into wooden boov presses to stamp these pastries, but I didn't think that was a practical thing to suggest and I don't know where to buy boov stamps. In addition, while the pastry is not bad, sort of like a heavy donut, it seemed to need something more. Mongolians stack them, two in one direction, then another layer in a crossways direction. The older and more venerable a family member, the more boov they get. Grandparents get seven. We would not want to eat nearly this many. Also, by tradition yogurt, hard cheese, and candies are piled on top. This did not seem appealing. But after much reflection I decided that vanilla ice cream would replace the dairy foods and a hard caramel sauce would replace the candy. I don't know what a Mongolian might think, but we loved this dessert.

We made one shoe per person. This is a three-shoe recipe.

1½ cups flour	1 cup water
1¼ cups sugar	½ cup canola oil
1 stick plus 6 tablespoons butter	6 scoops vanilla ice cream

In a mixer with a paddle, beat together the flour with ¾ cup sugar and 1 stick of butter. Beat in ½ cup water and paddle until it becomes a well-mixed dough. Divide the dough in thirds, making long rolls about the size of a child's shoe. Here is where the wooden stamp comes in, but you can use a rolling pin or your fingers. Flatten the center to about a ½-inch thickness and press out the sides to a thicker edge, as with a pizza.

Here again the Mongolian authenticity problem arises. You are supposed to fry these in mutton fat, but for reasons of health and availability we used canola oil (though mutton fat is tasty). Thoroughly fry on both sides in very hot oil. Drain on paper towels. Place one on each plate.

In a pot melt ½ cup sugar, 6 tablespoons butter, and ½ cup water on high heat and boil until the mixture becomes thick and brown.

Place 2 small scoops of ice cream on each shoe. Pour the hot caramel sauce over the scoops. The cold of the ice cream should cause the caramel to form a hard shell.

DRINK
◆ MONGOLIAN TEA

This is the most common drink in Mongolia. It has also become common in our household, because Talia loves it. Place the amount of loose green tea in a teapot that you would use for a full pot of green tea. Fill a third of the pot with hot water and allow it to steep for a few minutes. Then add boiling milk with whatever amount of sugar you prefer. Mongolians often make it with no sugar.

PERU NIGHT

HINT: A COUNTRY IN THE TROPICS THAT IS NOT TROPICAL.

Peru is in the tropics, between the Tropic of Capricorn and the equator, but with the exception of one corner that lies in the Amazonian rain forest, it is not tropical. This is partly because much of Peru is the high Andes, but also because the Humboldt Current that comes from the subarctic south of Chile sweeps the coast of Peru and cools it in the same way that the Caribbean Gulf Stream warms the coast of England.

I have always thought of Lima as the toughest town I have ever experienced. This is because in a lifetime of roaming rough neighborhoods in Hartford, where I grew up—and in New York; San Juan; Mexico City; Manila; Kingston; Jamaica; really some of the most infamous slums in the world—the closest I have ever come to having my wallet taken was in Lima. It was an old

trick. A man squirted some kind of liquid detergent on my shoulder, and as I turned to examine the spot, he stuck his hand in my pocket and took my wallet. What really angered me about this was the lack of artistry. He didn't even try to lift the wallet unnoticed, just jammed in his hand and ran. I started to run after him. I had spent the previous week in Cuzco in the Andes, with an altitude of more than eleven thousand feet, and I suddenly realized that in Lima, back at sea level, I had remarkable lung power. I chased this young man through the streets of the capital for a half hour until, exhausted, he screamed, "*Aye, que loco!*" and threw the wallet at me.

Before Europeans arrived, Peru was the center of a vast Incan empire. Its descendants are a significant part of the population and culture and this is reflected in the country's food.

Corn

APPETIZER
◆ CEVICHE

I have been making this dish for many years. It is probably of Peruvian origin and, in any event, is extremely popular there. The Spanish insist the name comes from an Arabic word and that the dish is of Andalusian origin, but the indigenous coastal Peruvians, the Moche, marinated fish in fermented passion fruit before the arrival of the Spaniards. The Incas, two thousand years ago, marinated fish in *chichi*, fermented corn or cassava. The limes were brought by the Spanish. I have always thought this was an ideal dish because it is rich in flavor, contains almost no fat, and in the right serving dish is colorful and beautiful.

Peruvians add to this recipe a yellow chili that is common in Peru. I used hot Hungarian paprika, which is about the same level of heat, although it's the wrong color. You could use a bit of minced Scotch bonnet, but keep in mind that this is a much hotter pepper.

3 sole fillets, cut into 2-inch pieces
fresh-squeezed lime juice
a pinch of coarse salt
2 cloves garlic, sliced

2 cloves shallots, sliced
1 small bunch fresh coriander leaves
    (cilantro), chopped
1 tablespoon red peppercorns

In a bowl, cover sole fillets with fresh lime juice, then add the salt, garlic, and shallots. Top with coriander leaves and a sprinkling of red peppercorns. Marinate about 12 hours or more.

SALAD
◆ PERUVIAN SALAD

This is a salad of beautiful colors but not much green. When I am in Peru I long for green vegetables. I asked a Peruvian friend in New York what green vegetables Peruvians eat. He thought for a moment and said, "None. We learn to eat them here." Even now that Peruvians have become major exporters of asparagus and other green vegetables, they still don't eat them very much.

Avocados are thought to have come from pre-Spanish central Mexico: the name is from the Aztec language. But Peruvians, who eat a lot of avocados, call them by an Incan name, *palta*. Does this mean the Incas were eating them before the Spanish arrived? This is an unsolvable debate. There are wild avocados growing in the Andes. But they are always found near worn trails, so they may have been cultivated or sprung from the discarded pits of travelers. In any event, while avocados are green, they are a fruit and not a vegetable.

Peruvians eat a lot of tomatoes, another name from the Aztec language, though tomatoes also may have been grown in pre-Spanish Peru. Any botanist will tell you that a tomato also is a fruit, not a vegetable, and in fact it is a berry. But in 1893, when an importer in the US tried to evade the vegetable tariff by claiming tomatoes were a fruit, the case went to the Supreme Court, which ruled that the tomato is a vegetable because it is used like a vegetable. Shows what they know.

Zapallo is a huge orange squash indigenous to Peru and hard to find elsewhere, but butternut squash is a close substitute. Potatoes were a wild Andean plant first cultivated in pre-Spanish Peru. The name comes from the Spanish *patata*, which comes from the word *papa* in Quechua, the language of the Incas. Onions are native to Peru and also most of the rest of the world. Corn and red pepper are also Peruvian. So with the exception of the lime juice, this is a truly Peruvian dish.

1 large slice from a butternut squash
1 medium-size thin-skinned potato
3 tomatoes, quartered
1 avocado, sliced
1 white onion, sliced thinly

¼ cup corn oil
juice of 1 lime
a pinch of salt
1 teaspoon cayenne pepper

Peel the squash slice, steam it until it is soft to a fork but not mushy (about 15 minutes), and cut into half-inch pieces. Boil the potato for 20 minutes, then slice but do not peel. Arrange the squash and potato on salad plates along with the tomato, avocado, and onion.

In a bowl, combine corn oil, lime juice, salt, and cayenne pepper. Mix well and pour over plates of salad.

MAIN COURSE
◆ DUCK AND YUCCA

This type of cooking with roots is from Iquitos—which, with a population of 400,000, is the largest city in the world not accessible by road. It is a port on the Amazon River surrounded by rain forest, a steaming, ramshackle kind of tropical place, and when I was there in the 1980s, it seemed much smaller. I had flown in, but once there the only way to get around was by riverboat. Being short of cash, I was relieved but distrustful when I saw the blue American Express sign on a weather-beaten piling by the rickety boat landing. I handed the man my card and without hesitating he pressed it against a carbon-copy form, rubbed it on a rough tropical tree trunk, and handed me a receipt to sign. The charge turned up itemized on my next American Express bill.

I used three boneless duck breasts because that was what the store had the day I went, but you could also use whole quartered ducks. There is a trick to boning a duck that works well for this recipe. Split the duck in half and roast it skin side up for twenty minutes. Then let it cool, and you can pull off the spine and the ribs starting with the spine side. You will still have the drumstick and wing on the bone, but the main body will be boneless.

¼ cup plus 1 tablespoon corn oil	7 garlic cloves
about ¼ cup coarse salt	2 tablespoons cumin powder
2 ducks	1 cassava (yucca) root
2 turmeric roots	2 cups water

Heat a small amount of corn oil in a skillet or casserole dish—use a pan that has a cover. Rub coarse salt on the skin of the duck and place it skin side down in the hot oil until the skin is browned. Then turn it over. In a food processor, grind turmeric roots with the skin scraped off (you could use 2 tablespoons of turmeric powder if the roots aren't available), the garlic, and the remaining 1 tablespoon of corn oil. Puree and add to the skillet with the duck. Add cumin powder. Peel the cassava root and slice it into ⅓-inch-thick disks. Cut the disks in half if it is a really thick root, and cook them on both sides in the oil with the duck. Add the water and cook slowly with the lid on for about 2 hours. Finish the last 15 minutes of cooking at a higher temperature with the lid off.

DESSERT
◆◆ CHOCLO CAKE

Choclo means corn, and *pastel de choclo*, literally corn cake, is sometimes stuffed with meat and is not a dessert. But this is a dessert choclo, a simple peasant's dessert.

½ cup raisins
¼ cup plus 1 cup sugar
about ½ cup pisco
3 eggs
2 cups cornmeal
1 cup flour

1 tablespoon baking powder
3 tablespoons powdered anise
1 stick melted butter
2 oranges
2 cups milk
1 cup grated coconut

Preheat oven to 350 degrees. Place the raisins in a pot and add ¼ cup sugar and enough pisco, a Peruvian alcoholic beverage, to cover the raisins. Bring to a slow boil, then remove from heat and let cool.

Lightly beat the eggs in a mixing bowl with the paddle attachment. Add the cornmeal, flour, baking powder, anise, and remaining 1 cup sugar. Then beat in the melted butter, the zest and juice of 2 oranges, the milk, the grated coconut, and the macerated raisins.

When the mixture is well beaten, pour it into an eight-inch springform pan that has been brushed with butter and dusted with flour. Bake for 1 hour.

DRINK
◆ PISCO SOUR

In the 1980s when I went to Peru as a journalist, a leftist band of guerrillas called Sendero Luminoso—Shining Path—was active. They were particularly popular among the indigenous peasants in the central highlands around the town of Ayacucho. They seemed to have some connection with the local utility, since they could cause electrical blackouts during their attacks, in which they sometimes killed dozens of people. The Peruvian government stationed a soldier outside my hotel room in Ayacucho, presumably for protection, but this did not make me feel particularly comfortable since the army had killed as many people as Sendero had. Worse, the soldier outside my door was a nervous eighteen-year-old. I could hear him fidgeting with the clips on his automatic weapon.

I couldn't sleep, so I went to the bar and ordered a pisco sour. The bartender was mixing it in a blender to get the egg whites to froth when suddenly the room went dark. The high-pitched whir of the blender slid an octave lower and stopped. In the dark I heard the bartender whisper, "Sendero."

I waited a few seconds and heard nothing more. So then I whispered to the bartender, "While we are waiting, could I have my drink?" I heard the glass being placed in front of me in the dark, silent room. The pisco sour was perfect.

Pisco is a distilled alcohol made from grapes in Peru. It is a white brandy similar to the drink called aguardiente in Spain. There are more arguments over the origin of the word *pisco* than even the word *ceviche*. It is named after a town, or an earthen jar, or a word in the local language for "bird." But most people agree that the pisco sour was invented in Peru in the 1920s by an American bartender named Victor Vaughn Morris, or was it by another bartender who worked for him in his Lima bar, Mario Bruiget? In Chile they say an Englishman invented it. I have heard Peruvians crediting an Englishman as well. *Somebody* deserves credit for this.

a little less than ½ cup sugar	2 cups pisco
1½ cups water	1 egg white
1½ cups freshly squeezed lime juice	Angostura bitters

Make a simple syrup: heat the sugar and 1 cup water on low heat, then cool. Mix the lime juice and ½ cup water, then mix with ¼ cup of the syrup. Chill the mix along with the pisco.

Mix the lime water with the pisco. Pour into a blender, add an egg white, and beat on high speed, hoping the foam will form before the Sendero cut the power. Pour into cocktail glasses and add a drop or two of bitters to each glass.

This makes an enjoyable drink for children without the pisco, but they may want it slightly sweeter.

SWITZERLAND NIGHT

HINT: THE WORLD'S MOST NEUTRAL COUNTRY IN THE MIDDLE OF THE WORLD'S MOST WARRING CONTINENT.

Europe, though relatively peaceful for the past fifty years, has been the site of almost nonstop war for several millennia. One war—the Hundred Years' War in the 1300s and 1400s—lasted more than a century as the British tried unsuccessfully to take over France. What is now Switzerland used to be immersed in the continental brawls as part of the aggressive Holy Roman Empire, a Germanic federation that, as most children learn in school, was neither holy, Roman, nor an empire. In 1648 the Holy Roman Empire recognized the independence of the breakaway provinces that became Switzerland. Then the very acquisitive Napoleon invaded and tried to take over Switzerland, but after he was defeated and removed, the 1815 Congress of Vienna that established the new European order recognized Switzerland as a neutral, nonaligned nation, and it has remained that way. It maintains a standing army, there to defend the country's neutrality, but the army may be best known for its excellent pocket knifes.

A land of spectacular alpine vistas, charming villages, and lush green mountain meadows, Switzerland has been somewhat out of the mainstream of Europe. It is known for its banking secrecy, which allows scoundrels from all over the world to hide unreported money, and its chocolate, which for many years has been too industrialized to truly rank among Europe's best. The country did not allow women to vote until 1971, though in 1999 Ruth Dreifuss became both the first female and the first Jewish president of Switzerland, and there have been other women presidents since. In 2002 Switzerland joined the United Nations, which to some meant that it was no longer officially neutral. Probably the most famous quote about Switzerland is from Graham Greene's brilliant screenplay for *The Third Man*, delivered with equal brilliance by Orson Welles while putting on his gloves: "In Italy for thirty years under the Borgias they had warfare, terror, murder, and bloodshed, but they produced Michelangelo, Leonardo da Vinci, and the Renaissance. In Switzerland they had brotherly love—they had five hundred years of democracy and peace, and what did that produce? The cuckoo clock."

But actually, they produced not even that. The cuckoo clock originated in the Black Forest region of Germany.

Officially, Switzerland has four languages: German, French, Italian, and Romansh. The last was the language spoken by the original Roman conquerors, a dialect of Latin, and despite its historic claim is spoken by only a small group of people. German speakers by far outnumber others in Switzerland.

I always used to imagine that because of its different cultures, you could put together the ideal meal in Switzerland, the best of all worlds—an Italian appetizer, a French main course, and a German dessert. But this was mostly a fantasy because, while the nations of Europe are increasingly integrated, the regions of Switzerland remain surprisingly distinct. This means that the meals you eat are usually entirely German, entirely Italian, or entirely French depending on which region you're in.

Also, the cooking in each of these regions is a uniquely Swiss take on the cuisine but not really matching that of France, Germany, or Italy.

For Switzerland Night, our dinner came entirely from the largest region, German Switzerland.

SALAD
◆ HAZELNUT SALAD

2 heads endive, chopped
1/2 head fennel, chopped
1/3 pound green beans
1 dozen whole hazelnuts

a large pinch of coarse salt
1/2 cup olive oil
2 tablespoons raspberry vinegar

Mix the endive and the fennel. Trim and lightly steam the green beans, then add to the endive and fennel along with the hazelnuts and salt. Whisk together the olive oil and raspberry vinegar and mix into the salad.

MAIN COURSE
◆ CHEESE FONDUE

Unlike many Swiss dishes, this one is truly national, recognized by all regions. It originated in Zurich, which is German, but the name *fondue* is French for "melted." The seventeenth- and eighteenth-century Swiss fondue included eggs, which made it into something like a cheese soufflé, which is also a French dish, and the dish known today as Swiss fondue clearly came from the French part of Switzerland from where Gruyère cheese, famous in the world as Swiss cheese, comes. For a family, this is a dish that cannot be overlooked on Swiss Night because most kids love it and because it is easy for children to make. It calls for a fondue pot, which is most any kind of pot that you can heat at the table.

1 garlic clove
2 pounds of assorted Swiss cheese,
    such as Emmentaler and Gruyère,
    aged and young
1/3 cup kirsch

1½ cups dry white fruity wine
2 tablespoons cornstarch
3 teaspoons fresh grated nutmeg
2 French baguettes, sliced in ½-inch
    rounds and cut in half

Before heating the pot, cut the garlic clove in half and rub the entire interior of the pot with the two halves. Grate the cheese and put it in the pot with the kirsch, white wine, cornstarch, and grated nutmeg. Stir the pot constantly with a wooden spoon as it is heating until—as Talia, who was doing the stirring, put it —"it looks like melted ice cream."

To eat, stick a piece of bread on a fork and dip into the fondue.

TALIA: On Fondue

It's nice that one of the more delicious International Night recipes is also one of the fastest and easiest to make. It doesn't take much more than ten minutes to prepare the pot, throw everything in it, and let it melt! Crusts of bread go great with the cheese. But I think boiled potatoes might be good, as well as endive leaves and red peppers. You can just have fun and experiment with different things. After all, what isn't good with gooey melted cheese? Well, gummy bears! So maybe not everything.

DESSERT
◆◆ ENGADINER NUSSTORTE

This translates from German as a nut cake from Engadine, which is in a mountainous, Romansh-speaking area in eastern Switzerland. I have made this cake for many years, and until now I've always made it more or less correctly: it was in my repertoire when I was a pastry maker back in the 1970s. But suddenly, for Swiss Night, I was overtaken by an irresistible urge to put chocolate on top instead of the top crust. This is wrong, and I apologize to the good people of Engadine, on whose tradition I have trampled. But dark semisweet chocolate and walnuts is just one of those great combinations.

THE CRUST

2 cups flour
1 cup powdered walnuts
1½ cups sugar
2½ sticks butter
¼ cup kirsch

2 eggs
2 tablespoons cinnamon
a generous pinch of salt
zest of one lemon

In a mixer with a dough hook, combine the flour, powdered walnuts (you can powder them in a food processor), and sugar. Cut the butter into 10 cubes and add one at a time while mixing. Add the kirsch, eggs, cinnamon, and salt. Mix until it comes together as a dough, then press into the bottom and sides of a 9-inch springform pan. Press the lemon zests into the dough, distributed evenly.

Walnuts

THE FILLING

1½ cups sugar
⅓ cup water
¼ cup kirsch

⅓ cup heavy cream
3 tablespoons honey
3 cups walnuts

Preheat oven to 350 degrees. Melt the sugar over low heat in the water and stir until it begins to caramelize. Add the kirsch, heavy cream, and honey. When it is well mixed and caramelly, stir in the walnuts and pour the mixture into the crust. Bake for 1 hour.

CHOCOLATE GLAZE

1 cup sugar
⅓ cup water
8 ounces high-quality dark bittersweet
    chocolate

12 ounces high-quality dark bitter
    chocolate

After the torte has cooled, melt sugar over low heat in the water. Add the dark bittersweet chocolate and melt. The quality of the chocolate is important, so use good chocolate. With a rubber spatula, spread the mixture on top of the torte so it makes a smooth surface and let chill in the refrigerator for at least 2 hours.

Melt the dark bitter chocolate in a double boiler. Spread it evenly on top of the semisweet chocolate glaze. Before it cools, place a few walnuts on top as a decoration.

DRINK

Black currant juice, preferably unsweetened so that you can adjust the sweetness. Add a little sugar so the bitterness does not overpower the flavor. Place the slightly sweetened juice in a third of a glass and fill with club soda, leaving a small space at the top for a handsome pink head of foam.

IRELAND NIGHT

The third of the six Celtic nations that Talia's roaming finger was to land on was also the largest and most influential. In 1169, by legend on May 1, Norman knights, the same people from northern France that had conquered England a century earlier, invaded Ireland, beginning an unwelcome, long-lasting English dominance. By the fifteenth century the Celtic Irish were regaining control, but toward the mid-1500s Henry VIII and his daughter Elizabeth I reestablished control. Irish resistance, British oppression, and economic deprivation have characterized Ireland's painful history and have driven the Irish people around the world. A crop failure leading to the Great Famine of 1840, in which one million Irish people starved to death, drove more than a million abroad, so that by 1850 half of the immigrants to the US, including a sizable part of the populations of New York and Boston, were Irish. The US is only one of many countries strongly shaped by Irish culture.

A violent struggle finally led to an independent Ireland in 1923. But the British still controlled the six Protestant counties in the north, which led to something like a civil war beginning in the late 1960s, known with Irish euphemism as the Troubles. These Troubles cost nearly four thousand lives until 2007, when the British finally began the permanent withdrawal of troops.

In all these struggles and sorrows, Ireland became a land of songs and poems and great writers and a people with very long memories. There is a popular song still sung about the death of Roddy McCorley, a leader in the local resistance in County Antrim who was executed by the British. The year was 1798, but the Irish don't forget how the British shot McCorley by the Ban at the bridge of Toome.

When I went to Ireland I immediately saw part of the problem, for the Irish—warm and often coarse, empathetic to the traveler or the vagabond, the poor and the marginal, crassly iconoclastic and irreverent—have much in common with Americans but almost nothing, except perhaps the love of words, with the English.

For many years I had wanted to go to Ireland, more than anything because of the beauty of its literature. I wanted to go to the land of Yeats, Synge, O'Casey, and Joyce to see what kind of a place produced all this great writing and not even in a language that it considers its own. Once, as I was eating lunch in a New York restaurant, my waiter told me he was Irish from Sligo. I recited a stanza of a favorite Yeats poem about Sligo, and he said that hearing Yeats made him quiver and he gave me a glass of champagne.

Ireland has the largest Celtic-speaking population, but most of its literature is in English, an adjective not well loved. I was invited to Ireland to participate in something called the

Electric Picnic. This was a very Irish affair. It spread over acres in open fields in Port Laoise and included food booths, a great deal of drinking, children's theater and children's games, rock concerts, and a tent or two for literature, bringing notable Irish writers such as Roddy Doyle as well as gifted newcomers. To hear an Irish writer give a reading is a worthwhile event because they are natural storytellers full of pathos and humor and their words pour out like music. This seemed true of many people in Ireland, though I think it was a little shocking to Talia that there was rarely a sentence without a word beginning with *F*.

SOUP
◆ COCKLE SOUP

This is a very Irish dish made with the little ribbed bivalve that often appears in Celtic food. It can also be made with mussels, or with both. Cockles and mussels are Dublin food, as in the celebrated song about Molly Malone.

> In Dublin's fair city,
> Where the girls are so pretty,
> I first set my eyes on sweet Molly Malone,
> As she wheeled her wheel-barrow,
> Through streets broad and narrow,
> Crying, "Cockles and mussels, alive, alive, oh!"

A true Irish story, it is completely made up and has a tragic ending. Young Molly, at the end of the song, succumbs to fever. For the 1988 Dublin Millennium a bronze statue was erected to ill-fated Molly, her wheelbarrow stuffed with shellfish and her low-cut dress stuffed with Molly.

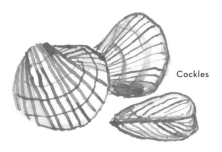

Cockles

1 pound cockles
about 4 tablespoons salt
2 cups whole milk

1 celery rib, minced
¼ cup parsley, minced

Thoroughly wash the cockles in their shells and then put them in salted water. Traditionally they should be cooked in seawater, but if no seawater is available, add salt to water. Seawater is at least 3 percent salt and you need enough water to cover the cockles, so a big spoonful of salt is required. Heat the water, and the instant all of the shells are open, cut off the heat.

With a slotted spoon, remove the shells and let cool. Pour out half the water from the pot. To the remaining water add the milk and celery. Remove the cockles from their shells and toss them into the soup. Heat it, add the parsley, and serve.

This is a small amount of cockle soup to start off a heavy meal with far to go. Serve with Irish soda bread.

BREAD
◆ SODA BREAD

This is a recipe for a small ball of bread. Not only is this a great textured crusty bread, but it is an easy bread to make.

2 cups flour
a generous pinch of salt

⅓ teaspoon baking soda
about ¾ cup buttermilk

Preheat oven to 400 degrees. In a mixer with a dough hook, work together on moderate speed the flour, salt, and baking soda. Mix in the buttermilk ¼ cup at a time until the dough becomes homogenous but not too wet. This will require about ¾ cup of buttermilk but could be a little more or less depending on the speed of the mixer and the mood of the gods.

Thoroughly dust your hands with flour so that you can scoop up the dough and form a ball. Place the dough ball on a baking sheet. With a knife, slash a large cross on the top—not so Jesus will bless the baking, but so the heat will distribute more evenly for even rising. Bake for about 40 minutes. Pierce the bread deeply with a wooden skewer, which should release steam, and if the bread is done the skewer will come out completely dry.

MAIN COURSE
◆ BEEF IN GUINNESS

Guinness, a black bitter beer with a nitrogen-injected creamy head, is the most popular alcoholic beverage in Ireland, and that's a market worth cornering. It has been brewed in the same place in Dublin since 1759. In the early twentieth century, at the time of the independence fight, it was the largest brewery in the world. Guinness is a style of beer called stout, and some say this dish was originally cooked with a different style called portman, which is no longer made. Some argue that portman and stout are the same thing and others say that portman was a milder form of stout. There is no lack of arguments in Ireland. This dish has a rich, slightly bitter black sauce that is softened by the sweetness of the prunes.

2 ounces unsliced bacon
about 1/3 cup olive oil
1 pound beef, cubed
1/2 cup flour
3 carrots, cut into 2-inch pieces
12 pearl onions, peeled

1 1/2 cups pitted prunes
8 hazelnuts
1–2 cans Guinness stout
water
6 mushrooms, halved

Cut the bacon into cubes and cook in olive oil over low heat. Dust the beef with flour and add to the pan with the bacon, browning on all sides. Add the carrots, pearl onions, prunes, and hazelnuts. Cover with a liquid that is 3 parts Guinness to 1 part water. Add mushrooms. Bring to a high boil and then reduce to a moderate bubbling simmer. Cook, covered, for about 2 hours until the sauce is thick and black.

VEGETABLE
◆ COLCANNON

This fine old dish, originally made with kale, has fallen on hard times and too often ends up a soggy mess of cabbage and mashed potatoes. But this is a better version, harking back to its roots. Colcannon is traditionally served around Halloween, which in Ireland is full of legends and traditions of druid rites and spirits. A gold ring, a button, a thimble, and an old Irish sixpence—I used a penny—are buried into the dish. If you find the coin you will be rich; if the ring, you will wed. The boy who finds the button or the girl who finds the thimble will never marry. Kids enjoy this game, though you might want to skip the thimble and button. Or hide your own food-safe amulets with meanings you choose.

1 large bunch kale
1 stick butter
1 leek, thinly sliced
1 green onion, chopped
1 medium-size thin-skinned potato,
    chopped

a large pinch of salt
3 turns of black pepper
½ pint light cream

Chop the kale, removing the stems, and sauté over low heat thoroughly in butter with the leek, green onion, and potato. After the ingredients are thoroughly sautéed add the salt, pepper, and cream. Cook slowly for another 10 minutes.

DESSERT
◆◆ APPLE CHARLOTTE

Many European cultures claim the charlotte, and though popular in Ireland, the Irish must face the possibility that its origin is English. The name may come from an Old English word for custard or from the wife of George III, who was German. There are other German claims to the dessert, and some historians think it was named after Charlotte of Prussia, the nineteenth-century wife of Czar Nicolas I, so there is also a Russian claim. I often make charlottes with a Bavarian cream filling surrounded by ladyfingers. But this is an older way to make a charlotte, and if you take care in how you arrange the bread, it can be a rustically handsome dessert. You can use soda bread or some other textured white bread with crust, but do not use the tasteless, spongelike, factory-made kind of white bread.

1 loaf textured white bread
1 stick melted butter, plus 1½ sticks butter
6 apples, peeled, cored, and sliced
1 cup sugar
1 lemon
3 egg yolks
½ pint light cream
¼ cup confectioners' sugar

Preheat oven to 350 degrees. Slice bread into ⅓-inch slices. Cut slices in half and dip one side in the melted butter, then place, butter-side down, side by side to cover the bottom of an 8-inch springform pan. Cut ½-inch strips of bread and dip one side in butter and place them vertically, butter side against the pan, along the outer rim at a height so that the crust end barely reaches over the top.

Sauté the apple slices in 1½ sticks of butter until soft, then add the sugar and juice of ½ lemon. Meanwhile, beat the egg yolks in a mixing bowl and heat the cream to a boil. Add the egg yolks to the cream and stir quickly over not too much heat until it thickens, being careful because too much heat will curdle the custard. Pour it over the apple mixture, then pour mixture into the springform. Dip more bread slices in the melted butter and arrange on top. Bake for 30 minutes.

After the charlotte cools, squeeze ½ lemon on top. Then lightly dust with confectioners' sugar and lemon zest.

SWEETS
◆◆ YELLOWMAN TOFFEE

A livestock fair has been held in Ballycastle every year for more than three centuries, and yellowman is always sold there. Almost every Irish cookbook has a recipe for yellowman, and it is always the same.

2 tablespoons butter
1 cup corn syrup
1 cup brown sugar

2 tablespoons cider vinegar
1 teaspoon baking soda

Melt the butter in a pot over low heat and add the corn syrup and brown sugar. The better the brown sugar, the better the toffee. Add the cider vinegar. Melt everything together and boil it until a drop placed in cold water turns fairly hard. Then add the baking soda, which will make the mixture fizz up and turn yellow. Take a glass of cold water and periodically put a small drop of mixture in the water and roll it with your thumb and forefinger. When the drip forms into a soft but firm ball, remove the mixture from heat. Pour onto a well-greased baking sheet, and before it is completely hardened, cut into squares. Cool and serve.

DRINKS
◆ IRISH ROSE

The original Irish Rose has Irish whiskey, which is always a good idea for adults, but this recipe can also make a pleasant nonalcoholic drink.

Use equal amounts of fresh-squeezed lemon juice and cherry juice and sugar to the sweetness you prefer. Since the cherry juice is sweet, you don't have to add any sugar if you prefer not to. Pour into glasses and add a splash of soda to each glass. Garnish with a maraschino cherry.

Adults might want to consider Guinness instead. There is something soothing about the creamy head. Or is it the nitrogen?

ARGENTINA NIGHT

HINT: ONE OF THE SOUTHERNMOST NATIONS ON EARTH.

Argentina is the third-most south-ern country in the world. The first, the nearby South Georgia and South Sandwich Islands, is actually not a country but a British protectorate inhabited only by British researchers and officials. Argentina narrowly loses the number-two spot to its neighbor Chile. But Argentina claims the South Georgia and South Sandwich Islands to be rightfully its own, and if the British were to concede this point, Argentina would then gain the claim to being the southernmost country in the world.

The great thing about being a journalist is not only that you get to go places, but that when you get there you have something to do, taking you to people and places that a tourist usually doesn't encounter. But the story on which you work can color your view of the country in strange ways. I did go to Argentina once as a tourist, but that trip is overshad-owed in my mind by the two trips I made as a journalist, neither of which provided very favorable views of the country. The first was in the mid-1970s when the military regime had been overthrown, and as bodies appeared in fields and rivers, the Argentines were trying to tabulate exactly how many thousands of people the former regime had quietly driven away and murdered.

The next visit was another grim story in the mid-1990s when Italy moved to extradite a Nazi war criminal, eighty-three-year-old Berlin-born Erich Priebke. Argentina was in-famous for hiding Nazi criminals, but Priebke was the first to be extradited.

But I have other memories, especially of natural beauty, such as the thrill of white-water rafting on a wide Andean river near the Chil-ean border. Most of my food memories involve beef, though I am sure I ate other things as well.

In 2012 Argentines ate 129 pounds of beef per person, which may seem like a lot. Ameri-cans who consider themselves serious beef eaters only consumed 57.5 pounds per person. But this is a cultural crisis in Argentina, where beef eating is considered their identity and consumption has plunged to little more than half of the 222 pounds per Argentine in 1956. Now Uruguay has surpassed them: Argentina is only the second-largest country when it comes to per capita beef consumption. But that's still a lot of beef.

In any event, Argentina Night was one of our simplest and most appreciated meals, especially the way Talia kicked it off dancing the tango in a long dress with a red flower in her hair.

APPETIZER
◆ CROQUETAS DE ZAPALLO

While the rest of Latin America pays homage to its Indian roots, Argentines endlessly assert their European-ness. We are told that Buenos Aires is a European city. It is no more European than many other cities in the Americas, but nevertheless the only region that still has a noticeable Indian presence and signs of indigenous culture is the region of Salta, wedged between the Chilean, Bolivian, and Paraguayan borders. Here the food traditions show the flavors of indigenous cooks such as these corn and squash fritters.

1 cup winter squash, peeled and
   chopped
2 eggs
1 cup milk
1 cup cornmeal
1 cup flour
a pinch of salt

2 teaspoons cinnamon
2 teaspoons ground cloves
2 teaspoons ground cumin
2 teaspoons ground allspice
2 teaspoons baking powder
3 tablespoons butter

Cook the squash in boiling water until soft, about 20 minutes, and then puree it in a food processor, blending in all the remaining ingredients besides the butter.

Melt the butter in a skillet until sizzling. With a wooden spoon, place dollops of the batter in the hot butter, cook for a few minutes, and then flip with a spatula and cook the other side. Both sides should be slightly browned.

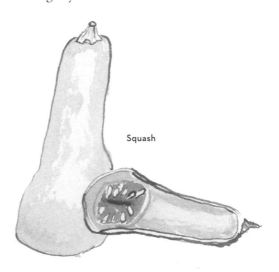

Squash

MAIN COURSE
◆ STEAK AND AJI ASADO

For this dish, buy the best grass-fed steaks you can find. We got two-inch-thick dry-aged New York strip steaks.

3 steaks	1 red pepper
coarse salt	olive oil
2 green peppers	a pinch of dry oregano
1 yellow pepper	1 teaspoon cayenne pepper

Grill the steaks with a little coarse salt.

For the aji, place the peppers one by one on the burner, turning all sides until the skin is completely blackened. Put them in a paper bag and seal it shut until the peppers have cooled. Then rub the blackened skin off the peppers, remove the seeds, and tear them into strips. Arrange the strips on a platter like the spokes of a wheel. Add olive oil, coarse salt, a pinch of dried oregano, and cayenne pepper.

DESSERT
◆◆ DULCE DE LECHE CREPES

With the possible exception of the tango, dulce de leche, literally a sweet made from milk, is Argentina's most celebrated invention. These days it is most often made by boiling a can of sweetened condensed milk. The can cannot be completely covered with water, but, on the other hand, if the water boils away too much, the can will explode. Exploding cans does not seem like a comfortable idea for family cooking, so we made it the old-fashioned way. The ingredients cook down to a fraction of their original volume, so don't hesitate to make a lot. Follow these proportions and make sure to use a good, thick-bottomed pot that has room for double the volume, because the ingredients expand in the early stages of cooking.

THE FILLING

4 cups whole milk

2 cups sugar

a generous splash of vanilla extract

1 teaspoon baking powder

Boil the milk. Lower heat and add the sugar, vanilla, and baking soda. Keep heat below medium, just enough for a few bubbles, and cook for about 3 hours until the mixture becomes a thick caramel sauce.

THE CREPES

3 eggs

1½ cups milk

2 tablespoons butter, melted

a pinch of salt

1 cup plus 2 tablespoons flour

whipped cream or vanilla ice cream

Beat the eggs with the milk, melted butter, and salt. After the mixture is well beaten, add the flour. Mix well until it takes on the consistency of cream. Let sit in the refrigerator at least 1 hour. Then, with a ladle, pour a small amount on a griddle or skillet with sizzling butter, wait a few minutes until the top side looks dry, and remove with a spatula (see Brittany Night, p. 167). Fill with dulce de leche. Fold the crepes over and place whipped cream or vanilla ice cream on top. There is also dulce de leche ice cream, although this seemed to me to be taking things a little too far. But it's up to you.

DRINK

Argentines love chamomile tea sweetened with honey. Not a tea but a flower—a relative of daisies and also ragweed—chamomile does not have caffeine.

PORTUGAL NIGHT

HINT: THE EUROPEAN COUNTRY CLOSEST TO NEW ENGLAND.

The short distance between Gloucester, Massachusetts, and Portugal explains why there is such a strong history of Gloucester-to-Lisbon sailing records.

When I first went to Portugal in 1975, it was an exciting place where decades of dictatorship were suddenly vanishing. It was also a very poor place, though for visitors a lack of economic development was not without charm. The beaches were brightened by fleets of fifteen-foot wooden-hulled fishing boats painted in bright yellows and reds with high wooden prows sticking up like hungry birds. Though a few of the boats had small outboard engines, most were still powered by oars made of rough-hewn branches with paddleboards nailed to the ends. Six or eight men would row to sea in these deep boats and fill them with either clams that they dragged nets for or sardines that they caught by circling shoals.

The fishermen were dressed in black with short pants, a black sash, sandals, and black cloth hats with a tassel that fell on one shoulder. At sunset they returned from sea and dragged their boats to the beach with a rope tied onto their high prows. Their sturdy women waited in plaid skirts and black blouses, and the fish were sorted. Fires were set up to grill sardines, and farmers came in donkey- and mule-drawn carts with leafy vegetables. Tents were set up. Children were playing. It was like everywhere else—families with good catches looked happy, and those with less fish looked sad or angry.

Portugal at the time was losing its long-distance fleet because nations all over the world were closing off their continental shelves two hundred miles from shore to reserve them for their own fishermen. The shelf of Spain and Portugal drops quickly into deep water and does not provide much in the way of off-shore fishing, but the Portuguese had been fishing the banks off Newfoundland for centuries, quite possibly since before Columbus's voyage. Theirs was known as the white fleet because the ships were white. They still fished the way they had in the nineteenth century: square-rigged sailing barks voyaged by sail power to Canada, where they dropped their fishermen into the sea in rowboats called dories. The fleets from other countries had two men to a dory—one to bait the hundreds of hooks on longlines, set them, and haul them in the high seas with their incredible weight once the cod and halibut were hanging from the hooks, and a second man to manage the boat against the rough chop of the North Atlantic. But in the white fleet, one man was sent out alone in each dory. Many dories were lost. The people of Portugal had harder lives than other Westerners.

The long history of the white fleet fishing the Canadian Grand Banks for cod, then salting and bringing it back for the European market, has made the Portuguese great salt cod eaters, even now, when they must import it. The Portuguese like to say that they have 365 salt cod recipes, one for every day of the year.

Maybe, but a lot of these dishes are very similar. If you serve salt cod in olive oil with tomatoes, onions, and potatoes, it is the celebrated Bacalhau à Gomes de Sá from Porto. But if you leave out the tomatoes and add beaten eggs, it is the nationally renowned Bacalhau à Brás. And if instead of beating the eggs you add hard-boiled eggs and include chickpeas instead of potatoes, it is Meia Desfeita com Grão. An Azorean fisherman in Provincetown, Massachusetts, served a combination with potatoes and chickpeas and hard-boiled eggs. I don't know what that one was called, but I liked it so much that I often make it. He had invited me on board to show me not his bacalhau but his dragging net, which he had cleverly rigged so that it would drag above the ocean floor to avoid destroying ocean habitat. His gear rig, like his salt cod, was impressive, but I was wondering who would ship out with him since his ancient bottom dragger had plywood patches on the hull that looked like they might spring out with an enormous *boing* if he hit a wave wrong. Still, the bacalhau *was* good, and, unusual in New England, he had a high-quality espresso machine bolted next to the wheel in the pilothouse. These "Portagees" were tough people to go to sea with, but their hard life had its amenities.

The Portagees—New England fishermen who were said to be Portuguese—in fact were from the Azores, Portuguese-speaking islands in the middle of the Atlantic. Their food has some similarities to that of Portugal, and they popularized Portuguese bread and sausages and some fish dishes in New England.

The White Fleet is gone, though the European Union does allow some modern Portuguese boats in Northern European waters. A few of the painted little wooden boats are still hauling clams or sardines, though now more often with outboard motors.

When I think about the food of Portugal I think of tomatoes, garlic, onions, clams, salt cod, and above all sardines. The acrid and sweet smell of grilled sardines is the smell of Portugal, from the beaches to the streets of Lisbon.

And so these were the foods of our Portugal Night.

———

The pork for the Pork and Clams must be marinated overnight, and even before that, you must first make a paste known as massa de pimentão (see p. 290). If you plan on doing more Portuguese cooking, you might want to make a greater quantity, as massa de pimentão is a common ingredient in Portuguese dishes.

These are the amounts just for Portugal Night. The suspiros part of the dessert (see p. 292) needs to be made the day before.

APPETIZER
◆◆ SARDINES

This very Portuguese dish is said to be from the coast just south of Lisbon. Similar dishes can be found as you go farther down the coast. This dish should be started several hours before dinner.

9 cleaned sardines
½ cup flour
a pinch of salt
¼ cup olive oil
2 large, ripe, unpeeled tomatoes, diced
3 garlic cloves, peeled and minced

½ yellow onion, chopped
3 bay leaves
a pinch of salt
3 turns of black pepper
2 tablespoons unsweetened cocoa powder
1 cup dry white wine

Dust the sardines in flour and a pinch of salt. Fry them for about 3 minutes on each side in a skillet with hot olive oil. Remove them from the skillet, lower the heat, and add the tomatoes, garlic, onion, bay leaves, salt, and pepper. Sauté for 20 minutes.

Add the cocoa powder and white wine. Simmer on low heat for 20 more minutes.

Fillet the sardines. (See Sicily Night, p. 85, and Aquitaine Night, p. 210.) Place the fillets skin side up in a clay baking casserole. Pour the sauce evenly on top and let sit 2 or 3 hours in the refrigerator.

Preheat oven to 350 degrees. Remove the casserole from the refrigerator 30 minutes before baking. Bake for 20 minutes.

MAIN COURSE
◆◆ PORK AND CLAMS

This dish, common in much of Portugal, is sometimes called Porco á Alentejana, but since both upper and lower Alentejo province, running along the Spanish border, produce a great deal of pork, there are numerous pork dishes with this name. Coming from New England, I am sensitive to the reality that clams are different everywhere. Portuguese clams are hard to find outside of Portugal; the closest I could come were littlenecks.

¾-inch-thick smoked slab bacon
¾ cup olive oil
marinating pork cubes from day
   before (see recipe below)
½ yellow onion, diced
4 garlic cloves, peeled and minced

2 cups white wine
1 cup tomato sauce #1 (see Basic
   Recipes, p. 25), or a good jarred
   tomato sauce
about 15 clams (littlenecks if available)
1 bunch Italian parsley, chopped

Dice the bacon and sauté in olive oil over medium heat. Remove cubed pork from marinade and add to pan, browning on all sides. Add onion and garlic. Sauté until the onions are wilted, then add the marinade from pork, white wine, and tomato sauce. Cover and cook over low heat for 2 hours. It should cook fast enough so the liquid is evaporating, but it shouldn't be a vigorous boil. It is done when the meat is tender but the sauce is still liquid enough to steam the clams.

Place the clams in the pot with the parsley. Cover and cook over moderately high heat until the clams have opened. Serve with crusty bread.

PORK MARINADE

1¼ pounds pork tenderloin, cubed
massa de pimentão (see recipe below)

3 bay leaves
1 cup dry white wine

Rub the cubes of pork thoroughly with the massa de pimentão. Put in a clay casserole or ceramic bowl with the bay leaves and white wine. Marinate overnight, stirring occasionally.

MASSA DE PIMENTÃO

4 garlic cloves, peeled and finely
   minced
a pinch of salt

3 tablespoons sweet powdered red
   pepper
2-3 tablespoons olive oil

Put the garlic in a bowl with the salt and powdered red pepper. I use the Basque pepper from Espelette, but Hungarian sweet paprika would also work. Add enough olive oil to make a moist paste. This can be ground in a blender or food processor, though most food processors do not take to this small an amount. I used a mortar and pestle, which worked well, and after all, how many opportunities do you have to use your mortar and pestle?

VEGETABLE

◆ FEIJAO VERDE COM COENTRO

This dish should be prepared 4 to 5 hours before serving.

1 pound green beans
2 large garlic cloves, peeled and sliced
1/3 cup chopped fresh coriander
    (cilantro) leaves
a generous pinch of salt

5 tablespoons olive oil
1 tablespoon lemon juice
2 tablespoons cider vinegar
4 turns of black pepper

Steam the green beans for 2 or 3 minutes until they are bright green. Place the garlic in an earthen casserole with the coriander leaves, salt, and olive oil. Dump the hot beans on top of the garlic-and-coriander mixture and let stand 10 minutes, then marinate in the refrigerator, covered, for 3 to 4 hours.

About an hour before serving, remove the beans from the refrigerator and leave on the counter, still covered. Just before serving, add the lemon juice, vinegar, and pepper. The acids—the vinegar and lemon—must be added at the last moment or they will ruin the color of the beans. Toss well, taste, and add more vinegar, olive oil, salt, and pepper, if you like, to taste.

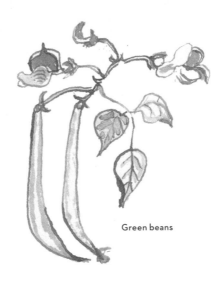

Green beans

DESSERT
◆◆ SUSPIROS E SONHOS (SIGHS AND DREAMS)

One of the great things about Portuguese desserts are the names. The sighs, *suspiros*, are meringues that make up half of the dessert. They need to be made the night before so they can thoroughly dry in the oven overnight.

SUSPIROS

The recipe for these meringues makes about twenty.

2 egg whites	¾ cup sugar
1½ tablespoons fresh lemon juice	⅓ cup water

Preheat oven to 300 degrees.

Beat the egg whites and the lemon juice in a mixing bowl and whip until white and opaque.

Heat the sugar and water. Stir gently until sugar dissolves. Over high heat and without stirring, cook until the syrup reaches a soft ball state: that is, if you put a drop from a spoon in a glass of cold water, you should be able to fetch it out and roll it into a gummy ball.

Then pour the hot syrup slowly into the egg whites while whipping them on the highest speed until they are stiff and fluffy. Spoon the mixture one dollop at a time onto a baking sheet lined with foil, shiny side down. Place in oven. Bake for 30 minutes, then reduce heat to 200 degrees and bake another 20 minutes. Then reduce heat to 100 degrees and bake another 30 minutes. Then turn off the oven but do not open the oven door until the following morning. Set aside until you assemble the sighs and dreams together.

SONHOS

Now make the dreams—*sonhos*. There are a lot of variations on *sonhos*, but these are my dreams. You learn from this dish that we all have different dreams, but our sighs are the same. This recipe makes about fifteen dreams.

1½ sticks butter	2 tablespoons orange-blossom water
2 tablespoons sugar	3 eggs
a pinch of salt	¼ cup canola oil
¾ cup water	½ cup sugar
¾ cup flour	4-5 tablespoons powdered cinnamon

Melt in a pot the butter with the sugar, salt, and water. After the ingredients are heated and well mixed, pour in the flour and beat the mixture together with a wooden spoon. Remove from heat. Put the dough ball in the mixer with the paddle attachment. Add the orange-blossom water and 1 whole egg and beat with the paddle until thoroughly mixed and silky. Add another whole egg and beat until smooth and silky again. Repeat with the third egg.

Pour close to an inch of oil into a skillet and heat until very hot. Start spooning in the batter so that you have dollops about the size of the suspiros. When puffed and browned, turn over to brown the other side. When all puffy and café-au-lait colored, remove to paper towels. Sprinkle generously with granulated sugar and then with powdered cinnamon.

Serve sighs and dreams together on a platter.

DRINK
◆ ICED LEMON TEA

With a zester, scrape off all the zest from three lemons and heat it in four cups of almost-boiling water with two tablespoons of honey. It is important to let this steep without the water ever coming to a boil.

Traditionally, this is drunk in a cup as a hot infusion, but because our Portugal Night fell on a very hot summer night, I decided to serve it chilled. Then Talia came up with a major improvement.

TALIA: *Improving Portuguese Lemon Tea*

This lemon tea is very good, but to go with the dishes we were eating, I felt it needed more . . . pizzazz. The flavor was so close to perfection; if only I knew what it was missing. It was like having something on the tip of my tongue . . . That's when I figured it out. Lemon juice. The drink was made with lemon peels; however, it had no actual lemon juice, and that's exactly what it needed. But only a small amount. You don't want it to be so sour that you need to add sugar, but just sour enough that it has a kick. The perfect amount would be somewhere between three hard squeezes of half a lemon and a whole half a lemon in the pitcher, depending on just how much sourness you like. For me, that was around three and a half hard squeezes of half a lemon. You'll taste the difference immediately.

NICARAGUA NIGHT

HINT: THE LARGEST COUNTRY ON ITS ISTHMUS.

Though tiny, Nicaragua is the largest country in Central America, that narrow strip of land between the Pacific and the Caribbean that connects North America to South America, Mexico to Colombia.

Like many international journalists of my generation, I went to Nicaragua to write about their civil war. In 1979 a brutal, long-standing dictatorship closely allied to the United States was overthrown. The new government, the Sandinistas, promised to work for democracy, but the new American president, Ronald Reagan, adamantly opposed them. In the end the Nicaraguan government proved themselves by holding a fair election, losing, and peacefully stepping down.

Reagan illegally armed and supplied an opposition faction in the east of the country with ties to the old dictatorship, even though Congress had voted not to support them. That unleashed a mean civil war.

From the outset, this was a strange setting for a civil war. Nicaragua was already one of the poorest countries in the Americas when, on December 23, 1972, the capital, Managua, was devastated by an earthquake, killing five

Pineapple

thousand people. The quake struck at 12:29. I know this because when I got there more than a decade after the earthquake, the clock in the steeple in the center of town still said 12:29. Like everything else in the capital, it had not been fixed since the earthquake.

Because of the war, American hostility, and poverty, there were shortages of almost everything, and the currency was worthless. We were required to buy a significant quantity of local money to enter the country. So the reporters would sit at the bar of the Intercontinental Hotel—which was called that but was no longer part of the chain—with five-inch stacks of bills arranged in front of them. If you wanted a drink, you slid one of the stacks toward the bartender.

One of the things that was hard to come by was gasoline. This was a problem for journalists, because the war was being fought mainly on the other side of the country, and it took a tank of gas to drive to the war and back to the hotel. The way to go was to find someone with a full tank of gas and ride with them. I had heard that there was a battle taking shape in the east. There was only one east-west road, and the rebels, known as the

Contras, were trying to cut it off. A couple of other journalists and I found a dubious character who seemed to have driven down from the States just for the fun of it and who somehow had a tank of gasoline and offered to drive us, so we went with him.

It was only a day-long battle. The government had Soviet helicopter gunships that could fire rockets that blew huge holes in the nearby mountains. I have no idea how many they killed, but by late afternoon the Contras had fled and the army was packing up their impressive array of equipment. We were going to drive back to the capital with the army, but someone had tipped me off that this town had *el mejor jugo de piña en el mundo,* the best pineapple juice in the world.

At an outdoor stand just off the main square of town, a man peeled the pineapple with a machete, placed it in a vertical press, pulled down on a lever, and the juice squeezed out. He peeled four pineapples, one glass for each of us. Worth the wait, it was indeed the best pineapple juice I have ever tasted.

But when we got back to our car, the army was gone. They were already on their way back to Managua. Now the sun was setting and we were in between the lines of the two opposing forces, a bad place to be. We made numerous inquiries about a place to stay for the night, but everyone shook their heads and looked very scared and did not want to speak to us.

So we decided to just spend the night in the car. To do this, we decided we needed some rum. Even in those hard times, Nicaragua made excellent golden rum, Flor de Caña. We bought a bottle, but while rum was plentiful, there was a scarcity of bottles, and the store would only give us the rum in a strong, clear, plastic bag.

For a few minutes we passed the bag around the car taking sips, but then someone said—I think it was me—"The hell with this. Let's take our chances driving back to Managua." Everyone agreed and for about forty minutes we nervously rode the dark road toward the capital.

Bright lights suddenly blocked the road. We had reached the rear guard of the army. They shined flashlights in our eyes and demanded press passes and then a young officer with suspicious eyes asked why we had not retreated with them. I explained in Spanish that we had planned to but we had stopped for this incredible pineapple juice. As soon as the young officer heard the words *jugo de piña,* he smiled. He repeated them, and soon all five soldiers were laughing and saying something about the wondrous quality of that *jugo de piña.*

We all agreed that it was the best in the world and he waved us past and we drove on to Managua. A block before the hotel, the car ran out of gas and we had to push it uphill the rest of the way. Next battle, I would have to find gas somewhere else.

Pastel de tres leches must be made the day before. Rice for the gallopinto must also be made the day before. Canned beans can work well, but if you prefer dried beans, they must be soaked overnight and then cooked for several hours with salt and garlic the day of the meal.

MAIN COURSE
◆ NICARAGUAN BEEF

Cattle ranching is one of the major economic activities in Nicaragua. For this dish, a choice beef fillet works best, though most any cut could be used.

1 pound beef, cut in ½-inch slices
1 bunch Italian parsley
6 garlic cloves
½ tablespoon salt
5 turns of black pepper

½ cup olive oil
2 tablespoons red wine vinegar
juice of ½ lime
6 corn tortillas

Cover each beef slice loosely in plastic wrap and tap with a wooden roller until it has doubled in size. Unwrap the pieces and place them in an earthen casserole.

In a food processor, grind the parsley, garlic, salt, black pepper, olive oil, red wine vinegar, and lime juice. Grind the mixture in the food processor. Put half the sauce on the meat, covering both sides of each slice. Let the meat marinate for 40 minutes in the refrigerator.

Heat a grill pan and grill each slice of beef for a few minutes on each side. Serve with gallopinto and a bowl of extra sauce to be spooned over the meat. Also serve with warm corn tortillas, which can be warmed in a steamer or in a microwave for 1 minute with a damp paper towel on top of the stack.

VEGETABLE
◆ GALLOPINTO

Gallopinto is as close as Nicaragua comes to having a national dish. It is commonly found most everywhere in the country. It is also made in Costa Rica and elsewhere in Central America, but it's believed to be Nicaraguan in origin. The Spanish brought rice, and the indigenous people grew beans. Rice-and-bean dishes in various forms are popular most everywhere in the Caribbean basin, but this is the Nicaraguan version. The Spanish-language name means "spotted rooster," probably a reference to the rice spotted with red beans. Make any quantity you like of this dish, but there must be at least twice as much rice as beans. Rice should be made the day before.

½ yellow onion, finely chopped, plus ½ yellow onion, chopped
½ cup olive oil
a pinch of salt
1½ pounds white rice, cooked

2 cups chicken stock (see Basic Recipes, p. 24, or use commercially made stock)
5 garlic cloves, peeled and chopped
1 15-ounce can small red beans, such as Goya's habichuelas rojas pequeñas

Sauté the finely chopped ½ onion in olive oil until translucent—about 5 minutes. Add salt and the cooked rice and stir gently until the rice is well sautéed—about 5 minutes more. Add the chicken stock. Bring to a hard boil, but do not stir. Cook until the liquid is all gone except for bubbles on the surface, then cut the heat down to as low as possible, cover the rice, and do not touch it for 15 minutes. Then remove the lid, transfer the rice to a container, and fluff it with a fork until it is cool. Refrigerate until the next day.

Sauté the remaining ½ chopped yellow onion and the garlic in olive oil over low heat. Drain the beans, but not thoroughly, add to the hot olive oil, and stir for 5 minutes. Then add the cold cooked rice and stir slowly for 5 minutes.

DESSERT
◆◆◆ PASTEL DE TRES LECHES (THREE-MILK CAKE)

This cake soaks in the three milks and has to be made the day before. Every recipe I could find calls for more of the milks than I used, and yet the cake could not soak up all the milk. So it becomes a very moist sponge cake with sauce—difficult to serve, but delicious.

9 eggs, separated
2½ cups sugar
2 drops vanilla
1 tablespoon baking powder
1½ cups flour
¼ cup Flor de Caña rum

1½ cups heavy cream
½ cup evaporated milk
½ cup sweetened condensed milk
a splash of vanilla extract
slightly sweetened whipped cream

Preheat oven to 350 degrees. Beat the egg whites in a mixer with ½ cup sugar until very stiff. Separately beat the yolks with 1 cup sugar and the vanilla until the ingredients make a thick, cream-colored paste. Carefully fold the whites into the yolks (see Chocolate Raspberry Soufflé in Provence Night for more on folding, p. 37). Then carefully fold in the baking powder and then the flour, a third at a time. Pour into an 8-inch springform pan and bake for 45 minutes.

Add the rum to 1 cup sugar and cook over low heat until the sugar melts. After the cake has thoroughly cooled (at least 2 hours), punch holes in it with a toothpick and pour the rum syrup on top, then the heavy cream, evaporated milk, and sweetened condensed milk with a splash of vanilla, and refrigerate. The next day, cover the cake with slightly sweetened whipped cream.

DRINK

Jugo de piña, of course. (See p. 296.) For the grown-ups, add a shot of Flor de Caña.

RUSSIA NIGHT

HINT: THE BIGGEST BICONTINENTAL COUNTRY.

Russia is both the largest country in Europe and the largest country in Asia. It is difficult to grasp just how large it is. If Napoleon and Hitler had grasped this, they might not have wanted to invade. To say that it is more than six and a half million square miles does not really make it clear, even if you point out that the United States is less than four million square miles. It is useful to realize that Russia has nine time zones. I do have a sense of the size because I crossed it by train, which took five days. Well, I didn't really cross it, because I started in Moscow, which is "central Russia," a long way from the European border, and I crossed the Siberian-Mongolian border, which is a lot closer than the Pacific Ocean. But staring day after day at rolling hills with white birch forests gave me some idea of the vastness of the country.

The scenery never changed. It was August, so even Siberia looked the same. The Ural Mountains produced no new, dramatic vistas. We rolled on and on, stopping in cities with names I never heard of where millions of people lived and the primary activity was manufacturing weapons for an arms race that had recently been canceled with the fall of Communism.

Russians like to make things large. Their wristwatches are large. They are proud of having built the world's largest airplane. Their statues are enormous, which creates a lot of work when there is a regime change and they have to

be torn down, but this has not happened that often in Russia. It did happen in 1991 with the fall of the Communist regime that had been in place since 1917. I was there in 1997. In Moscow, the problem was clear. Everywhere there were very large statue bases, some of them even lit at night, but with the statues missing. It was a society that had canceled all its heroes but didn't have new ones to replace them with.

Perhaps because of the size of the country, food has always been a problem. There has always been hunger. Before the Communists, a few people ate well and everyone else was hungry. After the revolution, living up to the egalitarian ideal of Communism, almost everyone ate badly and there was still hunger. Food under Communism was designed to conform to ideology. So private restaurants were closed and replaced with state cafeterias, which eliminated the greed and unfairness of private enterprise and also liberated women from cooking, especially since people were to eat there rather than in their homes. So in one stroke, restaurant food and home cooking were killed off. This was not done without reason. Even today in wealthy countries such as France and the United States, there are few industries with as great a disparity between the income of owners and workers as restaurants. But the state cafeterias had terrible food, and soon everyone did. This led some to buy food illegally on the black market, but due to unscrupulous merchants this food was even worse. Political ideology had replaced culinary thought. In 1922 a brochure from Siberia even suggested artificial food, certain manufactured amino acids that could be ingested intravenously in place of eating a meal.

Shortly after the fall of Communism, I had an opportunity to cook with Russians. These were Jews who had moved to Berlin, and I somehow ended up in charge of a staff of five Russians cooking a Passover seder for fifty Russians under the supervision of a bearded Hasid from London who insisted on the strictest standards of kosher observance. Kashrut was the least of my problems. The Russians insisted on putting mayonnaise on everything, which they squirted from plastic bottles that were, of course, very large. When I tried to stop the mayonnaise, their alternative was ketchup. In France, if you take overcooked chopped vegetables and bury them in mayonnaise it is called without irony "Russian salad."

In Moscow the restaurants tried to sell the foreigners extremely expensive sturgeon— nothing like near extinction to drive up the price of a species. So many of these prehistoric giants were being ripped open for their eggs, they had to do something with the white-fleshed bodies. But they didn't do anything interesting with them or with anything else.

On the train, my home for many days, there was no food in the dining car because it had been taken over by black marketeers who had it stacked floor to ceiling with boxes of booty to sell in Siberia. Instead, at every stop women would come on the platform and sell food that was familiar to me from my Central European grandparents. Stuffed pastries called pirogies, and smoked fish. These women who illegally went on cooking in their homes and illegally selling their food had been the best dining hope in Communist times, and they still were on my train trip.

There was one other source of food. I had a first-class cabin, which meant it was shared with one other passenger. A new cabin mate got on every morning. I do not speak Russian, but between German, French, and hand gestures we could communicate. Each one of these men wore a jacket and tie, carried a leather attaché case, and introduced himself as a businessman. He would remove his jacket and tie, sit on his berth, and open his case, taking out the exact same contents as the man before him: a knife, a sausage, a bread, and a bottle of vodka. He would offer to share with me, and we would not always finish the sausage or bread, but always the bottle of vodka.

Every night when the vodka was all gone, my cabin mate would pass out. In the morning he would get up, dust off his crumbs, put on his tie and jacket, grab his empty attaché case, and leave, and a new businessman with a new attaché case would get on.

When Talia's finger finally landed on Russia—surprising that it took so long, given how much space it takes up on a globe—I decided to delve into politically incorrect, prerevolutionary, pre-mayonnaise cuisine to see if it would lead me to better food than I had eaten in Russia. We would eat the food of nineteenth-century Russia.

Fortunately, there was the translation of Elena Molokhovets's *A Gift to Young Housewives* by Joyce Toomre, a Russian scholar and food historian. This book was first published in 1861—an enormous year for Russia, not because of the book, but because Czar Alexander

II, fresh from defeat in the Crimean War, by decree emancipated the serfs of Russia. These serfs' lives had been completely controlled by the aristocrats whose land they worked. They were virtual slaves. Alexander had said that it was better for him to set them free than for them to free themselves by an uprising. But it was an incomplete and unsatisfying emancipation in which their lives were still largely controlled by landowners, and in the midst of a growing anti-czarist movement Alexander was assassinated in 1881. This marked an end to all attempts at reform and the beginning of a huge migration to the United States, particularly among Jews who had hoped for reform. As Alexander had warned, as the repression grew after his assassination, so did the rebel movement, until the czars were finally overthrown in the 1917 Communist revolution.

During these dramatic times, Molokhovets's book for housewives was the leading cookbook in Russia, reprinted numerous times. The people who read it never cooked, but they would use it to instruct their household servants, who could neither read nor write. Anton Chekhov satirized Molokhovets, though really he was satirizing Russian dining, when he offered a typical Molokhovets menu:

1. glass of vodka
2. daily shsci with yesterday's kasha
3. two glasses of vodka
4. suckling pig with horseradish
5. three glasses of vodka
6. horseradish, cayenne pepper, and soy sauce
7. four glasses of vodka
8. seven bottles of beer

Is this a joke? It sounds like the Russia I know. But it is clear from Molokhovets's book that a few people in the nineteenth century were eating quite well. Most of the others, including the ones producing the food, were starving. And so there was a revolution, and that was the end of her book, because the revolution disapproved of housewives and other women staying at home cooking. At the time of the revolution 295,000 copies had been printed, which is not huge for a country Russia's size, but given how few people could read, let alone afford the cuisine she described, this was an enormously successful cookbook. At an unknown date, around the time of the revolution, Molokhovets died.

After the revolution, the book was an anachronism. Cooking was not seen as a gift to housewives. Just the word *housewife* was offensive. While Molokhovets devoted great space to the dietary requirements of religious observance, she seldom mentioned health and nutrition. The new Soviet cuisine was the exact opposite.

All of our recipes for Russia Night were based on recipes by Molokhovets, though all were modified. The closest to hers is the Stroganoff recipe.

The dough for the pirozhki and the borscht, the paskha and the pistachio water, should all be made at least 24 hours in advance, though 48 hours in advance would be preferable. This also makes the night of the dinner easy.

APPETIZER
◆◆◆ FISH PIROZHKI

According to Molokhovets, they are *pirog* if they are small and *pirozhkis* if large. Mine were in between, but large enough for one per person to be satisfying in this four-course meal. Molokhovets also says that this dish should be made with "any kind of dough that is handy," but one of her suggestions that intrigued me, because I had never tried it, was a brioche dough.

It is difficult to make a small amount of the dough or the filling, so this recipe will produce extra pirozhki and extra dough. The pirozhki can be frozen unbaked and used later, or baked and reheated the next day. Extra brioche dough is never a problem. We had fresh hot brioches and jam for breakfast the next morning, but you could also make sticky buns, cinnamon rolls, Alsatian kugelhopf, or challah.

THE DOUGH

¾ tablespoon dry yeast (¾ packet)
¾ cup lukewarm water
1½ sticks unsalted butter, softened
4 whole eggs

¼ cup sugar
1 tablespoon salt
3¾ cups flour

Mix the yeast into the lukewarm water until it dissolves. Then combine it in a mixer with the butter, eggs, sugar, and salt. Using the whip attachment, beat until foamy, then change to the dough hook and add the flour, mixing on medium speed until thoroughly incorporated. Then refrigerate overnight covered but not sealed.

THE FILLING

Molokhovets's recipe calls for sturgeon, which is very endangered and not commercially fished here. Most any freshwater fish would work. I chose trout.

1 small trout	1 white onion, halved
¼ cup rice	5 garlic cloves
2 cups commercially made vegetable stock, or:	3 tablespoons salt
	2 hard-boiled eggs, chopped
8 carrots, chopped	3 tablespoons finely chopped fresh dill
3 parsnips, chopped	3 tablespoons finely chopped chives
1 leek, chopped	half a stick of melted butter
3 bay leaves	5 turns of black pepper
1 rib celery	at least 3 tablespoons salt

Poach the trout, then peel and fillet it. Crumble the fillets into a mixing bowl. Put the rice in a pot and add vegetable stock to more than cover the rice.

There are numerous good commercial vegetable broths. If you prefer, simmer in a full stockpot of water the carrots, parsnips, leek, bay leaves, celery, onion, garlic, and 3 tablespoons of salt for 5 hours. Strain out the vegetables and keep the rest of the stock because you will need it for the borscht.

Do not stir the rice, but boil it until there is nothing left of the stock except a few bubbles on the surface, about 15 minutes. Turn off the heat. Cover the pot and leave it to sit another 15 minutes. Then fluff with a fork and add to the fish. Add the hard-boiled eggs, dill, chives, melted butter, pepper, and a generous pinch of salt. (Taste the filling: it needs a lot of salt to bring out these mild flavors.)

ASSEMBLY

dough	1 egg yolk

Preheat oven to 350 degrees. After the dough has been refrigerated for 24 or 48 hours, roll it out on a very well floured board. You could also just press it out with your fingers, but either the roller or your fingers will also need to be well floured. Cut 3 x 3-inch squares and put filling on one half. Gently fold over and press the edges. With a spatula, carefully lift each to the baking sheet. Beat the egg yolk with a little water in a bowl and brush it on the top of each pastry. Let rest about 30 minutes and then bake for about 1 hour or until golden.

SOUP
◆ BORSCHT

Molokhovets gives a number of recipes for this soup, some with meat. I have run into meat borscht before, but I prefer the vegetarian version. She gives one vegetarian recipe because the Russian Orthodox Church has days on which the eating of meat is forbidden. Eastern European Jews, including my family, prefer vegetarian borscht because if there is meat, by Jewish dietary law, sour cream cannot be added. But I did not care for Molokhovets's recipe because it called for frying the beets and then making a roux with flour, and this seemed unnecessarily heavy. So we made up our own variation.

4 large or 6 small beets, cut into
    halves or quarters
3 beet tops

1 tablespoon salt
3 cups vegetable stock
1 cup sour cream

Boil the beets in water for 20 minutes. Then plunge them in cold water and the skins will easily pull off. Grate the beets in a food processor and put them in a pot. Remove the grater and add the chopping attachment and puree 3 beet tops without their stems with some vegetable stock (see pirozhki filling for note on vegetable stock, p. 304). Add this to the pot with the beets, along with the salt and the rest of the vegetable stock. Bring to a boil. Simmer 5 minutes more. You can serve this hot with sour cream, but we preferred to make it a day in advance and serve it chilled with sour cream.

Beet

MAIN COURSE
◆ BEEF STROGANOFF

All of these Russia Night dishes have endured but greatly declined over the past century, but none have fallen so far from the original as this wonderful Stroganoff. It is important to understand that this is not a stew with hours of slow cooking to tenderize the meat; a very high quality of beef has to be used. Molokhovets was not talking about food for peasants—just cooked by them, of course.

Here Molokhovets's recipe calls for Sareptskaja mustard. This was a Russian style of homemade mustard with the dried seeds ground, the mustard strained, and honey added. Honey mustard, which is probably similar, is widely available. But I don't like sweet mustard. So I worked out a compromise. I added 2 tablespoons honey mustard and 3 of coarse French country mustard, the kind with whole seeds in it. This gives a more pungent flavor, a nicer look, and a better texture.

13/4 pounds beef tenderloin, cut into
    bite-size pieces
a large pinch of salt
1 tablespoon powdered allspice
2 sticks butter
3 tablespoons flour

2 tablespoons honey mustard
3 tablespoons coarse French country
    mustard
1 cup beef stock (see Basic Recipes, p.
    24, or buy it)
1 cup sour cream

Mix the tenderloin pieces, salt, and allspice, and let sit unrefrigerated for about 30 minutes. Molokhovets suggested 2 hours, but we found half an hour to be sufficient. The point is, as the great turn-of-the-century French chef August Escoffier cautioned, salted meat will not brown. You want this meat completely soft, like pats of butter adrift in the sour cream sauce.

Then sauté in the butter. When cooked lightly on all sides, so the beef is no longer red on the outside, remove it from the pan. Add the flour to the butter and stir over low heat until it becomes a smooth paste. Stir in the mustard, beef stock, sour cream, and beef cubes, plus any red juice that may have gathered on the plate. Cook over moderately high heat until the sauce thickens, and serve.

In Russia, Stroganoff was never served over noodles, as it sometimes is in the West, but instead over shredded potatoes. Russians put potatoes in most everything, but we didn't. There is a nice sauce, however, if you want to have some crusty bread or sauté some grated potatoes, but with four courses of this kind of cuisine we decided to keep things light.

DESSERT
◆◆ PASKHA

Traditionally, this dessert was made in a mold and served on religious holidays, notably Easter. The molds were originally made of hand-carved wood, though now they are plastic with Russian Orthodox religious patterns on the side. If you are more secular—revolutionary or otherwise—an unused clay flowerpot works extremely well.

1 lemon
2 limes
2 cups sugar
½ cup water
2 sticks unsalted butter
1 cup sour cream

2½ cups confectioners' sugar
5 egg yolks
2 pounds farmer's cheese
2 splashes vanilla extract
2 splashes almond extract

Dice the peel of the lemon and limes and place in a pan with the sugar and water. Cook over low heat for 30 minutes and then allow to macerate at a very low heat for another hour.

Melt the butter in a pot, add the sour cream, and mix well. Add ¼ cup of the syrup from the candied peel and the confectioners' sugar and mix well. Then add 5 egg yolks and stir briskly over medium heat. Be careful not to let the heat get too high or the eggs will curdle, and keep the mixture moving until it slightly thickens.

Then pour into a mixer with the farmer's cheese. Add the vanilla extract, almond extract, and the candied diced peel. Stir on medium speed with a paddle until well mixed. Cover the inside of the flowerpot with a double layer of cheesecloth. Pour in the mixture and place the flowerpot in a bowl to catch the runoff. Keep for a day or two, periodically pouring the liquid out of the bottom of the bowl. When ready to serve, pull it out of the pot by the cheesecloth and hold it up for any last drippings through the cloth. Place it upside down on a plate and remove cheesecloth. Serve small slices, as it is extremely rich.

DRINK
◆ PISTACHIO WATER

The pistachio was Molokhovets's idea; the soda was mine.

½ pound shelled pistachio nuts
2 cups water

1 cup sugar
1 bottle club soda

Cook the shelled pistachios in boiling water with the sugar for a few minutes. Then puree in a food processor. Boil again for a few minutes and then strain, but allow some of the pistachio mush to stay. Chill a day or two, and when you are ready, strain it again and fill half the glass. Fill the rest with soda.

JAMAICA NIGHT

HINT: THE BOTANICAL GARDEN OF THE BRITISH EMPIRE.

The eighteenth-century British experimented with transplanting tropical vegetation from the Pacific to the fertile ground of Jamaica. The primary goal of what Gandhi liked to call the Brutish Empire was to find cheap nourishment for slave labor. The HMS *Bounty*, commanded by Captain William Bligh, was a famous example. It set sail for Tahiti in 1787 to pick up breadfruit plants, which were then to be taken to Jamaica. Breadfruit trees provide many large fruits whose meat seems starchy and filling; hence the name. Would this not be an inexpensive way, the British reasoned, to fill the bellies of the Africans laboring in the cane fields? That particular shipment never made it to Jamaica due to a now famous mutiny, but lush, mountainous Jamaica did become home to an enormous variety of tropical plants. And in fact Bligh, turned loose in a launch, incredibly crossed the Pacific and captained other ships, persecuted other sailors, and ultimately brought breadfruit to Jamaica and Saint Vincent. Today the fruit is a staple across most of the English-speaking Caribbean.

Many of the plants Jamaicans eat, and much of the food of our Jamaica Night, is not indigenous to the island. Neither the mango, the coconut, the sugar, the rice, the beans, the ginger, the lemons and limes, nor most of the spices are native to this small island. But they grow there now and are such a part of Jamaica that when Jamaican-born Claude McKay, a leading writer of the Harlem Renaissance, wanted to express

how he missed his island, he wrote about how the fruit in Harlem markets reminded him of home.

Of all the islands of the Caribbean that I visited regularly for the decade when I covered the region for the *Chicago Tribune*, there isn't one that I miss more than Jamaica. I was always based in Kingston, the port capital that is as tough a city as anywhere in the world. I spent a great deal of time on those burning-hot streets, meeting great musicians and hopeful young musicians and with the gangs that backed the JLP and the gangs that backed the PNP. That was the way it worked in Jamaica. A neighborhood was fiercely loyal to its party. I happened to be particularly friendly with a JLP street-gang gunman named Chubby, a sad man who never had any money or any hope or ever owned anything but a gun and often talked about how he wished he could be doing something else. One dark election night in Kingston when the pat-pat-pat of gunfire echoed through the city, the silhouette of a gang member with an M16 approached me with a menacing swagger. How glad I was to realize it was my friend Chubby. Since I left, I am told he died in a shootout, which is how most of the gang leaders end up.

I also knew the two party leaders, Edward Seaga and Michael Manley—a study in opposites. Seaga was part Scot, part Lebanese, rumored to have a black ancestor somewhere, but very white looking, which is unusual in

Jamaica. He was stiff and nervous and generally uncomfortable. I went with him to the slum that was his district in Kingston, Tivoli Garden, to attend all-night African religious ceremonies that he loved, where passionate African drumming lead people to become possessed by spirits while Eddie stiffly clapped his hands, never looking more white than there.

Manley was one of the most charming men I ever met, a natural politician, in fact born into it because his father, Norman, is considered the founding father of independent Jamaica. I used to go on the campaign trail with Michael. His car had a driver who could careen at ninety miles per hour on narrow winding country roads. Michael came to a town and got out of the car and it seemed that all of Jamaica screamed. No advance men to whip up enthusiasm were needed here. He walked through the village looking for shy people hiding behind doors and trees, tried to touch everyone in town—they would kiss his hand—and then he would be driven to the next town. I have met or covered a number of politicians with true charisma, including Spain's Felipe Gonzalez and Cuba's Fidel Castro, but Michael was one of the best, and when I reflected on what charisma is I concluded that it is an absolute and unshakable belief in yourself and your own ability to seduce.

Whenever I had enough of hot and tough Kingston I would explore Jamaica, one of the world's most beautiful islands, with its thickly forested mountains and fishing villages and farming communities and a coastline of thrilling beauty. Jamaica is one of the few islands—and the largest of them—that is completely surrounded on all sides by the smooth, warm, blue Caribbean Sea and is never touched by the open Atlantic. There is one long stretch of beach that is tourism at its most horrible and I rarely went there, but the rest of Jamaica has an incomparably beautiful coastline, some of it so remote that it still is home to the descendants of runaway slaves whose reinvented African culture still survives.

In 2008 *Food & Wine* magazine sent me back to Jamaica with chef Bradford Thompson and his Jamaican wife, Kerry-Ann Evans Thompson, to travel the back roads, shop for food, cook, and explore Jamaican cooking so that Brad could develop recipes. For our Jamaican Night, the crab rundown and the rice and peas were influenced by Brad's recipes, though with a few differences. The sauce for the jerk was based on Brad's, which in turn was based on a recipe from Kerry-Ann's family.

The jerk must marinate for 48 hours in the refrigerator, so make it two nights before. When you are ready to cook the evening of the dinner, open two coconuts. The water will be used for the rundown and rice and peas, and you can grate the coconut meat for the dessert.

BREAD
◆ BAMMY

This is the most Jamaican recipe here, because long before Europeans brought their flour and fruits there was cassava root. This is the original Jamaican bread. In Jamaica I usually eat it for breakfast. No matter, it was good with the rundown. This recipe will make six or seven bammy. If you have leftovers, you can store them for a few weeks. If they get hard, soak them in milk and heat them in a frying pan with melted butter.

1 thick, foot-long cassava root, peeled
    and grated

1½ tablespoons salt
¼ cup canola oil

Grab the grated cassava a fistful at a time and squeeze the juice out. Mix in the salt. Heat the oil in a frying pan. Grab the grated cassava, again a fistful at a time. This of course means that Talia makes smaller bammies than I do. Squeeze it again to remove a little more juice. Place it in the frying pan. In Jamaica, they have metal rings to make circular bammies, but you can make them free-form. They should be about 5 to 6 inches in diameter and between ¼ and ⅓ inch thick. You can do this by gently pressing on the blob you put in the pan with a Mexican bean masher until the desired thickness. When the bottom is a little golden, the root will start to steam. Turn it over with a spatula and lightly brown the other side.

Apparently the bammies reminded Talia of potato latkes, and she requested apple sauce with them. This would be good, but is not at all customary.

APPETIZER
◆◆ CRAB RUNDOWN

Rundown refers to the sauce being reduced; there are many types of rundown in Jamaica. Black crabs can be found along the south coast there, but most any kind of crabmeat would work. The curry in this recipe should be the colombo mixture (see columbo and curry, pp. 10–11, in On Sugar and Spice and French Guiana Night, p. 249).

¼ cup coconut oil (or canola oil if you want to be healthier, but it will have less flavor)

1 yellow onion, chopped

1-inch piece of ginger root, peeled and chopped

5 garlic cloves, peeled and chopped

1 tablespoon curry powder

1 tablespoon allspice

5 white cardamom seeds

1 tablespoon turmeric powder

1 tablespoon salt

4 turns of black pepper

2 large tomatoes, chopped

½ Scotch bonnet pepper (or a whole one if you like it hotter), veined, seeded, and minced

leaves from 3 sprigs oregano

1 coconut

1 14-ounce can of unsweetened coconut milk

1 pound crabmeat

Heat the oil in a frying pan and sauté the onion, ginger, and garlic for 5 minutes, stirring and not burning or browning. Add the curry powder, allspice, cardamom, turmeric, salt, and black pepper. Sauté and mix for a few minutes and then add the tomatoes and Scotch bonnet pepper. Continue sautéing until the tomatoes have softened a little and then add the oregano.

Add the water from the coconut along with the unsweetened coconut milk. Bring to a hard boil for 3 minutes and then turn down the heat to a slow simmer for about 20 minutes until the sauce has been reduced to about ⅓ the original volume.

Just before you are ready to serve, add the crabmeat and stir on low heat for about 3 minutes.

MAIN COURSE
◆◆ JERK CHICKEN

One of my favorite meals in Jamaica was at the Chelsea Jerk Center. Although in a relatively middle-class neighborhood of Kingston, this was a dreary place at night—a dark lot surrounded by chain-link fences and always full of people, cars, and long lines. Worth it, mon, worth it. There are two windows, one for chicken and one for pork, and at either window you could also get the corn fritters called festivals that are similar to what is known in the American South as hushpuppies. At the Jerk Center they wrap it all in newspapers, preferably the *Daily Gleaner*, which, whatever else may be said about it, is excellent for wrapping jerk. The other necessary ingredient is a cold bottle of Red Stripe beer, which is everywhere in Jamaica, though the street gangs prefer Guinness.

Jerk was originally and traditionally cooked in an open-pit fire. That's how it is made in the various jerk centers around the island—with a very spicy dry rub, and then it is barbecued, a method that appears to have come from West Africa and was preserved by the runaway slaves in the island's interior. Most people don't have an open-pit fire in their home, so this modified recipe will work better. It has that nice restaurant trick: it's really cooked ahead of time in the oven, so all you need to do before serving time is a quick grilling.

But you do need a two-day head start.

1 Scotch bonnet pepper, veined and seeded	3 garlic cloves
4 sprigs oregano	¼ cup dark brown sugar
4 green onions, chopped	¼ cup water
1 cup gold rum	1 tablespoon salt
1 tablespoon soy sauce	5 turns of black pepper
	6 chicken quarters

In a food processor puree the Scotch bonnet pepper with the oregano, green onions, rum, soy sauce, garlic, dark brown sugar, water, salt, and pepper.

Rub the mixture thoroughly on the chicken quarters. This is enough sauce for about 8 pieces, though actually we made 6. One piece per person is enough, but we cooked extra because it's always good the next day too. Place the chicken in an earthen or Pyrex baking dish, pour the rest of the mixture over it, and let it sit in the refrigerator for 2 nights, covered.

About 2 hours before you are serving the jerk, preheat the oven to 400 degrees, take the chicken out of the refrigerator and let sit for 10 or 15 minutes, and then bake it for 1 hour. Let it cool at least 10 to 20 minutes. Then put the chicken on a grill pan at the hottest temperature possible and grill on both sides so there are a few blackened marks.

VEGETABLES
◆ CALLALOO

There are two plants, both central to Caribbean cooking, that are often confused because they are both called callaloo. One refers to the broad thick leaves of the same plant that produces the dasheen root, which is also widely eaten in the Caribbean. While hiking on a volcano on the island of Montserrat that later erupted and buried the island in ash and lava, a local taught me how to fold the leaf to make a cup that could be used to scoop up drinking water. This plant, *Colocasia esculenta*, is more typical of the eastern Caribbean, from Antigua down to Grenada and Trinidad, than Jamaica. In Jamaica, callaloo usually refers to *Amaranthus viridis*, which has a more delicate leaf used in Jamaican cooking. Just a small side dish of callaloo lets you know you are in Jamaica. If you don't live near a Jamaican market, spinach is a good substitute.

½ pound callaloo or spinach
4 tablespoons butter
a pinch of salt

4 turns of black pepper
¼ teaspoon fresh grated nutmeg

If you have callaloo, discard the seeds from the top of leaves, wash thoroughly, boil for a few minutes until tender, drain thoroughly, toss in hot butter, and add the other ingredients.

If you use spinach, wash thoroughly, drain carefully, toss in hot butter until tender, and add other ingredients.

Callaloo

◆ RICE AND PEAS

This dish is everywhere in the Caribbean. Sometimes it is called peas and rice. I have been in restaurants where they actually gave you a choice between rice and peas and peas and rice, but I could never grasp the difference. The peas are sometimes beans and sometimes pigeon peas, an African transplant. Every country has its own variation on this dish, but Jamaican rice and peas is particularly nice because of the addition of coconut.

½ white onion, chopped
1-inch piece of ginger root, peeled and minced
¼ cup coconut oil
1 cup white rice

8 ounces canned red beans
½ Scotch bonnet pepper, seeded and deveined
1 coconut
8 ounces unsweetened coconut milk

Sauté the onion and ginger in coconut oil over low heat. After a few minutes add the rice and stir and sauté for 5 minutes. Add the canned beans. Goya's habichuelas rojas pequeñas work well. Add the Scotch bonnet pepper, the water from the coconut, and the coconut milk. (Save the coconut meat for the dessert.) This should be enough liquid to completely cover the rice; if not, add a little water, but not too much. The liquid should extend no more than ½ inch above the rice. Cook without stirring, covered, until all that remains of the liquid is a few bubbles on the surface. Turn off the heat, do not stir, and cover the pot. Wait 10 minutes, then discard the pepper and fluff the rice with a fork.

DESERT
◆◆ COCONUT LIME MANGO TART

Talia was passionate about this dessert. I basically made it up. The lemon-lime coconut custard is based on a recipe from Caroline Sullivan's 1893 cookbook, *The Jamaica Cookery Book*, the first book of Jamaican recipes ever published. She suggested that the custard would be good in a crust, and I decided to bake it in a French tart pan with a ripe mango on top.

THE CRUST

2 sticks butter, cut into 8 pieces
2 cups flour
1 tablespoon salt
1 cup sugar

1 cup grated coconut
a splash of vanilla extract
1 whole egg

In mixer with a dough hook, add the butter to the flour and work on medium–high speed until the flour has the texture of coarse meal. Add the salt, sugar, and coconut. When thoroughly mixed, add the vanilla and the egg and keep the hook turning until a dough ball forms on it. Press the dough into a 9-inch tart pan, pressing it thin on the bottom and pushing it against the ridges of the outer ring so that it sticks out above it. Curl the edges back into the pan.

THE FILLING

2 sticks butter
2 cups confectioners' sugar
4 eggs
1½ cups grated coconut

2 limes
1 lemon
1 ripe mango, peeled and cut into long
    strips

Preheat oven to 350 degrees. Melt the butter with the confectioners' sugar over low heat and pour the mixture into a mixer with a whip. Beat it thick and add the eggs one a time while continuing to beat until the mixture is thick, whitish, and frothy. Pour into a mixing bowl and add the grated coconut. Mix well and add the zest of 2 limes, the zest of 1 lemon, and the juice of 1 lime. Mix thoroughly and pour into crust. Arrange the mango strips around the tart in a sunburst pattern.

Bake for about 40 minutes or until custard is solid and crust is lightly browned—but not too dark.

DRINK
◆ GINGER ALE

Melt equal parts sugar and water over moderate heat with about six slices of fresh ginger root. Let the mixture steep for a few minutes on the heat, then remove from heat and let it slowly cool. Mix this syrup with cold club soda—ice if you like—and stir.

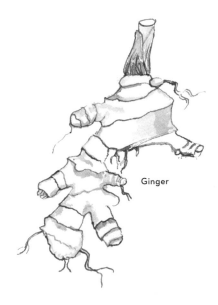

Ginger

SRI LANKA NIGHT

HINT: A TEA ISLAND.

This hint was too easy: Marian got it on her first guess. She said Ceylon, which is what this island was called when it was a British colony. In 1972 it reverted to its ancient name, Sri Lanka. It is the oldest continuously Buddhist nation in the world. The name Ceylon has been associated with tea since 1824, when the British brought the plants from China. One million people out of a population of twenty million earn their living in the tea industry, which is the leading export for this island nation.

Their food has much in common with parts of southern India, with coconuts and spices being central ingredients.

The green chili pepper used in the following recipes is a small, medium-hot type favored in this part of Asia. You could substitute a small Mexican serrano, or part of one, according to taste. A number of these recipes were based, with significant variations, on the recipes of Peter Kuruvita from his handsome book *Serendip: My Sri Lankan Kitchen*.

Green chile

APPETIZER
◆◆ FISH BALLS AND MINT SAMBAL

Consider substituting toasted sesame oil for the cooking oil in this dish. It is not authentic but gives a wonderful flavor. Fresh curry leaves are used a lot in Sri Lankan food and are available in Asian stores or online. They impart a subtle flavor, good if you can find them, but it's okay to omit them if you can't. Mint Sambal should be made first so fish can be served hot.

FISH BALLS

½ pound yellowfin tuna or boned
    bonita, cut into slices
2 medium-size thin-skinned potatoes,
    quartered
a generous pinch of salt
4 turns of black pepper
½ yellow onion, minced
¼ cup sesame oil

4 curry leaves
1 teaspoon powdered cumin
1 long green chili pepper, deveined
    and seeded
1 cup flour
3 eggs, beaten
1 cup bread crumbs
½ cup canola oil

Place the fish in a steamer with the potatoes. Steam for about 10 minutes until potato is soft, then mash the mixture in a bowl with salt and black pepper.

While the fish is steaming, sauté the onion in oil. Add the curry leaves and cumin. Sauté a few minutes, then remove curry leaves and add onion mixture to mashed fish along with the chili pepper. Mix well and form little patties 1½ inches in diameter and ½ inch thick. Dredge them in flour, dip them in beaten eggs, coat them with bread crumbs, and fry in hot canola oil until golden on both sides. Serve hot with a small bowl of mint sambal.

MINT SAMBAL

1 cup fresh mint leaves
½ white onion, chopped
3 slices fresh ginger root, peeled and
    chopped
2 garlic cloves, peeled

1 long green chili pepper, deveined
    and seeded
¼ cup grated coconut
1 lime
2 tablespoons water

Place all ingredients in a food processor. Spin blade until mixture is well minced but not pureed.

MAIN COURSE
◆ SQUID CURRY

1 pound squid
½ teaspoon fennel seeds
1 tablespoon powdered cumin
2 tablespoons powdered turmeric
1 teaspoon red chili powder
3 long green chili peppers, minced
2 teaspoons powdered coriander
½ teaspoon fenugreek seed

5 turns of black pepper
½ cup ghee (See On Fats and Oils, p. 6, and India Night, p. 238)
½ yellow onion, sliced in thin rings
5 curry leaves
juice of 1 lime
6 ounces coconut milk

Slice squid bodies into rings and put them, along with the tentacles, into a bowl. Add the fennel seeds, cumin, turmeric, chili powder, chili peppers, coriander, fenugreek, and black pepper.

Pour ghee into a skillet and heat. Add onion and curry leaves. Sauté for a few minutes and then add squid and spices. Sauté while stirring with a wooden spoon for 5 minutes. Then add lime juice and coconut milk. Cook on high heat while stirring until liquid is reduced by half. Remove curry leaves and serve.

Squid

VEGETABLE

◆ STIR-FRIED SNOW PEAS

¾ pound snow peas
½ cup ghee
½ yellow onion, chopped
5 curry leaves
2 garlic cloves, chopped

1 long green chili pepper, deveined
  and seeded
2 tablespoons Madras curry (see On
  Sugar and Spice, p. 11)
juice of 1 lime
2 generous pinches of salt

Snap the ends off the peas and pull downward on the straight side to remove stems and strings.

In a skillet of hot ghee, sauté all the ingredients except for the snow peas for a few minutes. Then add the snow peas and stir just a few minutes, until they become bright green.

DESSERT
◆ WATALAPPEN

This is a Sri Lanka classic. You cannot make this dish without palm sugar, a dark sugar made from coconut palms, which is surprisingly easy to find in stores that carry a variety of sugars, Asian specialty stores, or online. (See sugar in On Sugar and Spice, p. 15.)

1 pound palm sugar
¾ cup water
¼ teaspoon freshly grated nutmeg
¼ teaspoon powdered green
    cardamom
¼ teaspoon powdered cinnamon

¼ teaspoon ground cloves
a splash of vanilla extract
5 eggs
6 ounces coconut milk
1 handful raw cashews

Preheat oven to 350 degrees. Dissolve the palm sugar in ¾ cup water, stirring on low heat. Remove from heat when completely dissolved and add nutmeg, cardamom, cinnamon, ground cloves, and vanilla extract.

In the mixer, beat eggs with whip attachment, slowly adding sugar mixture. Add coconut milk. Pour into an ovenproof dish. Place in a roasting pan so that the baking dish is about half covered with water. Bake for 20 minutes.

While it is baking, chop well a handful of raw cashews. A cashew, by the way, is not a nut but the seed of an edible fruit. Put the chopped cashews under a broiler and watch closely. Take them out when they brown and before they blacken. Sprinkle on top of the custard. Continue baking until set, about 40 minutes more. Serve hot or cold.

Cashew
fruits

SWEETS
◆ COCONUT ROCKS

A children's favorite, these are a bright pink by virtue of industrial food coloring, a product that always makes me nervous. Ours are dyed with a slightly less bright but less toxic beet juice, which can be made simply by boiling a cut-up red beet.

1 pound sugar
7 ounces whole milk
1 teaspoon cardamom powder

1 pound grated coconut
beet juice

Dissolve the sugar in the milk by stirring gently over low heat. When completely dissolved, add cardamom. Then boil the mixture over high heat, stirring occasionally, until a drop in a glass of cold water forms a soft ball that you can roll on your fingertips. Then quickly add coconut and mix well. Cut off the heat. Take half the mixture, pile it on a well-greased baking sheet, and with the gentle tapping of a Mexican bean masher (a greased spatula would also work) level it to a half-inch slab. Add enough beet juice to the remainder so that when mixed it turns pink. Place it on top of the flattened mixture and again gently tap it flat. After it cools, cut into squares.

DRINKS
◆ KOTHAMALLI

I hesitated to serve this with a meal since in India and Sri Lanka it is considered a cold remedy. Why drink medicine to accompany a meal? But it seemed a delicious concoction. And then the night before Sri Lanka Night (Sri Lanka Eve?), Talia came down with a cold. She reported feeling better after sipping kothamalli, but Marian and I also found it to be a very pleasant infusion.

3 tablespoons coriander seeds
2 sticks cinnamon
3 slices ginger root

water
honey

Combine ingredients in a small pot of water. Simmer at a low boil for about 20 minutes. Serve with honey.

◆ EARL GREY TEA

Earl Grey is a black tea mixed with oil from bergamot, a citrus related to an orange. It was invented in Ceylon about 1830 and named after the prime minister of England at the time. The best Earl Grey is made from orange pekoe leaves, a black tea, picked from a single Sri Lanka estate and mixed by hand with bergamot oil. Beware of teas blended from various estates—these teas generally don't specify the estate—and sprayed with synthetic citrus oils.

Bring ¾ cup of water to just under a boil. Pour into a teacup with a large basket of loose tea leaves to give the tea lots of room. Let steep a few minutes, according to taste. Too long and the tea will become bitter. Remove the basket and save. It can be used again to steep a second cup.

BELGIUM NIGHT

HINT: A COUNTRY MANUFACTURED TO CREATE A NEUTRAL SPACE BETWEEN POWERFUL WARRING NATIONS.

Americans often love Europe for its age, its history, the sense of ancient nations with long-standing traditions. But Belgium as a nation is younger than the United States. The Romans had a province of its colony of Gaul called Gallia Belgica in what is now Belgium, but there was never a separate nation of Belgium until 1830, when the Catholic southern part of the Netherlands rebelled against the Protestant north and broke away. With the strong encouragement of the British, a new nation was created. To the British, who had often been at war with both the Netherlands and France, the idea of a nearby foothold on the Continent that was not controlled by either of its adversaries was very appealing. The new state was to be a buffer to keep the French from invading northward, as Napoleon had done until his final defeat in Waterloo in what is now Belgium.

But there was a problem. The Belgians were not one people but three. In the north are the Flemish, who speak a dialect of Dutch. The Dutch say that Flemish is far more "pure" than their own evolved language, which has incorporated many words from French and German and English and even Yiddish. In the south is Wallonia, where people (known as Walloons) speak a dialect of French. But in eastern Wallonia, they speak German. Belgium was divided into four regions: German speaking, French speaking, Flemish speaking, and Brussels, the capital city that is in the Dutch region but is officially bilingual—French and Flemish.

The Flemish have kept their dialect of Dutch, but Wallonian French has almost vanished and been taken over by French, though with a slightly different accent. There is open animosity between the French and Flemish speakers. The French ran the country for more than a century, during which time the French language was a prerequisite for government jobs—that is, most good jobs. But the Flemish have a far faster-growing population and there are far more Flemish today, which has put them in a position of power.

Although a fairly new country, Belgium has a lot of very old folk festivals, parades, and processions such as one featuring the Gilles, costumed characters in the town of Binch who throw oranges. But the darkest, most embarrassing annual event happened in Diksmuide. Belgium has a troubled history with Germany. Invaded in World War I, forty thousand Belgians died holding the trenches outside of Diksmuide, a Flemish town that was destroyed in the battle. The fact that Flemish soldiers were led to this slaughter by French-speaking officers who could not even communicate with them is one of the most bitter roots of a hostile Flemish nationalist movement. In World War II the Nazis played the Flemish card, telling Flemish nationalists that they were "Aryans" like them, and pro-Nazi rituals were held in Diksmuide.

In contemporary times this town holds an annual remembrance of the World War I battle that has become the site for an annual gathering of neo-Nazis.

I believe I was one of the first reporters to cover it—or at least to make it to the end unharmed. Previously journalists had been severely beaten and chased out of town. But strangely, these journalists had always chosen to argue with the Nazis, which is an odd approach to journalism. Not only out of professional comportment but because some of these Nazis were extremely large and had tattoos on their shaved heads and were generally scary looking, I resolved not to argue with them and it turned out they loved a journalist who would actually listen to them and take notes on their unbelievably ignorant, outrageously racist, and, to be honest, very stupid theories. There were not only Flemish at the Diksmuide event but also Walloons, as well as people from France, Holland, Britain, Spain, Italy, and even a few from the United States. Just a big international Nazi beer fest.

I lived in Belgium for a few months in 1980, after living in Paris, where I wrote for the *International Herald Tribune*. I was starting a new job as an investigative reporter. Brussels was not Paris. Its most famous statue was of a boy urinating, pissing on Brussels. The city had been largely ruined years earlier to accommodate the 1958 World's Fair. Highways crisscrossed the city, making driving efficient but destroying neighborhoods, most of which were concentrated on a single ethnicity. There were French neighborhoods and Flemish neighborhoods and immigrant neighborhoods. I lived in Saint-Gilles, a Spanish neighborhood near the center of town, where even the commerce in the shops and markets was conducted mostly in Spanish, and since I had no desire to get embroiled in the French-Dutch feud, I also spoke Spanish in the neighborhood.

You could not tell by looking or even by knowing someone's name whether they were Flemish or French. If you spoke to people in the wrong language, they would be offended and might refuse to do the interview. A handy trick for an American: I would explain in French that I was an American and ask if they spoke English. It they were Wallonian, they would say that they didn't, and they would be pleased that I spoke French. If they were Flemish, they almost always did speak English and were pleased that I did not propose French. But all this was going to get tiresome.

The principal employers in Brussels were the European Union—then the European Economic Community, whose capital was in Brussels—and the North Atlantic Treaty Organization, also headquartered in Brussels. A city of bureaucrats—Eurocrats, in fact—and highways. I was missing Paris.

My small apartment in Saint-Gilles had a wood-burning fireplace, the only one I have ever had, and I thought I would enjoy it but I found that after buying the logs it bothered me to burn them up—some kind of urbanite confusion, no doubt.

My favorite neighborhoods, though, were Flemish, because they had dark wooden taverns where people drank thick local beer, more sour than bitter, and ate french fries dipped in variously seasoned mayonnaises, occasionally with mussels or sausage. These cafés reminded me of Vincent Van Gogh's first great painting, *The Potato Eaters*. The cafés looked dank and poor but also exuded a warmth and sense of family.

About french fries—they are Belgian, probably Flemish, and known everywhere as frites. The French are contemptuous of Belgians and like to tell jokes in which they are shown as dumb and backward. These are called frite jokes, and the French pejorative for a Belgian is a *frite*. When somebody French uses this pejorative, I like to point out that in America we call frites "*french* fries."

For an article I was working on, I had to make regular trips to Mons—or was it Bergen? In Belgium most towns have a French name and a Dutch name that do not necessarily resemble each other. So when I left Brussels I was in the Flemish region and followed signs to Bergen, but eventually I crossed into Wallonia, where there were no signs to Bergen but only signs to Mons.

When I finished the article, the managing editor told me the paper couldn't publish it because "it would get us in a lot of trouble." They didn't seem to know it, but they did not want an investigative journalist. With great joy I got on a train for Paris's Gare du Nord. I had only spent a little more than three months living in Brussels and I have not been back since.

My best memory of Belgium is the food—not just frites, although there are great frites and sauces—but game from the Ardennes and fish from the coast and pastry and the best handmade filled chocolates, *pralines,* in all the world. So while I might not jump at another chance to go to Belgium, I was very happy when Talia's finger landed at that spot on the globe.

APPETIZER
◆ MOULES AUX CHICON

I may have completely invented this dish, but cooked endive, butter, and mussels are ubiquitous staples in Belgium. Like a Belgian town, Belgian endive (escarole) has a completely different name in Wallonia and in Flanders. In Flemish it is *witloof,* which means "white root," referring to the pale color that the escarole plant takes on when grown shaded and picked young, before the leaves have a chance to curl. In Wallonia but not in France, it is called *chicon,* "little chicory." Chicory is also used to refer to the mature plant with green curly leaves and roots that used to be ground up to stretch cheap coffee, an unfortunate budget saver that has vanished from Europe but is maintained as a local treat in New Orleans.

Before steaming, discard mussels that are open, and after steaming. discard the ones that haven't opened. Both are signs that the mussel has died—of what, you don't want to know.

1 pound mussels
juice of 1 lemon
4 garlic cloves, peeled and chopped
3 tablespoons butter

4 heads endive (5 if small), root
    ends cut off, sliced vertically in
    spaghetti-like strips
a large pinch of salt
5 turns of black pepper
leaves from 3 sprigs of thyme

Steam the mussels, then remove them from their shells and put them in a bowl with the lemon juice.

Sauté the garlic in the butter in a skillet. Add the endive, salt, pepper, and the thyme leaves and sauté until the endive is wilted. Add the mussels and stir well, sautéing for another few minutes.

Endive

MAIN COURSE
◆ WATERZOOI

This does not have two names, only a Flemish one that means "boiling water." The dish is from the charming Flemish city of Ghent—or, if you are following signs from Wallonia, Gand. Ghent is a medieval city where the Lys River meets the Scheldt. Waterzooi originally was made from the freshwater fish caught in those rivers. But since Belgium was the first industrialized nation on continental Europe, its rivers became polluted, and soon the river fish became rare and waterzooi became a chicken dish. But it is also frequently made from the white-fleshed bottom fish of the Atlantic. We chose halibut, which technically made this dish *Gentse Waterzooi van Tarbot*—halibut waterzooi in the Ghent style. The fish stock takes a few hours to cook, so you may want to make it the day before. By any name it is a colorful dish, white with orange and green.

FISH STOCK

3 tablespoons butter
2 small porgies or other small fish, whole but gutted and scaled
3 shrimp, whole with heads if you can get them
2 cups dry white wine
5 garlic cloves

4 sprigs thyme
3 carrots, scraped
1 yellow onion, cut in half
1 leek, well washed and chopped
3 tablespoons salt
5 turns of black pepper
6 mussels

Sauté the porgy in butter at the bottom of a stockpot. When browned on both sides, add the shrimp and white wine and bring to a strong boil for 3 minutes. Reduce heat. Add the remaining ingredients and simmer for 3 or 4 hours. Strain. Discard the leftover solids; the flavor will be cooked out of them. Our cat, Duende, though, enjoys a bit of the fish. In fact, if you make fish stock often, you really should have a cat.

WATERZOOI

1½ pounds halibut
2 tablespoons butter
1 leek, chopped
1 large shallot, peeled and chopped
2 cups dry white wine
1 pint light cream

3 egg yolks
1 celery root, scraped and cut into
    narrow strips
4 carrots, peeled and cut into narrow
    strips
1 bunch parsley, chopped

Sauté the pieces of halibut in butter. Add the leek and shallot, then after a minute add enough fish stock to cover and poach the fish.

Remove the poached fish from the stock. Add the white wine and boil until somewhat reduced. Add the light cream and boil until reduced by half. Then add the egg yolks, whisking rigorously over low heat until the sauce thickens. Add the celery root and carrots and continue heating the sauce over low temperature, moving it with the whisk for about 3 more minutes until the vegetables are bright and lightly cooked. Pour over the fish and sprinkle with parsley.

DESSERT
◆ TART AU SUCRE

This is a very popular Belgian dessert. Make it with the darkest brown sugar you can find.

1 batch short pastry dough (see Basic Recipes, p. 23)
3 eggs
1½ pints heavy cream
a splash of vanilla extract

1½ cups muscovado (see On Sugar and Spice, p. 15)
¼ cup turbinado (see On Sugar and Spice, p. 15)
4 tablespoons butter

Preheat oven to 350 degrees. Press the dough into a 9-inch pie plate. In a mixer, whip together the eggs, heavy cream, vanilla, and muscovado. Whip thoroughly and pour into the pie crust. Dot the top with butter and sprinkle with turbinado, which is not the darkest but has large, tough crystals that will preserve a little of their crunchiness in baking. Bake for 1 hour or until the pie, when jiggled, is solid.

DRINKS

Belgium has very distinct beers known as lambic, made in or near Brussels. They are cloudy and sour. Supposedly they are fermented with wild yeast from the valley in which Brussels is situated, then refermented in the bottle. My personal favorite is Geuze, a thick sour beer that I could not find in the US. I could find Krick, which is made with morello cherries. This is the only traditional fruit lambic; others that have appeared on the market, such as currant, peach, apricot, plum, raspberry, et cetera, tend to be made with fruit syrups and are best avoided.

Since we were drinking cherry beer, I thought Talia should have a fizzy cherry drink as well, so we mixed a quart of cherry juice with the juice of 1 lemon and filled a glass halfway with the mixture, then topped it off with club soda.

ETHIOPIA NIGHT

HINT: THE WORLD'S MOST POPULOUS LANDLOCKED COUNTRY.

This surprising fact has only been true since 1993 when, after thirty years of war, Eritrea became an independent nation and Ethiopia lost its coastline.

Ethiopia Night came about when Talia and I were visiting my old friend, publisher George Gibson, in his office in the prow of the Flatiron Building. In addition to its unique shape and dramatic urban vistas, George's office had a great globe that spun not only east-west but north-south, so that spinning it afforded a perfect random chance. He asked to choose a country and his finger landed not far north or far south but near the equator, on Ethiopia.

I have never been to Ethiopia, though I have eaten Ethiopian food on a number of occasions. There is a similarity to the food that might make it tiresome day after day: red onions, garlic, ginger, nigella seeds, and berbere (see On Sugar and Spice, p. 8) are included in almost everything.

But for one meal it offers in a single course a rich variety of seasonings, deep flavor, wonderful color, and assorted textures. This meal combines a chunky deep maroon color, a mushy bright orange, and a crisp, bright green. It is a beautiful table. There is no dessert because, though I searched far and wide, I failed to find any dessert in the least bit Ethiopian.

MAIN COURSE
◆◆◆ INJERA

The only difficult thing about cooking Ethiopian food is making injera. It is also the most important, because it is served with all food, which is scooped up with these spongy pancakes instead of flatware. The sour taste of the injera adds a flavor accent to all the food.

Injera is made with teff, a grain grown in northern Ethiopia. The word *teff* comes from a word in Amharic, the Ethiopian language, meaning "lost," because the grains are so tiny that if dropped they are impossible to find. This makes it a highly portable grain, since enough to seed an entire field can be carried in a very small pouch. Teff, a staple in Ethiopia for perhaps as long as six thousand years, was largely unknown outside of Ethiopia for most of this time. But because it is gluten-free and rich in protein, it has become a star of the health-food industry and is now easy to obtain in health-food stores or online.

4 cups teff	3-4 tablespoons butter
5 cups water	

Mix the teff and water in a bowl and beat with a whisk until well mixed and foaming. Cover the bowl tightly and let sit unrefrigerated for about 24 hours. This leads to the fermentation process that creates the sour taste.

Melt the butter in a large skillet and cover with a thick layer of ladled batter. Once it starts to form bubbles, which should take less than 1 minute, cover the skillet and cook another 30 seconds so that the surface is not liquid but still has a sheen. Then turn the skillet upside down over a plate to drop out the pancake and begin another one.

◆ SEGA WAT (MEAT)

1 red onion, thinly sliced
3 tablespoons olive oil
6 garlic cloves, peeled and chopped
1½ pounds boned leg of lamb, cubed
a generous pinch of salt
5 turns of black pepper
1 sprig fresh rosemary
3 sprigs fresh thyme

2 plum tomatoes, chopped
1 red bell pepper, chopped
1 shallot, chopped
2 cups red wine
2 tablespoons coarse seed mustard
juice of ½ lemon
1½ tablespoons berbere
2 hard-boiled eggs, halved vertically

Sauté the red onion in the olive oil. Add the garlic, lamb, salt, and pepper. Brown the lamb on all sides. Add the rosemary pulled apart off the main stem, plus the thyme, tomatoes, red pepper, and shallot. Add the red wine, mustard, lemon juice, and berbere and simmer for 40 minutes over medium heat. Before serving, add the hard-boiled eggs.

◆ MISER WAT (VEGETABLE)

1 red onion, chopped
3 tablespoons olive oil
6 garlic cloves, peeled and chopped
2 tablespoons ginger root, peeled and
    minced
2 tablespoons berbere

1 teaspoon nigella seeds
2 teaspoons powdered cardamom
a generous pinch of salt
5 turns of black pepper
8 ounces red lentils
6 cups water

Sauté the red onion in olive oil. Add the remaining ingredients. Simmer over medium heat, stirring occasionally until the lentils are soft, about 30 minutes.

◆ ZELBA GOMEN (VEGETABLE)

½ red onion, thinly sliced
¼ cup olive oil
3 garlic cloves, peeled and chopped
3 tablespoons fresh ginger root,
    peeled and minced

½ jalapeño pepper, veined and
    seeded
a large pinch of salt
5 turns of black pepper
1 large bunch kale, big stalks removed
    and well chopped

Sauté the onion in olive oil. Add the garlic, ginger, jalapeño, salt, and pepper, and then the kale. Stir until the kale turns bright green and begins to wilt.

DRINK
◆ ETHIOPIAN SPICE DRINK

1 quart water
8 cardamom seeds
2 tablespoons nigella seeds

4 thick slices fresh ginger root
juice of 1 lemon
honey

Combine ingredients and simmer 30 minutes. Add honey to taste. Strain and chill.

AUSTRIA NIGHT

HINT: THE EASTERN KINGDOM.

The name of Austria in German, Öster-reich, means "eastern kingdom." It has never been entirely clear if Austria is western or central European. While the country is mostly German speaking, Croatian, Slovenian, and Hungarian are also recognized as official languages. Austria was the only country to negotiate its way out of the Soviet bloc, and during the Cold War it was a kind of neutral territory where the two superpowers could meet. The capital, Vienna, a city of great music and gorgeous pastry, has a darker side of intrigue. For me Carol Reed's 1949 film noir *The Third Man*, written by Graham Greene, captures the city better than anything else. When I find myself in a dark cobblestone passageway I can't help hearing that zither music in my mind . . .

Pretzel

Away from the plains, the rolling green hills and high glacier-studded peaks of the rest of Austria look like a different world, though it is still the land of Mozart, pastry, and whipped cream. Salzburg and neighboring towns such as Hallein and Halstatt all have names meaning "salt town," and ancient salt-mining equipment as well as ancient salt miners themselves have been found in the area perfectly preserved in the mines, trapped in cave-ins dating back thousands of years. One of the mines is such a curiosity that its owners have decided there is more money to be made selling tickets to tourists than in mining salt, so it is open to the public but closed to mining. Among the stops of interest in that particular cavernous, dark, underground maze are slides that the workers used to drop from one level to another. Slipping down these slides, some with a drop of a hundred feet, is deemed such a delight that a trip wire sets off a camera and you can buy pictures of yourself descending. The descent filled me with such horror, which apparently showed on my face, that the tour operators refused to even sell me my photo.

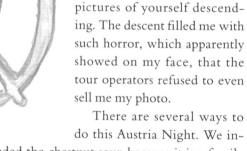

There are several ways to do this Austria Night. We included the chestnut soup because it is a family favorite and a great Austrian dish, but we did not make it on Austria Night because there was too much food. But you could make it as an alternative to the fish. Or you could do salad, soup, and fish and then skip the meat course and go straight to dessert. Or if you made small portions you could have an Austrian feast with salad, soup, fish, meat, and dessert.

The pretzel needs to be started the day before.

BREAD
◆◆ LAUGENBREZEN (BOILED PRETZEL)

These thick pretzels are boiled like a bagel, with a similar result, but then crisped on the outside in the oven. They are a wonderful accompaniment to almost anything. The following recipe makes four or five large pretzels.

When dishes call for coarse salt, Americans have the habit of using kosher salt, which has large, flat crystals for kosherizing meat. But in recent years large, round crystal salts from Britain, France, Spain, and many other countries have become available.

3 tablespoons olive oil
2½ cups tepid water
a generous pinch of salt
3½ teaspoons sugar

4¼ cups flour
1 tablespoon dry yeast
1 tablespoon baking soda
coarse salt

Mix the oil and water in a bowl. In a mixer, combine the salt, sugar, and flour, then add the yeast. With a dough hook attachment at a moderate speed, add the oil and water to the flour mixture. After a few minutes, increase the speed and keep mixing until it becomes a ball.

Roll the dough out about 1 inch thick on a baking sheet. Dust it lightly with flour and cover it with a moist towel. Leave it in a warm place and let it rise, which should take about 1 hour. Then cover with plastic wrap and refrigerate overnight.

The next day, cut the dough into strips about 1½ inches wide. On a floured counter, roll each strip until more than 2 feet long. Make a loop in the center about midway, crossing the 2 ends, and then take each end down and press it into the bottom of the loop.

Cover a baking sheet with parchment paper. Boil a large open pot of water with the baking soda added. Place each pretzel in, one at a time, boil it for a few seconds, and then turn it over and continue boiling until it floats to the surface. This complete process should be less than 30 seconds.

Remove each pretzel with a slotted spoon and place on the baking sheet. Let them rise for about 1 hour.

Preheat oven to 350 degrees. Sprinkle the pretzels with coarse salt and bake them until brown, which should take less than 30 minutes. You can serve them cold, but if you can time it right, they are very nice still warm.

SOUP
◆ MARONENSUPPE (CHESTNUT SOUP)

This is a favorite dish of Talia's, which we order in the wintertime at Café Sabarsky, Chef Kurt Gutenbrunner's charming Viennese restaurant in Neue Galerie, the little museum to Austrian and German art near the Metropolitan Museum of Art in New York. We have greatly simplified Gutenbrunner's more elegant recipe to make this an easy dish to make. We did not use whole raw chestnuts because roasting and peeling them is a recipe for madness.

½ pound mixed mushrooms, such as oyster, shiitake, crimini, or chanterelle
1½ cups water
2 tablespoons butter
1 cup celeriac, peeled and chopped
½ pound peeled canned or jarred chestnuts
a pinch of salt

3 turns of ground black pepper
½ tablespoon sugar
2½ cups chicken stock (see Basic Recipes, p. 24, or buy)
1 cup 2 percent milk
1¼ cups heavy cream
a pinch of freshly grated nutmeg
1 sprig fresh Italian parsley

Cover the mushrooms with water, slowly simmer for 1 hour, and then strain to get the broth. Save the mushrooms for later, perhaps for an omelet in the morning.

In a large pot melt the butter and add the celeriac. Sauté, stirring, for a few minutes but don't brown. Then add the chestnuts, salt, pepper, and sugar. Continue stirring until mixture starts to caramelize. Add the mushroom and chicken stocks, bring to a boil, and then immediately slow the heat to a simmer, add milk and cook for 15 minutes. Then add the cream and the nutmeg and cook for another 5 minutes. Ladle into soup bowls and add one or two parsley leaves for color.

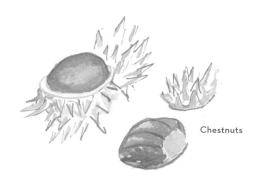

Chestnuts

APPETIZER
◆ FORELLE MIT SCHNITTLAUCHEN (TROUT WITH CHIVES)

3 trout
½ cup flour
3 tablespoons butter
a large pinch of salt

juice of 1 lemon
½ cup dry white wine
1 stick cold butter, cubed
fresh chives, chopped

Dust the trout fillets in flour and sauté them in 3 tablespoons butter with a pinch of salt and a sprinkling of fresh lemon juice. Lightly brown the fish on both sides and remove the fillets to plates. Add the white wine to the remaining butter and cook it down on high heat. Then turn off the heat and let it cool a few minutes. Add the cubed cold butter and stir with a wooden spoon until it has melted and formed an opaque sauce. Pour the sauce over the fish and sprinkle with chopped fresh chives.

SALAD
◆ CELERIAC AND APPLE SALAD

Celeriac, sometimes called celery root, is in the celery family but is not the root of the celery we eat. It is a different vegetable, cultivated for its bulbous root. It is good raw and crispy, but for some reason Austrians almost always cook it.

1 lemon
1 cup celeriac, peeled and cut into matchstick-size pieces
1 teaspoon sugar
1 large crisp apple, peeled and cut into matchstick-size pieces

1 cucumber, peeled and split horizontally
a pinch of salt
2 turns of ground black pepper
¼ cup grape-seed oil
1 sprig parsley

With a zester, scrape the zest off the lemon and set it aside.

Place the cut-up celeriac in a pan covered with water with the juice of ½ lemon and sugar. Simmer for about 3 minutes. It should not be cooked completely limp. Let it cool.

Add the celeriac to a bowl with the cut apple. Scrape the inside of the cucumber with the tip of a spoon to remove seeds, then slice the 2 halves into crescents and add them to the bowl. Add salt, black pepper, grape-seed oil, a few parsley leaves, and the lemon zest.

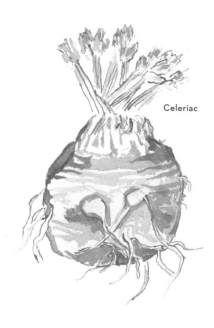

Celeriac

MAIN COURSE
◆◆ GEFÜLLTE KALBSBRUST (STUFFED VEAL)

1 pound chestnuts, roasted and peeled
    (or jarred)
1 sprig fresh rosemary
1 sprig fresh thyme
1 sprig fresh oregano
1 shallot, minced
5–6 wild mushrooms
a generous pinch of salt
½ pound stale bread, chopped
about 1 cup light cream

3 whole eggs
5 turns of black pepper
about 8 brussels sprouts
about 8 pearl onions, peeled
about 5 carrots, peeled and cut into
    strips
a 5-pound breast of veal, deboned by
    the butcher, leaving a pocket for
    stuffing

Preheat oven to 400 degrees.

Slash, roast, cool, and painstakingly peel the chestnuts—or you can get the same results by buying a jar of roasted and peeled chestnuts. Add them in a large mixing bowl to the leaves of the rosemary sprig, the thyme, and the oregano. Add the shallot, wild mushrooms (whatever is available—I used chanterelles), salt, and the chopped stale bread. Add enough light cream to cover the bread. Let soak 30 minutes and mix well with your hands. Add the eggs and pepper. Mix well and pack tightly into the veal's pocket.

Place the stuffed veal in a roasting pan and arrange around the meat the brussels sprouts, onions, and carrots. Roast for 2 hours.

DESSERT
◆◆ LINZERTORTE

It was not easy for us to decide on a dessert, because Austria is truly the land of desserts. I have tasted linzertorten in Vienna, in Salzburg, even in Linz, where it was created. It is always a little different. I have seen it with red currants, with the raspberry preserves mixed with applesauce, with almonds instead of hazelnuts. When I was a pastry maker I did a lot of experimenting with this dessert and I truly think this is the best linzertorte, although whether it is the most authentic . . .

½ pound hazelnuts
2 cups flour
3 tablespoons powdered cinnamon
1 teaspoon powdered cloves
2 sticks cold butter, cubed

2 cups sugar
2 eggs
6 ounces fresh raspberries
about 8 ounces raspberry preserves

Roast the hazelnuts on a sheet in an oven or, better, in a toaster oven with a window so you can watch. Set to broil and as soon as the skins brown—do not let them blacken—take them out and let them cool.

Preheat the oven to 350 degrees. Rub off the hazelnut skins by placing 4 or 5 at a time on your flat palm and rubbing your hands together in a circular motion. Powder them in a food processor, then place with the flour, cinnamon, and cloves in a mixer with a dough hook. Mix in the cold butter cubes until the dough takes on the texture of coarse meal. Add the sugar. Mix well. Add the eggs one at a time, continuing to mix.

After thoroughly mixed, flour your fingers and press half of the dough into a tart pan. Place the raspberries inside the tart, then completely cover with raspberry preserves.

Take the remaining dough and roll it into strips. Place one diagonally across the top. Place the next diagonally from the opposite side. The next runs parallel to the first. The next is parallel to the second. Alternate in this way to create a woven pattern. Do not put the strips too close together, because the dough expands in baking.

Bake for 40 minutes.

DRINKS

◆ ELDERFLOWER SYRUP AND CLUB SODA

Mix about one part syrup to four parts soda. The syrup is made in Austria and available in gourmet shops or online. A leading maker of the syrup is Darbo.

Grüner Veltliner wine is also very agreeable as an adult beverage.

Elderflower

TURKEY NIGHT

HINT: A 97 PERCENT ASIAN COUNTRY.

My view of Turkey is dominated by Istanbul, because it is the only part of Turkey I know. When you are in Istanbul, a city half in Europe and half in Asia, it is hard to believe that only 3 percent of Turkey is in Europe. Istanbul is a European city. True, it is a Muslim European city and is filled with mosques, which is unusual for Europe, but the feel of the cobblestone back-streets, the main boulevards, the lifestyle is clearly European. Even the relationship to Islam often resembles the modern secular or indifferent European approach to Christianity. Turkey's Nobel Prize winner, Orhan Pamuk, writes in his book *Istanbul: Memories and the City*—which may be the best book about the city—about how the people he grew up with never fasted or observed the holiday of Ramadan, but always threw lavish feasts to celebrate the end of the fast.

Istanbul, whether on the European or Asian side of the Bosporus, is a great walking city. Pamuk wrote:

> Why, instead of the sun-drenched postcard views of Istanbul that tourists so loved, did I prefer the semi-darkness of the back streets, the evenings and cold winter nights, the ghost people passing through the light of the pale streetlamps, the cobblestone views, their loneliness?

In Istanbul there is always a sense of the possibility of being surprised. Why, I wondered, did they have a number of Starbucks when the coffeehouse is a Turkish invention and the city has been famous for them since the sixteenth century? Men had no answer, but then women explained to me that they did not feel welcome in Turkish coffeehouses. That was when I noticed that the Starbucks were always packed with women.

Turkey once had one of the great empires, which, like that of the Austrians, was destroyed by World War I. Its cultural influence, most especially its food, has spread from Hungary to Saudi Arabia to Morocco. All of the Arab world eats some Turkish food, especially desserts. Much Greek food shows some Turkish influence, though Greeks assert it is the other way around. The Turkish yogurt-and-cucumber dip cacik is the Greek tzatziki, and Turkish börek is Greek spanakopita.

Olives

I found all my meals in Turkey to be treats, including breakfast, which consisted of Armenian string cheese and black olives. Tables were always set with bowls of things to nibble on, so for Turkey Night we started with a bowl of black olives and a bowl of Turkish dried apricots, which are the best dried apricots in the world.

To make this meal well, make the vegetable salad, the rose sherbet, and the baklava a day in advance.

APPETIZERS
◆◆ ISPANAKLI BÖREK

It would be very un-Turkish to have only one appetizer.

Börek is a stuffed pastry, of which there are many kinds. Ispanakli is spinach.

THE FILLING

1 pound spinach, well washed
1½ cups soft goat cheese

2 tablespoons chopped fresh dill

Steam the spinach. Drain it in a colander for 30 minutes. Chop it. Add the goat cheese and the dill. Mix well.

VERSION 1: USING YUFKA

Börek is often made with a dough called yufka. For the ambitious, here is the recipe.

2 cups flour	1 tablespoon melted butter
1 egg	a pinch of salt
½ cup water	6 tablespoons soft butter

Preheat oven to 325 degrees. Combine in a blender with a dough hook the flour, egg, water, melted butter, and salt. When well mixed, cover with a light dusting of flour and damp cloth and let stand for 15 minutes.

Flour a table and roll the dough to about a ¼-inch thickness. Spread 3 tablespoons of the soft butter on the dough. Cut the dough into thirds and stack the layers on top of each other, buttered sides in. Roll out again. Butter with the remaining 3 tablespoons. Cut in thirds and stack and roll again. Put back in mixing bowl and knead for a few minutes with the dough hook. Roll out a little thinner than ¼ inch thick. Let dry before using.

Place spinach in middle. Roll into a log and cut into 2-inch pastries. Bake for 20 minutes or until only slightly brown.

VERSION 2: USING PHYLLO

Making the börek with phyllo dough may seem like more work, but it is actually much easier because you can buy ready-made sheets of phyllo frozen. Just remember to take them out of the freezer the night before making the börek. Once you open the package, try to work quickly so the sheets don't dry out and become brittle.

Preheat oven to 325 degrees. Butter a baking sheet. Place a phyllo sheet down and brush it with butter. Repeat with 2 more sheets. Place the spinach filling in a long thin column vertically. Wrap the dough around it and roll it to one side of the sheet. Place a sheet of phyllo next to it. Brush with butter. Roll the log in the buttered sheet. Repeat with 4 more sheets.

Cut the log into 1½- or 2-inch pieces. This should make about 6 börek. Bake for 20 minutes or until only slightly brown.

◆ KOFTE WITH YOGURT SAUCE

THE MEATBALLS

½ pound ground lamb
½ cup white onion, finely chopped
2 tablespoons powdered cumin
a generous pinch of salt

8 turns of black pepper
1 teaspoon cayenne pepper
¼ cup olive oil

Mix the ground lamb with the onion, cumin, salt, black pepper, and cayenne pepper. Roll into small balls less than an inch in diameter. Cook in hot olive oil.

THE SAUCE

2 cups Greek-style yogurt
1 teaspoon powdered cinnamon
½ teaspoon powdered allspice
a pinch of salt
½ teaspoon cayenne pepper

3 garlic cloves, peeled and finely
   minced
⅓ cup finely chopped mint
1½ teaspoons zest from a fresh lemon
2 tablespoons honey

Mix the—forgive the expression—Greek-style yogurt with the cinnamon, allspice, salt, cayenne pepper, garlic, mint, lemon zest, and honey. Serve with the kofte meatballs.

MAIN COURSE
◆ BAKED FISH

In Istanbul, surrounded on three sides by water, Turks eat fish. It is prominently featured in the best restaurants. This dish can be made with many possible kinds of fish. But it is nicest if the fish is small enough to serve a whole fish to each person, such as the small sea bass sometimes called European sea bass, branzino, or loup de mer—a succulent, handsome, silvery fish with large bones that makes it easy to eat.

4 garlic cloves, minced	1 tablespoon powdered cumin
1 small red onion, minced	1 teaspoon powdered turmeric
1 cup Italian parsley, chopped	a generous pinch of coarse salt
1 cup fresh coriander leaves (cilantro), chopped	1 teaspoon cayenne pepper
	juice of ½ lemon
½ cup chives, chopped	½ cup olive oil
1 tablespoon sweet paprika	3 small branzinos

For three small fish: Combine the garlic in a bowl with the red onion, Italian parsley, coriander, chives, paprika, cumin, turmeric, salt, cayenne pepper, and lemon juice. Add enough olive oil to cover and let it sit about an hour.

Preheat oven to 350 degrees. Spread some of the mixture in a baking pan. Place the fish on top. Place additional mixture inside the fish cavities, then sprinkle the remainder on top of the fish. Bake for 1 hour.

Branzino

VEGETABLE
◆ KÖZLENMIS SEBZE SLATASI (ROASTED VEGETABLE SALAD)

Preserved lemons from North Africa are not normally used in Turkey, but so much North African food is found in Turkey and so much Turkish in North Africa that we took this liberty.

3 small tomatoes
1 red bell pepper
1 small eggplant

½ Vidalia onion
½ preserved lemon (see Basic
    Recipes, p. 24)

Grill (if you don't have a real grill, a grilling pan with ridges at high temperature works well) the tomatoes, red pepper, eggplant, and onion on all sides. When thoroughly grilled, let the eggplant cool and chop the tomatoes and pepper into bite-size pieces. Coarsely chop up the onion. Peel the eggplant and tear it into bite-size pieces. Add the preserved lemon, cut into small pieces. Put the chopped vegetables in a bowl, let sit an hour, and then drain off the juices.

DRESSING

3 garlic cloves, minced
½ cup Italian parsley, chopped
a generous pinch of salt

1 tablespoon red pepper flakes
1 cup olive oil

Combine the garlic, Italian parsley, salt, red pepper flakes, and olive oil. Pour over the vegetables just before serving.

DESSERTS
◆◆ ROSE WATER SHERBET

Old Turkish cookbooks, such as Turabi Efendi's English-language book published in London in 1865, often have sorbet recipes. Unfortunately, there are no tips on how they chilled the syrup to actually form the sorbet. I suspect these cookbooks are referring to something like what we call an Italian ice or snow cone, which is not the same thing. Another nineteenth-century Turkish cookbook by Mehmed Kamil called *The Sanctuary of Cooks*, published in 1844, suggests chilling the syrup and pouring it over shaved ice. Kamil even gives a recipe for rose sorbet, which starts with collecting fresh rose petals. Ice creams and sherbets are made by whipping a liquid at freezing temperatures. We have an ice cream maker, a low-technology one by Cuisinart, which works very well and was not expensive. If you don't want to get an ice cream maker, whip this cooled syrup in a mixer at high speed for a few minutes. Then freeze for 20 minutes, then whip again, then freeze another 20 minutes, and continue until you have a thick slush. Then freeze it overnight. Or make an old-fashioned ice by chilling the syrup and pouring it over shaved ice.

SYRUP

½ cup rose water
½ cup sugar

⅔ cup 2 percent milk

Rose water is easily found in specialty shops or online. Combine it with the sugar in a pot and melt them into a syrup. Add the milk and let the syrup cool.

◆◆ BAKLAVA

The thicker yufka was originally used for baklava in medieval Turkey. The thinner pastry that we call phyllo came later. The word *phyllo* is Greek, but phyllo is a Turkish invention. Before the Ottoman Empire collapsed in World War I, the grand palaces of the wealthy used to have two phyllo makers, one for the thin sheets we call phyllo for baklava, and one for the thicker yufka for börek. In the earlier days of the empire, soldiers used to go to the Palace of the Sultan known as Topkapi on the fifteenth day of the Ramadan festival to be presented with baklava.

Baklava still has considerable standing in Turkey. Baklava bakers are specialists, and their pastry is sold in shops that sell nothing else. Gaziantep, sometimes called Antep, is an ancient town in the southeast famous for its baklava, which is why most shops in Istanbul claim to be from there.

There are many different baklavas. In Gaziantep, the pistachio center of Turkey, it is made with pistachios. Others make it with almonds. Along the Black Sea they make it with hazelnuts. Some have sugar syrup, others honey, some honey and lemon. The baklava that is found outside of Turkey that is so sweet that you gasp for oxygen when you taste it bears only a vague resemblance to the delicate pastry made in Turkey. This Black Sea version is light and not overly sweet and, accompanied with rose water sherbet, is one of the best International Night desserts we made.

1 cup hazelnuts	3–4 tablespoons melted butter
½ cup sugar	about 22 sheets of phyllo dough
a splash of vanilla extract	

Roast the hazelnuts for about 10 minutes until they are brown, but watch them to make sure they don't start to burn. Cool and rub the skins off by placing 4 or 5 at a time on your flat palm and rubbing your hands together in a circular motion. Grind them briefly in a food processor so they are well chopped but not powder. Mix in the sugar and vanilla.

Preheat oven to 325 degrees. Brush butter on a baking sheet. Spread out 1 phyllo sheet. Brush it with butter and fold it in half vertically. Brush the top again with butter. Place another sheet half on top. Brush it. Fold it over and brush the new top with butter. Repeat with 4 more sheets, then place ⅓ of the nut mixture on top. It should not be an extremely thick layer.

Place another sheet half on top. Brush it with butter. Fold it. Brush the top. Continue with 4 more sheets. Spread another ⅓ of the nut mixture. Continue with 5 more buttered and folded sheets and then the last ⅓ of the nuts, but save the sugar and nut powder that has fallen to the bottom of the bowl. Fold and butter 5 more sheets. Butter the top and sprinkle with the remaining sugar and nut powder. Cut into triangles. Bake about 40 minutes. When it comes out of the oven, pour syrup (recipe below) over it.

SYRUP

½ cup water
½ cup honey

juice of ½ lemon
1 tablespoon powdered cinnamon

Combine ingredients over medium–low heat.

DRINK
◆ TURKISH ORANGE TEA

Coffee is a Turkish tradition. Coffee drinking originated in Ethiopia, was carried to Yemen, which was part of the Turkish Ottoman Empire, and by the sixteenth century Istanbul was a city of coffeehouses. But despite Turkey's leading position in coffee history, the Turks are great tea drinkers. They drink mostly black tea, which is domestically grown along the Black Sea. It is served in a small hourglass-shaped glass placed in a little saucer.

Even if you go to Turkey and bring back the black tea sold there, it is hard to reproduce its rich flavor. Part of the secret is to wash the leaves in cold water and dry them before brewing. Turks brew their tea in a kind of double boiler like a Russian samovar, though more compact, called a *çaydanhk*. This makes a very strong tea in the pot on the top, brewed with hot water from below. It is a demanding craft to get exactly right. In a Turkish tea glass the hot water goes to where the glass begins to indent, and the rest is filled with strong black tea. You can make your own version using a teapot and a kettle.

If you do not want to load your kids with caffeine, you can serve an apple tea and an orange tea, made in Turkey and available online. I am convinced that these teas are made solely for tourists, since I never saw a Turk drink them and they only seem to be sold in tourist shops. But it is very pleasant nonetheless. Talia loved the orange tea with a touch of honey.

EMILIA-ROMAGNA NIGHT

HINT: THE RICHEST VALLEY IN A GREAT FOOD NATION.

The river is the Po and the valley around it is the richest agricultural area of Italy. Its wheat fields produce pastas such as tortellini, its cows grazing in sweet grass produce Italy's greatest cheese, Parmigiano-Reggiano, its grapes make balsamic vinegar, and the well-fed pigs outside Parma give Italy its greatest ham. The region is connected from Piacenzo to Parma to Bologna to the Adriatic not just by the Po but by an ancient Roman road, the Via Emilia, now an eight-lane highway. When Talia's finger landed just north of Bologna, the capital of Emilia-Romagna—locals will point out that the city is in Emilia and not Romagna—the question was how to incorporate Talia's absolute favorite dish in the world, pasta with Bolognese sauce, with a meal including some of the other great regional products, and so Emilia-Romagna Night was born.

I spent some time in this region when working on my book *Salt*, not only because of the ancient saltworks of Salsomaggiore near Parma, but because Parmigiano-Reggiano cheese and prosciutto di Parma, both made near the saltworks, are two of the world's most celebrated salted foods. By Italian and European law, for cheeses to be labeled Parmigiano-Reggiano or hams to be labeled prosciutto di Parma, they must be made in Emilia-Romagna.

Balsamic vinegar is another matter. It is made in many places. The original, made since the Middle Ages in the town of Modena, is not a true vinegar but a reduction of the local Trebbiano grape juice and is labeled "Aceto Balsamico Tradizionale di Modena." The best of this has been aged twenty-five years. A less closely supervised but also high-quality product is *salsa di mosto cotto*. Another acceptable Modena product is *salsa balsamica*. But many of the bottles simply labeled "balsamic vinegar" or even "Balsamic from Modena" are not from Modena, and are simply artificially colored wine vinegars with gums added for thickener. A real balsamic should be not only dark and thick but should have a flavor much more complicated than that of wine vinegar and a woody taste of the barrels in which it was aged.

The dessert, tiramisu, should be started two days in advance.

TALIA: On Bolognese

My favorite dish is spaghetti Bolognese. Actually, that's not true, I also love fettuccine Bolognese and tagliatelle Bolognese. During a trip my family took around Italy we went to five cities, and in those five cities we ate three meals a day. Of those three meals, two of them had pasta. I looked at the choices on the menu. There were raviolis and gnocchis and many other kinds of pasta. That's when the hard part came. Choosing. Which one should I order? I mean, each restaurant makes each dish differently, so you don't want to miss out on something! It took some time, maybe too much time, but in the end I would decide. Spaghetti Bolognese. Or fettuccine Bolognese. Or tagliatelle Bolognese. For the entire trip, I ate Bolognese twice a day. Surprisingly, I never got sick of it, and to me, every time it seemed different. I didn't want to miss out on what might be the world's best Bolognese. What if the one night I had something different was the night we went to a restaurant that made the best ever? A special ingredient in the sauce, maybe? I don't know. But I do see why Italy is famous for pasta, at least Bolognese.

APPETIZER
◆◆ TAGLIATELLE BOLOGNESE

This recipe makes enough for an appetizer for six people. It is difficult to make less, so if you do not have six people, set some aside for another day.

We used a pasta machine to make the tagliatelle, but you can make pasta well with just a rolling pin and a knife—it just won't be as even and probably won't be as thin, which is important because pasta thickens as it cooks. It can be made with white flour and water. But the best pasta is made with eggs, durum wheat, and no water.

THE PASTA

about 1½ cups white flour
about 1½ cups durum wheat

5 whole eggs

Combine the white flour and the durum and mix in the eggs to make a dough that is soft and malleable after kneading. If the dough seems too brittle, add more egg; if it is sticky (you don't want it to be sticky), add more flour. Roll the dough to a thickness of about ⅛ inch, then cut it into ¼-inch strips. Remember that as it cooks, the thickness will increase. You'll also need somewhere to hang the fresh pasta to dry. In China, along the roads, you see it drying on strings between tree branches. Invent your own rig, or you can buy a pasta rack.

THE SAUCE

Classic recipes are like the game called telephone that we used to play when I was a child. Five or six kids sit in a circle. One kid mumbles something in the ear of the kid to his right. They keep passing it on, and finally the last kid says it out loud to the first kid, who is next to him. They see if the last kid's statement resembles the original one. In her excellent book on Emilia-Romagna cooking, *The Splendid Table*, Lynn Rossetto Kasper gives an authentic original Bolognese sauce recipe. I have made some changes to it. But Lynn may have included a few changes of her own, and the culinary historians in Bologna who gave her the recipe may have had their own improvements. So while I can't say that this is the original one-and-only Bolognese recipe, I am confident it is close to the original idea and a wonderful old-fashioned sauce from the days when cooks took time to make things well.

Before the grinders of the industrial revolution—one of the really bad things that happened to modern cooking—meat finely chopped with a knife was often used instead of ground meat. Finely chop the hanger steak yourself for a much better sauce.

5 ounces pork fatback
3 tablespoons olive oil
½ cup fresh carrot, minced
½ cup celery, minced
½ cup yellow onion, minced
¾ pound hanger steak, finely
    chopped

1 cup tomato sauce #1 (see Basic
    Recipes, p. 25)
1 cup beef stock (see Basic Recipes, p.
    24, or buy it)
1 cup Trebbiano or other northern
    Italian dry white wine
½ cup whole milk
⅓ cup heavy cream

Sauté the fatback until rendered. Add the olive oil, carrot, celery, and onion and sauté until onion is translucent. Add the hanger steak. Brown the meat. Add tomato sauce, beef stock, and white wine. Simmer over low heat for 2 hours. Periodically add a spoonful of milk and stir with a wooden spoon so that by the end of 2 hours you have added the ½ cup of milk. Put the heavy cream in a pan and reduce on high heat to half and stir it into the sauce. Take the amount of sauce and the amount of boiled pasta you are using and toss together in a bowl. Serve with grated Parmigiano-Reggiano.

MAIN COURSE
◆ GRILLED VEAL CHOPS IN BALSAMIC VINEGAR

Put veal chops on a hot grill and drizzle balsamic vinegar on them. After 12 minutes, turn and drizzle on the other side. Grill for another 12 minutes.

VEGETABLE
◆◆ ROASTED FENNEL PARMIGIANO-REGGIANO

1 large bulb fennel, or 2 small
½ cup beef stock (see Basic Recipes, p. 24, or buy it)
½ cup olive oil
3 garlic cloves, peeled and minced

1 sprig of fresh rosemary
a pinch of salt
3 turns of black pepper
1 piece Parmigiano-Reggiano cheese for shaving

Preheat oven to 300 degrees. Cut fennel into 1-inch-thick wedges and place in an earthen casserole. Add beef stock and drizzle thoroughly with olive oil. Add the garlic, the needles from the sprig of rosemary, and salt and pepper. Bake for 40 minutes. Before serving, shave Parmigiano-Reggiano cheese on top.

DESERT
◆◆◆ TIRAMISU

Another one of Talia's favorite dishes, tiramisu, now served everywhere in Italy, has only a fifty-year history. It was not invented in Emilia-Romagna but slightly to the north in Treviso. A key ingredient, mascarpone, is associated with the Milan area, marsala comes from Sicily, and the whole idea seems to come from zuppa inglese, a rum-soaked cream-covered cake that is from late-nineteenth-century Emilia-Romagna. Tiramisu needs to be made in several stages and should be started a day or two in advance.

STAGE ONE: FILLING

6 eggs
3 tablespoons sugar

½ cup sweet marsala

Beat 6 egg yolks with the sugar and marsala. Rest the mixture in a metal mixing bowl over a steaming pot so that the bowl does not touch the boiling water underneath, and whip until the mixture becomes thick. Set aside to cool for at least 4 hours.

STAGE TWO: SYRUP

2 cups sugar
1 cup espresso

¼ cup dark rum

Make a syrup by melting the sugar over low heat with the espresso and rum. Let chill.

STAGE THREE: FILLING, CONTINUED

8 ounces mascarpone
⅔ cup heavy cream

1 tablespoon sugar
a splash of vanilla extract

Put the mascarpone in a bowl and beat it smooth with a wooden spoon. In another bowl, whip the heavy cream with a little sugar and vanilla to soft peaks and fold thoroughly into the mascarpone. Then mix in the marsala mixture from stage one.

STAGE FOUR: LADYFINGERS

You can make your own ladyfingers, though the packaged ones (you'll need about sixty) are perfectly usable.

5 eggs, separated
3/4 cup sugar
2 small drops vanilla extract

1¼ cups flour
3/4 teaspoon baking powder

Preheat oven to 350 degrees. Cover three 11 x 17 baking sheets with parchment paper. Fit a pastry tube with a plain round nozzle.

Beat the egg whites to a soft slight peak, add a few spoonfuls of sugar, and beat until stiff. Add the rest of the sugar and the vanilla to the egg yolks and whip until pale and thick.

With a rubber spatula, very gently fold the whites into the yolks, a bit at a time. Mix the flour and baking powder and sift a little onto the egg mixture. Gently fold it into the egg mixture. Continue a little at a time until completely folded and there is no flour showing in the mixture.

Put the mixture in a pastry bag and pipe out lines of dough slightly longer than the height of the springform you are using. Bake for about 10 minutes.

STAGE FIVE: ASSEMBLY

1½ tablespoons unsweetened cocoa
    powder

½ cup heavy cream

Brush a 9-inch springform pan with melted butter. Cut a straight edge at the bottom of each ladyfinger long enough so the other curved end will stick out above the edge of the springform. Stick the ladyfingers in a border vertically along the edge of the springform. You can use a little of the syrup to help stick each one to the edge.

Cover the bottom with two layers of ladyfingers. Spoon the coffee-rum syrup from stage two onto the ladyfingers. Add a layer of half the filling. Then add a single layer of ladyfingers. Spoon syrup onto this as well. Then add the rest of the filling. Whip the heavy cream and spread it on top, then sprinkle with unsweetened cocoa sifted through a strainer—a light dusting. Chill overnight. Release the pan's side ring and serve.

DRINK

We all started with a glass of blood orange juice, a drink Marian and I are sentimental about because we had it every morning on our honeymoon in Rome and Sicily. The adults can also have a hearty red Sangiovese wine from Romagna.

TALIA: *My Confession*

After Emilia-Romagna Night, we still had one slice of tiramisu left in the fridge. It was still there the next day and I was home alone, so I took a knife and cut off a tiny shaving of the slice. An hour later, another sliver. It was just that good, even after the Night! Eventually, the remaining slice turned into a remaining sliver and then plop, it was gone. I ate the last bit. Then months later, it was my birthday and my dad created a cake, as usual. That year I had chosen a tiramisu-flavored cake because I loved it so much. The next day we went on a vacation and so we froze the leftover cake to have when we came back. A guest was staying in our apartment. When we came home, only a sliver of the cake was left . . . So here's your final tip before creating an International Night: never, ever, leave someone home alone with tiramisu!

ACKNOWLEDGMENTS

Thanks to José Abete and Wafaa Amagui in Marrakech; Kikuo Yamamoto, Yoko Clark, Louisa Rubinfien, Satoru Urabe, and Akira Tanaka in Japan; and Hasegawa Shigeki in Tokyo for sharing his recipes. I also want to thank my great editor, Nancy Miller, who worked so hard on this fun little thing that turned out to be a huge project, and to my wonderful friend and agent Charlotte Sheedy; Ana Maria Cecelia Simonetti dos Santos for her Brigadeiro recipe for Brazil Night; Mih-Ho Cha for a lot of help on Korean Night; my dear old friends Ginette and Bernard Diederich for help in Haiti; and Carlos Cristobal Marquez for sharing recipes in Havana.

And a special thanks to my great love, Marian, for dining and playing with us.

BIBLIOGRAPHY

These are books that helped us, giving us ideas about the culinary culture of the countries we were celebrating. All of these books came from our family food library.

GENERAL
Artusi, Pellegrino. *La Scienza in Cucina e L'Arte Di Mangiar Bene.* Milan: Sperling & Kupfer Editori, 1991 (original edition, 1911).

Boni, Ada. *Il Talismano Della Felicità.* Rome: Casa Editrice Colombo, 1997.

Castelvetro, Giacomo. *The Fruit, Herbs & Vegetables of Italy.* London: Viking, 1989.

Cost, Bruce. *Bruce Cost's Asian Ingredients: Buying and Cooking the Staple Foods of China, Japan and Southeast Asia.* New York: William Morrow, 1988.

Davidson, Alan. *The Oxford Companion to Food.* New York: Oxford University Press, 1999.

———. *North Atlantic Seafood.* London: Penguin Group, 1980.

Escoffier, Auguste. *La Guide Culinaire: Aide-Mémoire de Cuisine Pratique.* Paris: Flammarion, 1921.

Harris, Jessica B. *The Africa Cookbook: Tastes of a Continent.* New York: Simon & Schuster, 1998.

Hertzberg, Jeff, and Zoë François. *Artisan*

Bread in Five Minutes a Day: The Discovery that Revolutionizes Home Baking. New York: St. Martin's Press, 2007.

Kiple, Kenneth F., and Kriemhild Coneè Ornelas. *The Cambridge World History of Food.* New York: Cambridge University Press, 2000.

Lenôtre, Gaston. *Lenôtre's Desserts and Pastries.* New York: Barron's Educational Series, 1977.

Pellaprat, Henri-Paul. *L'Art Culinaire Moderne.* Castagnola, Switzerland: Éditions René Kramer, 1972.

Sitole, Dorah. *Cooking from Cape to Cairo.* Cape Town: Tafelberg, 1999.

Wolfe, Linda. *The Cooking of the Caribbean Islands.* London: Macmillan Publishers, 1985.

ANDALUSIA
Centeno Roman, José Maria, and Francisco Zarza Toboso. *Cocinando a la Española, Volume 2.* Bilbao: Editorial Cantabrica, 1974.

AQUITAINE
Conseil National des Arts Culinaire. *Aquitaine: Produits du Terroir et Recettes Traditionnelles.* Paris: Albin Michel, 1997.

ARGENTINA
Brooks, Shirley Lomax. *Argentina Cooks! Treasured Recipes from the Nine Regions of Argentina.* New York: Hippocrene Books, 2001.

AUSTRIA

Gutenbrunner, Kurt, with Jane Sigal. *Neue Cuisine: The Elegant Tastes of Vienna*. New York: Rizzoli, 2011.

Scheibenpflug, Lotte. *Specialties of Austrian Cooking*. Innsbruck: Penguin Verlag,1980.

Witzelsberger, Richard. *Das Österreichische Mehlspeisen Kochbuch*. Vienna: Verlag Kremayr & Scheriau, 1979.

BRAZIL

De Andrade, Margarette. *Brazilian Cookery: Traditional and Modern*. Rio de Janeiro: A Casa do Livro Eldorado, 1985.

BRITTANY

Charlon, Raymonde. *Savoureuse Bretagne*. Rennes: Editions Ouest-France, 1993.

Conseil National des Arts Culinaire. *Bretagne: Produits du Terroir et Recettes Traditionnelles*. Paris: Albin Michel, 1994.

Du Pontavice, Gîlles and Bleuzen. *La Cuisine des Chateau de Bretagne*. Rennes: Editions Ouest-France, 1997.

CHINA

Anderson, E.N. *The Food of China*. New Haven: Yale University Press, 1988.

Cheng, F.T. *Musings of a Chinese Gourmet*. London: Hutchinson, 1954.

Simoons, Frederick J. *Food in China: A Cultural and Historic Inquiry*. Boca Raton, Florida: CRC Press, 1991.

Young, Grace. *The Wisdom of the Chinese Kitchen: Classic Family Recipes for Celebration and Healing*. New York: Simon & Schuster, 1999.

Zee, A. *Swallowing Clouds: A Playful Journey through Chinese Culture, Language and Cuisine*. Toronto: Douglas & McIntyre, 1990.

CORNWALL

Kittow, June. *Favorite Cornish Recipes*. Sevenoaks, England: J.Salmon.

Mason, Laura, and Catherine Brown. *The Taste of Britain*. London: Harper Press, 2006.

CUBA

García, Alicia, and Sergio García. *El Aljibe: un Estilo Natural*. Havana: Editorial Si-Mar, 2004.

Lluriá de O'Higgins, María Josefa. *A Taste of Old Cuba*. New York: HarperCollins, 1994.

EMILIA-ROMAGNA

Kasper, Lynne Rossetto. *The Splendid Table: Recipes from Emilia-Romagna, the Heartland of Northern Italian Food*. New York: William Morrow and Company, 1992.

Rangoni, Laura. *Laceto Balsamico Modenese*. Lucca, Italy: Maria Pacini Fazzi Editore, 1999.

Tiocchi, Giuseppi. *La Cuciniera Bolognese*. Bologna: Arnaldo Forni Editore, 1990 (original printing, 1843).

FRENCH GUIANA

Désormeaux, Emile. *La Cuisine Creole Traditionnelle*. Fort-de-France (Martinique):

Editions Emile Désormeaux, 1995.

Rose-Rosette, Robert. *Le Punch Martiniquais.* Fort-de-France, Martinique: Editions Trois Rivieres, 1993.

GREECE
Archestratus, *The Life of Luxury.* Totnes, Devon, England: Prospect Books, 1994.

Skoura, Sophia. *The Greek Cookbook.* New York: Crown Publishers, 1967.

HAWAII
Laudan, Rachel. *The Food of Paradise: Exploring Hawaii's Culinary Heritage.* Honolulu: University of Hawaii Press, 1996.

HUNGARY
Koerner, András. *A Taste of the Past: The Daily Life and Cooking of a 19th Century Hungarian Jewish Homemaker.* Lebanon, New Hampshire: University Press of New England, 2004.

Lang, George. *The Cuisine of Hungary.* New York: Bonanza Books, 1971.

INDIA
Achaya, K.T. *A Historical Dictionary of Indian Food.* Dehli: Oxford University Press, 1998.

Sahni, Julie. *Classic Indian Cooking.* New York: William Morrow, 1980.

IRELAND
Irish Bread Recipes. Dublin: Tony Potter Publishing, 2004.

FitzGibbon, Theodora. *A Taste of Ireland: In Food and Pictures.* London: Weidenfeld and Nicolson, 1968.

Irwin, Florence. *The Cookin' Woman: Irish Country Recipes.* Belfast: The Blackstaff Press, 1949.

JAMAICA
Benghiat, Norma. *Traditional Jamaican Cookery.* London: Penguin Group, 1985.

Sullivan, Caroline. *The Jamaican Cookery Book.* Kingston: Aston W. Gardner & Co, 1893.

JAPAN
Tsuji, Shizuo. *Japanese Cooking: A Simple Art.* Tokyo: Kadansha International, 1980.

MEXICO
Nuevo Cocinero Mexicano en Forma de Diccionario. Mexico City: Miguel Ángel Porrura, 1986 (original printing, 1888).

Farga, Amando. *Historia de la Comida en Mexico.* Mexico City: 1968.

Kennedy, Diana. *The Cuisines of Mexico.* New York: Harper & Row, 1972.

Solís, Janet Long, Manuel Álvarez, and Aranzazú Camarena. *El Placer del Chile.* Mexico City: Editorial Clío, 1998.

MOROCCO
Benayoun, Aline. *Casablanca Cuisine: French North African Cooking.* London: Serif, 1998.

(Madame) Guinaudeau. *Traditional Moroc-

can Cooking: Recipes from Fez. London: Serif, 2003.

Hal, Fatema. *Authentic Recipes from Morocco*. Singapore: Periplus Editions, 2007.

Huica Miranda, Ambroosio, trans. *La Cocina Hispano-Magrebí Durante La Época Almohade: Según un Manuscrito Anónimo del Siglo XIII*. Asturias, Spain: Ediciones Trea, 2005.

Koehler, Jeff. *Morocco: A Culinary Journey with Recipes from the Spice-Scented Markets of Marrakech to the Date-Filled Oasis of Zagora*. San Francisco: Chronicle Books, 2012.

Wolfert, Paula. *Couscous and Other Good Food from Morocco*. New York: Quill, 2001.

NAPLES

Porcaro, Giuseppe. *Sapore di Napoli: Storia della Pizza Napoletano*. Naples: Adriano Gallina Editore, 1985.

Scully, Terence. *The Neapolitan Recipe Collection*. Ann Arbor: University of Michigan Press, 2000.

NEWFOUNDLAND

Newfoundland Christmas Cookbook. St. John's, Newfoundland: Hillcrest Publishing, 1992.

Jesperson, Rev. Ivan F. *Fat-Back & Molasses: A Collection of Favorite Old Recipes from Newfoundland and Labrador*. Printed by the Jesperson family, 1974.

NEW ORLEANS

Christian Women's Exchange of New Orleans, *Creole Cookery*. Gretna, Louisiana: Pelican Publishing Company, 2005 (facsimile of an 1885 edition).

The Picayune's Creole Cook Book: Sesquicentennial Edition. New Orleans: The Times-Picayune, 1987.

Prudhomme, Paul. *Chef Paul Prudhomme's Louisiana Kitchen*. New York: William Morrow, 1984.

Scott, Natalie V. *200 Years of New Orleans Cooking*. Gretna, Louisiana: Pelican Publishing Company, 1998.

PERU

Marks, Copeland. *The Exotic Kitchens of Peru: The Land of the Inca*. New York: M. Evans, 1999.

THE PHILIPPINES

Gelle, Gerry G. *Filipino Cuisine: Recipes from the Islands*. Santa Fe: Red Crane Books, 1997.

PORTUGAL

Anderson, Jean. *The Food of Portugal: Recipes from the Most Original and Least-Known Cuisine of Western Europe*. New York: William Morrow, 1994.

Vieíra, Edite. *The Taste of Portugal*. London: Grub Street, 1995.

PROVENCE

Conseil National des Arts Culinaire. *Provence-Alpes-Côte d'Azur: Produits du Terroir et Recettes Traditionnelles*. Paris: Albin Michel, 1995.

Reboul, J.B. *La Cuisiniére Provençal*. Marseille: Tacussel, 1910.

QUEBEC
Couillard, Suzette, and Roseland Normand. *Cuisine Traditionelle d'un Québec Oublié*. Montmagny, Quebec: 1981.

RUSSIA
Glants, Musya, and Joyce Toomre. *Food in Russian History and Culture*. Bloomington: Indiana University Press, 1997.

Toomre, Joyce, trans. *Elena Molokhovets' "A Gift to Young Housewives."* Bloomington: Indiana University Press, 1998.

SENEGAL
Thiam, Pierre. *Yolele! Recipes from the Heart of Senegal*. New York: Lake Isle Press, 2008.

SRI LANKA
Kuruvita, Peter. *Serendip: My Sri Lankan Kitchen*. Sydney: Murdoch Books, 2008.

SICILY
Correnti, Pino. *Il Libro d'oro della Cucina e Dei Vini di Sicilia*. Milan: Grupo Ugo Mursia, 1976.

Simeti, Mary Taylor. *Pomp and Sustenance: Twenty-five centuries of Sicilian Food*. New York: Alfred A. Knopf, 1989.

Wright, Clifford A. *Cucina Paradiso: The Heavenly Food of Sicily*. New York: Simon & Schuster, 1992.

TURKEY
Algar, Ayla. *Classical Turkish Cooking: Traditional Turkish Food for the American Kitchen*. New York: William Morrow, 1991.

Efendi, Turabi. *The Turkish Cookery Book: A Collection of Receipts, from the Best Turkish Authorities*. Whitefish, Montana: Kessinger Publishing (facsimile of London: William H. Allen, 1865, edition).

INDEX

A NOTE ON THE AUTHORS

MARK KURLANSKY is the *New York Times* best-selling author of *Cod, Salt, The Basque History of the World, 1968, The Big Oyster,* and *The Eastern Stars,* among many other books. He was awarded the 2011 National Parenting Publications Gold Award for *World Without Fish,* the 2007 Dayton Literary Peace Prize for *Nonviolence, Bon Appetit's* Food Writer of the Year in 2006, and the 1999 James Beard Award for Food Writing and the 1999 Glenfiddich Award, both for *Cod.* His children's books, *The Cod's Tale* and *The Story of Salt,* received the Orbis Pictus award from the National Council of Teachers of English and the ALA Notable Book Award, respectively. He lives in New York City. Visit his website at www.markkurlansky.com.

TALIA KURLANSKY, who often cooks and travels with her father, is in the ninth grade. This is her first book.